Lift Up Your Hearts

Homilies for the "A" Cycle

James A. Wallace, CSsR
Robert P. Waznak, SS
Guerric DeBona, OSB

Paulist Press
New York/Mahwah, N.J.

Cover design by Sharyn Banks
Book design by Lynn Else

Library of Congress Cataloging-in-Publication Data

Wallace, James A., 1944–
    Lift up your hearts : homilies for the "A" cycle / James A. Wallace, Robert P. Waznak, and Guerric DeBona.
        p. cm.
    ISBN 0-8091-4288-0 (alk. paper)
    1. Church year sermons. 2. Catholic Church—Sermons. 3. Sermons, American. I. Waznak, Robert P. II. DeBona, Guerric, 1955–. III. Title.

    BX1756.A2W35 2004
    252'.6—dc22

                                                                                2004011443

Published by Paulist Press
997 Macarthur Boulevard
Mahwah, New Jersey 07430

www.paulistpress.com

Printed and bound in the
United States of America

Contents

Introduction

This collection of homilies comes out of a vision of preaching voiced in the twenty-one-year-old document *Fulfilled in Your Hearing The Homily in the Sunday Assembly* (hereafter, *FIYH*).[1] Preachers were reminded in that profoundly pastoral work that "the function of the Eucharistic homily is to enable people to life up their hearts, to praise and thank the Lord for his presence in their lives" (25). How the homily will do this is suggested in the preacher's understanding of the nature and function of the homily as "a scriptural interpretation of human existence which enables a community to recognize God's active presence, to respond to that presence in faith through liturgical word and gesture, and beyond the liturgical assembly, through a life lived in conformity with the Gospel" (29).

A homily can function in a variety of ways—as proclamation, instruction, exhortation, and witness, to name a few; in *FIYH* the accent falls on the homily as an act of interpretation.[2] The understanding voiced there has three parts worthy of reflection. The homily is, first of all, envisioned as offering a "scriptural interpretation of human existence." We can hear the influence of the Pastoral Constitution on the Church in the Modern World *(Gaudium et Spes)*, which stated "In every age, the church carries the responsibility of reading the signs of the times and of interpreting them in the light of the gospel, if it is to carry out its task" (#4)."[3]

Preachers fulfill this charge in the homily when the biblical and liturgical texts serve as a lens on the life of the community of faith in the world.

---

1. Bishops' Committee on Priestly Life and Ministry, National Conference of Catholic Bishops, *Fulfilled In Your Hearing, The Homily in the Sunday Assembly* (Washington, DC: USCC, 1982). Numbers within parenthesis indicate page numbers.

2. See Robert P. Waznak, *An Introduction to the Homily* (Collegeville, MN: Liturgical Press, 1998), especially Ch. 2.

3. *Vatican II Constitutions, Decrees, Declarations*. Gen ed. Austin Flannery, OP (Northport, NY: Costello Publishing Co., 1996) 165.

Thus, "the homily is not so much *on* the Scriptures as *from* and *through* them" (*FIYH*, 20). And while the homily is to flow from the Scripture, "the preacher does not so much attempt to explain the Scriptures as to interpret the human situation through the Scriptures" (20).

Fulfilled in Your Hearing casts the homilist not so much as a teacher, though this is not say that good homilies are not instructional, but rather as a "mediator of meaning." On one side is the Word of God found in the Scriptures and undergirding the other liturgical texts. On the other side is the community of faith. From the location of being "in the middle," the preacher listens to both God's Word revealed in Scripture and tradition and to God's Word revealed in the lives of the people and what is happening in the world. And from that location, "the preacher then speaks a word that helps the community to know itself and to act as the People of God, the Body of Christ, the dwelling place of the Holy Spirit.

Fulfilled in Your Hearing recognizes that people hunger for meaning in their lives. "For a time they may find meaning in their jobs, their families and friends, their political or social causes. All these concerns, good and valid as they are, fall short of providing ultimate meaning. Without ultimate meaning, we are ultimately unsatisfied" (7).[4] What the Word of God in preaching can offer is "a way to interpret our human lives, a way to face the ambiguities and challenges of the human condition, not a pat answer to every problem and question that comes along" (15). And it is more likely to do this when preachers perform the preaching task "by offering a Word which has spoken to their lives and inviting these people to think and ponder on that Word so that it might speak to their lives as well" (15).

An understanding of the homily as a "scriptural interpretation of human existence" then leads to how it functions in the liturgy as an integral part. When God's people gather for Eucharist, they are there to give thanks and praise and to renew their commitment to the covenant they have entered at baptism. The homily serves a crucial function in the Eucharist when it enables the community 1) to recognize God's active presence in the world,

---

4. See also James A. Wallace, *Preaching to the Hungers of the Heart* (Collegeville, MN: Liturgical Press, 2002) for some of the hungers that the homily can feed.

and 2) to respond to the divine presence in this act of liturgy and in the way life is lived beyond the church doors. A few words about each of these goals.

A homily is to help people to recognize God's active presence, that is, to call the community to a vision of faith that knows the God revealed in Jesus Christ as a God who is truly God-with-us, Emmanuel. The homily is to evoke that faith that knows the risen, crucified Lord and the Holy Spirit as being at work in us, for us, and through us. This recognition of the living God happens when the homilist engages in the work of "making connections between the real lives of people who believe in Jesus Christ but are not always sure what difference faith can make in their lives, and the God who calls us into ever deeper communion with himself and with one another" (*FIYH*, 8).

The second purpose of the homily flows from the first and itself moves in two directions. In a word, the homily aims to evoke a response to the God whom people have recognized as active and present. And this response is both immediate and ongoing. The homily should move them toward the act of Eucharist, toward giving praise and thanks here and now, and then toward and beyond the church doors, out into the world to take part in the mission of the Church. It should help fuel the ongoing response to the final words of every Mass "Go in peace, to love God and serve one another."

This approach to the homily as an act of interpreting life through a biblical lens justifies the statement that the homily is integral to the liturgy. It helps to link the liturgy of the Word with the liturgy of the Eucharist. When the presider says, "Lift up your hearts," and the people respond, "We have lifted them up to the Lord," this has something to do with the homily having done its work. When the homily has evoked the necessary dispositions of gratitude and desire to give praise, it has done part of its job. God's Word spoken through the Scriptures and the homily works to bring the people into a communion of minds and hearts ready and able to thank and praise God for the many gifts we have received, even during those times when the world and our hearts have been battered and bruised by so many sorrows and so much senseless violence. The work of the homily is complete when it also serves to move the community out to that world, "to live a life in conformity with the gospel." The homily thus also serves to help motivate God's people to work for the transformation of the world to a world of peace and justice, reconcil-iation and love.

The homilies found here are the efforts of three preachers to address a word that interprets the lives of a community of faith and leads them more deeply into liturgy and life. Bob Waznak and I preached most of our homi-lies at Holy Trinity Parish in Georgetown, Washington, DC, where we have presided regularly. The communities at the 9:30 and 11:30 a.m. Sunday cel-ebrations especially were sources of inspiration and support for us. Guerric DeBona preached most of his homilies in the seminary and at various parishes near St. Meinrad's Archabbey in southern Indiana. We are happy to share our work with you, not as perfect examples of what a homily should be, but as sincere efforts to bring God's Word and life together on a particular Sunday. We offer them to both those who are preaching and those who are the recipients of preaching, to those who like to see what oth-ers have done with texts they themselves are working with and to those who might like to hear what another voice might say on a particular Sunday. You will find references in the homilies to events that were "of the day." I have changed few of these since all of the authors believe that homilies are meant to be disposable, spoken to the community at hand about the passing events of our lives, and drawing on these events when possible. Yet while such specificity situates a homily in a certain context, we hope you find that underneath the particularities of time and place, a reader might find a mes-sage that crosses over into the present.

Bob Waznak died on December 5, 2002. He was my colleague and friend for almost twenty years at the Washington Theological Union. The homilies presented here include some of the last he preached. Bob had the ability to bring together culture and proclamation in a way that was wise, witty, and warm. We shall miss his voice.

Guerric DeBona and I hope these homilies may help to open the Word for you on a day you need to hear it and in a way that will prove beneficial. May the Word of the Lord, rich as it is, lead us all ever more deeply into the mystery of our loving God.

James A. Wallace, CSsR
All Saints Day
November 1, 2003
Washington Theological Union
Washington, DC

ADVENT

You Visit Me by Night
FIRST SUNDAY OF ADVENT

Readings:
Isaiah 2:1–5; Romans 13:11–14; Matthew 24:37–44

There is nothing more powerful than that moment
>   when it dawns on us that Jesus was right about everything.

On the First Sunday of Advent a few years back, some dear friends of mine
>   went through a heartbreaking, life-changing experience.

Their son, Ethan, was walking back from a social event
>   one evening in Chicago with his friend.

The young college student was just about to reach
>   his parents' house when he was accosted by four men demanding money,
>   one of whom had just been released from jail.

After trying to reason with them, Ethan was shot several times.

His father ran out of the house to find Ethan
>   dying and his son's friend
>   lying in a confused, helpless heap on the ground, unharmed.

I can tell you that when I heard the awful news about this violent death,
>   Jesus' parable, told that very Sunday, about one man being taken
>   and one left in a field took on a stunning new meaning.

I grew new ears after hearing that Gospel for the First Sunday of Advent.

The course of our personal lives, the incidences surrounding our often-savage,
>   brutal culture, and the Word of God collided to spark a new meaning.

Advent is meant to wake us up to these very things:
> the life that we take for granted, the world that needs conversion,
> and the Word that ignites them both.

And it seems that Jesus himself deploys these very tools
> of personal insight—
> a prophetic look at culture and the Scripture that interprets them.

It is fascinating to see Jesus interpret his own tradition
> given to him in the Hebrew Scriptures.

The Word unfolding the Word.

Noah is a kind of biblical lens for Jesus, an analogy for how
> he interprets his own role as Son of Man.

Just as the flood came unawares in the days of Noah,
> so the Son of Man will come.

Without warning, he comes.

It must have been a real shock to some of those people in Jesus' time.

They were used to observing the same religious practices for centuries,
> using the same Law to justify their behavior.

Some of them probably stood there, much as we stand,
> our arms folded, as if to dare anything or anybody to move us,
> or even worse, as if we were asleep or uncaring,
> something that every airline attendant must see every day
> when he or she explains the safety features
> to a plane full of apathetic, even hostile, passengers.

They thumb the magazines, talk to friends:

"I have heard all this before."

But then:
> suddenly comes the preacher.

Jesus is reminding us not only of the Second Coming,
> but of his coming as Word,
> that which will break through and announce the kingdom of God.

Yes, this Advent, too, can catch us unawares.

Only those who are keen to listen with open ears will be made new.

How many "Second Comings" we might experience
    in the course of our lifetime, if only we would be open to the Word
    and its majestic revolution in our lives and in those around us.
Perhaps we have been a little dormant, a little complacent,
    even a little numb.
No wonder Paul, the great prophet for the Gentiles, says:
    "It is the hour now for you to awake from sleep.
    For our salvation is nearer now than when we first believed."

This is a day, then, for prophets and preachers and poets
    to point to God's inbreaking rule of justice for all people.
There is no more perfect penitential rite for this day
    than the one suggested in the Roman Missal:
    "Lord Jesus, you came to gather the nations into
    the peace of God's Kingdom; Lord, have mercy."
The celebrant is the prophet on the First Sunday of Advent
    and cries out for a habitation for all God's people.
Do we realize this wake-up call as an announcement of endless charity?
This is a sobering thought:
    All God's children, no matter what their color,
    or their faith or the numerous other diversities in our humanity
    can cry out with one voice:
    "Come, let us climb the LORD's mountain,
    to the house of the God of Jacob."
And so all of us are gathered here to witness what might be,
    what could be, what will be.
We are treading on the edge of a dangerous mystery.
The kingdom is coming—now.

It is hard to imagine what the crashing of the kingdom
    into our midst will be like as imagined by Jesus,
    the bringer of that Reign.
We have a clue since that Reign has already begun.

Jesus has ushered in that kingdom and given us
      the hope of its fulfillment.
The time has begun, although we don't know the hour.
We stand and wait in prayerful vigil;
      we long and search.
As one of the Prefaces for the Advent Season reminds us,
      "Now we watch for the day,
      hoping that the salvation promised us
      will be ours, when Christ our Lord will come again in his glory."
Whatever God's future for us may be,
      the coming of the Son of Man is going to be
      outside the box of even our most pietistic imaginings.

In Flannery O'Connor's short story, "The Displaced Person,"
      an elderly priest was standing on the back porch
      in a Southern household that owned a few peacocks.
The priest suddenly noticed that, without warning,
      one of the peacocks had opened his feathers into full splendor.
The peacock stood there beaming like the sun at high noon and
      "he raised his tail and spread it with a shimmering timbrous noise."
Then the priest said,
      "Christ will come like that."
Christ, who can resist your truth or your beauty?
Come, Lord Jesus.

GD

Questions for Reflection

1. How do I keep vigil for the Lord? Am I too busy? Do I let time, instead of God's mercy, overtake me?

2. Do I think of myself as a pilgrim or as someone who has already arrived? What is the difference?

3. Do I live out at night what I proclaim during the day?

Other Directions for Preaching

1. On that promised day, God will gather all nations together, even as we come together in Word and Sacrament.

2. There will never be peace on the earth until God's justice reigns.

3. The kingdom of God is beyond our imagining, yet is made manifest by Christ's saving power in the world.

The Voices of Advent
SECOND SUNDAY OF ADVENT

Readings:
Isaiah 11:1–10; Romans 15:4–9; Matthew 3:1–12

I sometimes think that there is a Catholic on the staff of *Jeopardy*.
Who else would come up with categories like "Saints,"
      or, as in last week's show, "Cardinals"?
That's why I'm waiting for the category on "Liturgical Seasons" to appear
      one day.
If it does, one of the trickiest questions will be about this season we now
      celebrate: Advent.
In the secular world, it is a word we never hear.
In the Church, we are celebrating Advent,
      but since Thanksgiving, society is celebrating Christmas.

Christmas Muzak is heard at the mall.
The commercials on kiddy shows tell your kids that Christmas won't be
      Christmas if they don't have a certain something from Toys R Us.
And once again, adults are told that they must buy a "salad shooter"
      for Christmas.
Oh, once in a while, once in a great while, you might find the makings of
      an Advent wreath
      amid the clutter of holiday decorations.
But mostly Christmas, not Advent, is in the air.
The voices of Christmas, especially a commercial Christmas,
      drown out the voices of Advent.

There are three Advent voices in today's scripture readings,

    three Advent voices that we all need to hear

        if we are to make any sense of our lives or the season we now celebrate.

The first is that of Isaiah,

    who lived in a time when Israel had some awfully weak

    and wicked kings.

Isaiah is a prophet who hopes that one day

    a new shoot of life will sprout from the old stump of Israel's kingdom.

He hopes for a king like David, who will rely not on political advisors

    but on God alone,

    a king who will bring justice and peace,

    especially to those who are poor and afflicted.

Isaiah's voice is a voice of hope.

The second Advent voice we heard today was that of St. Paul,

    who tells the Christian community in Rome

    that all the Jewish and Gentile Christians will live in hope

    and accept one another so that they will live in harmony and peace.

Paul's voice is a voice of hope.

The third Advent voice we heard today is a voice crying out in the wilderness:

    "Prepare the way of the Lord,

    make straight his paths."

Now, we can concentrate on how shaggy-looking John the Baptist was,

    or how strange his diet (grasshoppers and honey were not something

    you could fix up to look pretty even in a casserole dish with lots

    of parsley).

Or, we can remember how tough as nails he was when he told the Pharisees

    and Sadducees off

    by calling them a brood of vipers, which was as close as a prophet

    could get to a curse in those days.

But there must have been something more about this prophet with the
    strange clothes, strange diet, and nasty metaphors.
There must have been something about him that led all those people to go
    out to the wilderness
        to hear him and to be baptized by him in the river Jordan.
There must have been something about him that led people to hope.

After all, Matthew calls him a herald.
A herald in the ancient world was a special soldier to the king.
The king and his soldiers would go off to battle, while the people
    stayed at home.
When the victory was won, the king would tell the herald,
    "You ride back home ahead of us and tell the people the good news."
The people would stand, waiting, and the herald would gallop as fast as his
    horse would go.
As soon as he saw the people waiting in the distance, he would cry out,
    "Good news, good news, we have won, the victory is ours!"
John was God's herald.
    which is why he cried out at the top of his lungs,
    "Repent, for the kingdom of heaven is at hand!"
Repent, reform—for John this meant literally a turning around.
It was like going in one direction on a road and making a sudden U-turn.

It is an unfortunate but real fact that this season is one of the most anxious
    times of the year.
What to buy for her? For him? For them?
How will I find time to do my Christmas cards?
Should we invite them for Christmas dinner or not?
How can I put on my Christmas lights when I haven't yet raked the leaves?
'Tis the season to be very anxious.
There are more suicides, more family fights, more cardiac arrests
    than at any other time of the year.
We owe it to ourselves to live Advent not just in church but also in our
    daily lives.

A true Advent will bring us a true Christmas.

A true Advent will allow us to hear not just voices of anxiety
 but voices of hope.

A true Advent will help us to make a U-turn, a change in our lives,
 a turn to the One we are expecting and who is already in our midst,
 Immanuel, God with us.

RPW

Questions for Reflection

1. What voices do I hear competing with the voices of Advent? What are they saying?

2. Where do the voices of hope found in today's readings lead me? What is it they address in my life?

3. How can I add my voice to theirs as a voice of hope in our world? Who needs to hear this voice?

Other Directions for Preaching

1. Isaiah offers a profile of the one who is to come and draw together all nations. How do the prophet's images and the attributes he ascribes to the messianic king speak to our hunger for God's rule?

2. The reading from Romans offers a vision of the all inclusiveness of God's plan of salvation in Christ. How does that speak to our regard for all faith traditions?

3. What do we do with John's expectation of the one whose "winnowing fan is in his hand" and who will "gather his wheat into his barn, but the chaff he will burn with unquenchable fire"?

Word Never Broken
THIRD SUNDAY OF ADVENT

Readings:
Isaiah 35:1–6a, 10; James 5:7–10; Matthew 11:2–11

Gaudete ("Rejoice") Sunday, like the readings that inhabit this day,
    seizes upon the joy that the Lord is near.
The reading from Isaiah this morning presents us
    with a vivid contrast to that same prophet's message only last week.
The Second Sunday of Advent focused the eyes of the Christian community
    upward, toward that Holy Mountain and its swift magic:
    the wolf entertaining a lamb;
    the laughing adder dancing in a child's eyes;
    and most of all, the messianic infant's charge
    over a peaceable kingdom in a future, unfathomable place.

By contrast, the text of Isaiah today discovers
    the reality of God's saving power
    in the cracked contours of the present:
    the desert bursts into gorgeous flowers;
    pale hearts become strong; the lame jump and exult.
What was smashed has been rendered whole;
    what was broken has been restored to full power.
The God of all creation enters history.
The glory of Lebanon will be given them,
    the splendor of Carmel and Sharon.

12

And if the Isaiah text this week reveals a different vision
 of the God who urgently wants
 to liberate creation from bondage now,
 then we uncover another kind of Baptist this Third Sunday of Advent.
Where once he stood ecstatic at the shores of the Jordan,
 crying in the desert about a future way of the Lord,
 we find John now bound up in prison.
The John we met at the river was yoked
 to the dreamscape of the world waiting to be born.
We find John in another space this day—
 the unavoidable present moment—and in another kind of desert.
With no sight of a messianic presence,
 he appears seemingly without hope as he desperately
 searches the night from his prison grill
 for the once and future King.
So the cry of John is linked with the search for the Messiah
 when the Baptist sends his own messengers to ask Jesus:
 "Are you the one who is to come, or should we look for another?"
John finds his answer in the God
 that comes not as a vision of the future, but as redeemer,
 healer and sanctifier in the present moment.

Yet that was already a promise made by God, wasn't it?
It was announced by Isaiah
 and waiting to be fulfilled in Christ.
It is as if the prophet was told something in mystery
 that is now awaiting John in truth, far outside his prison fortress:
 "Here is your God," says Isaiah;
  "he comes with vindication;
 With divine recompense
  he comes to save you.
 Then will the eyes of the blind be opened,
  the ears of the deaf be cleared;

Then will the lame leap like a stag,
    then the tongue of the dumb will sing."
Once again, God's Word comes to free the captive,
    this time in the flesh:
Here is Jesus coming to God's people not as a dream child
    but as the Son who redeems his wandering brothers and sisters
    and sets prisoners free.
Here is Jesus charging human history electric with grace,
    restoring the natural world into a supernatural state.
Here is Jesus, born of a sinless woman
    and healing all he touches from corruption.

It is striking that, with as much as Our Lord would accomplish
    in his person in the Gospel, his words of comfort
    and liberation come to John not by Jesus' physical presence
    but through proclamation.
Indeed, these disciples of John must act *in the person of Christ*, in his place:
    "Go and tell John what you hear and see."
We have an echo of the commissioning of the Twelve
    that took place only one chapter earlier in Matthew's Gospel (10:7).
"As you go, make this proclamation," he tells his disciples.
    "The kingdom of heaven is at hand."
Yes, he now tells John's followers,
    "Go and tell...what you hear and see."
Human language, "Gospel-speak,"
    becomes the instrument of God's saving work,
    made possible by the living Word.
The holy child has come down from Mount Zion
    to become one of us.
    "How beautiful upon the mountains
        are the feet of him who brings glad tidings,
    Announcing peace, bearing good news,
        announcing salvation" (Isa 52:7).
Evangelization is the Word become visible.

That activity makes John's liberation possible and ours as well:

    God's saving intervention in human history.

Our God is near, we say today.

Where the Lord cannot be present, his works are told

    again and again and again.

Jesus spreads the Good News to John

    and evangelizes the Baptist's disciples in the process.

The Word comes near to John and to all those who were trapped,

    confined, and waiting for a messianic king.

So it is that Jesus reckons John as both the greatest and the least.

In the world of the past,

    where prophets announced the final coming of the Lord in the last days,

    there was no one greater than John the Baptist.

But in this new order, one in which God

    will sanctify all time by the servant King,

    the crucified Lord, John is the least.

Indeed, John lies on the fault line between

    the prophets waiting for a utopian transformation of Israel,

    on the one hand, and the disciples proclaiming God's healing,

    saving power in Christ, on the other.

The King is nearer than we think because the Word is alive,

    ready to be unleashed.

    We shout "Gaudete!" ("Rejoice") this Sunday not only because

    Jesus' entry into John's life is an image of the Word made flesh,

    now tumbling into redeemed human history—

But even more,

    we acknowledge that the Word has become Word:

    our liberation is possible by the very process of telling—

    and, beyond that, listening to—the Gospel.

This evangelization makes transformation actual

    if we allow ourselves to be converted by the Word.

Receiving the Word should come as no surprise to those
    who keep vigil and are attentive to the God that the author
    of the Letter to the Hebrews calls "a consuming fire."
Receiving the Word calls forth the solitary in us all, the Baptist in us all.
There was a devout monk in our monastery who died some years back.
Brother David typically took this season of Advent as a time
    to spend in his hermitage up in Monte Cassino,
    a small shrine not too far from the monastic grounds.
Brother David had a moderate-sized etching in his cell
    that depicted a man standing upright and being partially
    consumed by fire.
It was a powerful scene, this man seemingly
    imprisoned by a crowned knot of fire.
But far from being harmed, the man was clearly in a state of exaltation
    and joy.
As far as I know, the picture was without a title,
    and yet this depiction of someone in the throes
    of divine evangelization might well have claimed
    a question from a well-known story from the desert fathers:
    "Why not be completely changed into fire?"
For these flames are nothing less than the white heat
    of divine love, the Word, that consumes any barrier—
    from the fortress of Jericho,
    to John's damp prison, to those thick walls of our own making.
And suddenly, astonishingly, we have crossed the great divide
    into a joyful mystery.
No longer in a self-fashioned prison,
    we stand near a faithful maiden in Nazareth.
The expanding heart is also the open ear
    that receives the annunciation of the Word of God
    with fullness and joy.
"May it be done to me according to your word" (Luke 1:38).

And all flesh shall see what has been spoken:
  that His Word is never broken.

GD

Questions for Reflection

1. What has been my response to the new evangelization proclaimed by Pope John Paul II in the beginning of the third millennium?

2. Patience comes with great difficulty for many. Am I patient even in suffering?

3. What has John the Baptist to say to our contemporary world?

Other Directions for Preaching

1. Those who are patient will inherit not only the earth but the fullness of time as well.

2. Real proclamation begins when we can rejoice in the midst of hardship.

3. Those who wait accomplish far more than those who act.

Breaking the Silence
FOURTH SUNDAY OF ADVENT

Readings:
Isaiah 7:10–14; Romans 1:1–7; Matthew 1:18–24

Certain people had key roles in the early life of Jesus—
    among them are those we might call the "Advent people."
They show up every year in the Scripture readings for the final days
    of the season: Zechariah and Elizabeth, Joseph and Mary.
All but one speak to us—the silent one is Joseph, who never speaks a word
    in Sacred Scripture.
I thought tonight I would hand over the pulpit to him and give him a
    chance to talk.

(Pause)

Good evening.
I am Joseph, son of Jacob, son of Matthan, son of Eleazar—
    our family line goes back to King David, through his grandson
    Rehoboam.
Such a crowd here tonight....
I did not think there would be so many of you.
I am not used to such crowds—I am not like my son.
He was something in front of a crowd, you know.
I call him my son, but you know what I mean.
The story you just heard makes it clear how I fit in.
It was not a role I planned to have in life—it was both unexpected and
    unwanted.

You know, many artists have portrayed me to look like Jesus' grandfather.
Only El Greco got close. He made me young and vibrant.
I was so in love at the time all this happened.
When Miriam sent word she was pregnant, I felt pain, physical pain.
Tears came to my eyes, and I could not speak.
I loved her from the moment I first saw her.
We were betrothed, engaged—this was something a little different from
   today.
To be engaged in our day meant that formal words had been spoken.
A sacred commitment had been made.
In the Law of Moses, in the eyes of our people, Miriam was my wife.
But I had not yet gone to the house of her parents in procession and
      brought her to my home, to our bridal chamber, and consummated the
      marriage.
Now—with this message—that could never be.
The Law of Moses was clear: infidelity was adultery;
      an unfaithful woman was to be cast aside, stoned.
I could not do that to her, but neither could I dismiss the Law of the Lord,
      so I decided to divorce her quietly.
My heart was breaking.

For two nights I could not sleep.
Then on the third night, finally I slept. And I dreamed.
In the dream was this figure like an angel speaking to me:
"Joseph, Son of David,
do not be afraid to take Mary your wife into your home.
For it is through the Holy Spirit that this child has been conceived in her."
But I *was* afraid.
The Law of Moses told me to put her aside. That was God's Law.
But the angel went on:
      "She will bear a son and you are to name him Jesus,
      because he will save his people from their sins."
Later it was understood that all this was to fulfill the words
      of the prophet Isaiah:

"The virgin will conceive and bear a son, and they will name him
Emmanuel."
But that was only later; at the time it was not easy to hear, let me tell you.

I was afraid. I shared the same fear as King Ahaz.
When King Ahaz heard the words from Isaiah about a virgin
conceiving and having a son who was to be called Emmanuel,
he was afraid, too.
But for a different reason.
He was afraid of the kingdoms of the north,
which were threatening his kingdom, Judah.
The prophet Isaiah was calling Ahaz to trust in God—even to ask for a sign.
When he said, "I will not tempt the Lord," Ahaz was being more political
than pious.
Ahaz wanted to put his trust in Assyria.
But God was having none of it and answered Ahaz
that a child would be born of a young woman and that
he would be called Emmanuel, which means "God is with us."
Ahaz was being called to trust God, but he couldn't.

Now *I* was being called:
either to put my trust in the law given by God to Moses
or to put my trust in something new God was about to do;
either to put Miriam aside, or to take her into my home
and name the child Jesus.
Part of me said, "It's just a dream!"
But then I remembered my ancestor Jacob; he had dreams;
and my namesake Joseph, another dreamer;
and his dreams saved our people.

Well, that is my story. You know my decision.
What does all this have to do with you, you are asking?
Well, now it is your turn to choose to respond to some challenges:
Will you listen for the God who continues to speak to us?

What this often means is to wrestle with the complexity of your own life,
to listen to the wisdom of tradition, to the law of the Lord handed
down, *and* to be open to any new initiative God might be attempting
in you, through you.
*Will you put your trust in the living God who continues to work
new wonders?*
You live in an age when you can be tempted to put your trust
in many other things:
People are buying more guns than ever; "for security," they say!
Your leaders want to invest in more sophisticated missile-defense
systems.
From such ways, a new arms race is born. And more destruction.
And more despair.
Finally, *will you make this child Jesus, Emmanuel, central to your life?*

It will not be simple. It's not a one-shot deal, ending with a single response.
It wasn't for me and it won't be for you.
For me, the dreams continued to come:
"Joseph, wake up—Herod wants to kill the child—take him to Egypt."
"Joseph, wake up—Herod is dead—take the child to Nazareth...."
But, in the end, it was worth all the anxiety and all the gut-wrenching fear.
The child grew in wisdom and strength and grace.
And at the end, *my* end, that is, my son was there, and Miriam.
Not for nothing am I called the patron saint of a happy death.
And I can assure you, that you will find this as true now as it was then:
If you put your trust in God, you will surely discover
it's a wonderful life.

JAW

Questions for Reflection

1. How has God called me in my lifetime to put my trust in God?

2. Are there times when I have dismissed an inner prodding or invitation of grace as being "just a dream," having little substance or import?

3. What is central to my life? Who is at the center of my life? What role does Jesus Christ play there?

Other Directions for Preaching

1. The season of Advent calls us to let God be born in us and through us. Ahaz reminds us of the ability we have to resist giving our lives over to God and the capacity we have for concealing our real motives from God, others, and even ourselves. But God is faithful, God remains *Emmanuel*—"God with us."

2. Paul's beginning to the Letter to the Romans presents him as a slave, an apostle, and one set apart. All three titles reveal him as being aware of God's initiative in his life and conscious of a call to submit to Christ. Advent invites us to enter more deeply into the same awareness, but what forms can submission take today?

3. Matthew's account of the annunciation to Joseph reminds us as we approach the great feast of Christmas that this child came from God and invites us to share in the dawning of a new age. What might that new age look like?

CHRISTMAS

The Ordinariness of Holiness
THE NATIVITY OF THE LORD (MASS AT MIDNIGHT)

Readings:
Isaiah 9:1–6; Titus 2:11–14; Luke 2:1–14

This year many have declared boldly:
> "I'm not going to let a couple of fanatic hijackers ruin my Christmas!"
I find that an admirable statement of faith, and yet I think we have to admit
> that, while our Christmas celebration will be the same as it always is,
> this year, after the 9/11 attacks on America,
> we do come to the Christmas crèche with a different perspective
> about some of the most profound habits of our hearts.

For the past 104 days, reporters, theologians, preachers,
> and just ordinary folk have had to face one of the most
> perplexing features of human existence:
> evil itself.
Our president and his administration have unequivocally told us
> that our campaign against terrorism is a war against evil.
Others are not that sure.
They had come to believe in their cozy American lives that evil is a myth left
> over from the Middle Ages when people were not enlightened enough.
There is no such thing as evil, they said, only a mental condition that can
> surely be fixed with pills and psychoanalysis.
This preacher believes that there *is* something called evil,
> but that it is not easy to define.

25

I don't think we should use the word loosely or ascribe it to entire groups of
    people just because they are different from us.
And I certainly don't believe that evil is stronger than good.
That is a heresy condemned long ago by the Church.

What is so peculiar about evil is that it is quite often very ordinary in looks
    and intentions.
Essayist Lance Morrow reminds us that the videotape of Bin Laden and his
    cohorts who laugh at the Twin Tower disaster shows not the onstage,
    full makeup of a super devil, dazzling in lurid lights,
        but the backstage evil of mafiosi thugs.
Even the imagination of these criminals should not be praised;
        believing that, if they commit suicide, they would enjoy the instant
        Paradise of seventy-two virgins,
        is not imaginative; it is dim-witted.

Somehow we forget how ordinary evil can be.
Hannah Arendt pointed out years ago that Adolph Eichmann,
        the Nazi bureaucrat who managed Hitler's killing machine
        was a small, milquetoast kind of guy,
        nothing out of the ordinary.
And yet this evil man sent millions of people to the gas chambers simply by
    getting to work each day and doing what he was told to do.
There is a practical theological lesson here for all of us:
we, too, are capable of evil,
especially when we make evil something we think is inaccessible to us,
whenever we think evil is a monster bigger than life, living far away in a
    distant land.
No, it is in our very ordinariness, our getting to work on time, our lack of
    reflection and imagination, our dull minds and our refusal to finally
    do the right thing, that we are all capable of sin and evil.

Yes, we come to our Christmas crèche tonight knowing that evil
    can be ordinary,

but we also come knowing that holiness can be found in the most
ordinary of places and events of our lives.
Sure, there are angels and heavenly hosts praising God and saying:
"Glory to God in the highest."
But these angels were different.
They were not gazing into the clouds.
They were angels who were *bending near the earth* to touch their harps of
gold.
They were speaking to ordinary working people, shepherds.
And the sign the angels gave them was that of an infant wrapped in swad-
dling clothes.
In those days every child was wrapped in swaddling clothes,
which were strips of cloth to keep the child's limbs straight.
God came to us as a child held in restraint, vulnerable,
held back from even appearing as a god
but glimpsed only as an ordinary child.

In Luke's Gospel, Mary and Joseph travel a treacherous path because of the
census.
But once again, it is a story that reminds us that Mary and Joseph shared
the ordinary pain and suffering of so many others living in a country
occupied by military foreign forces.

Christmas reminds us that despite the evil in our world, grace abounds and
holiness is found in what is most ordinary in our lives.
Just as we have the tendency to make evil a superhero,
we do the same with holiness.
We think that only God and the saints are holy.
We forget that God came to us as one of us, an ordinary child, restrained,
whimpering, exposed to all of life's cruel humiliations.
Dorothy Day used to get furious when someone would call her a saint.
"You are trying to get yourself off the hook. I'm just an ordinary person.
You can do the same thing and live the same way as I do."

These past few months, the *New York Times* has carried a series called
"A Nation Challenged: Portraits of Grief."
Each day they have run the stories and photos of victims of 9/11.
The stories have left a powerful impact on those who have read them.
They are not just the stories of the superhero firefighters and police personnel,
but the ordinary persons lost in that disaster.

What is most impressive in these stories
is that loved ones and friends remembered how quiet and ordinary
these people were and yet also how good and generous and loving.
They lived temperately, justly, and devoutly, and were eager to do
what was good.
One wife said of her husband: "He never left the house without kissing
everyone goodbye. He made a trip to each of the girls' rooms to say
goodbye. And then he came to me."
Another tells the story of Antoinette Duger, who rose at 5:30 each morning
before work to spend time with her eight-year-old daughter, Megan:
"Each year she would gather with her mother and sisters to press their
own tomatoes and bottle a year's worth of sauce for each."
Antoinette's sister-in-law adds to this, writing, "It was a simple life well lived."

Evil, as we have seen, is not easy to define,
neither is goodness and holiness.
But we know it when we see it and experience it.

This silent night we find goodness and holiness in a scene so ordinary
that we might miss it
if it were not for our brothers and sisters who came before us.
They left us with a faith that is capable of knowing that in the very
ordinariness of our lives and times, goodness is more powerful than
evil, faith is stronger than death.

A stable can be a cathedral.
Bread can be God.

Our lives can be Godlike—
> All because of Christmas.

RPW

Questions for Reflection

1. When have I found evil in the everyday, and holiness in the humdrum?

2. The child presented to us as "wrapped in swaddling clothes and lying in a manger" reminds us how we are to understand who he is. What do these images say to you?

3. Who are the saints in our world today? Do you see yourself as one? As someone called to be one?

Other Directions for Preaching

1. Isaiah's people walking in darkness who "have seen a great light" continue to journey through time. Christmas proclaims the One who has brought justice and joy into our dark world.

2. In the Letter to Titus, the author proclaims that "the grace of God has appeared, saving all and training us to reject godless ways and worldly desires to live temperately, justly, and devoutly." How does this relate to our lives? What does this feast ask of us in response to God's initiative?

3. The opening words of the angel to the shepherds express the most common command in the New Testament: "Do not be afraid." How does the birth of this child take away our fear? What are the fears this birth speaks to?

God's Wondrous Word
THE NATIVITY OF THE LORD
(MASS AT DAY)

Readings:
Isaiah 52:7–10; Hebrews 1:1–6; John 1:1–18

Friends sent me a fax the other day, offering a listing of what familiar
    Christmas carols might have been called had they been written
    by government officials.
For instance, "Deck the Halls" becomes "Embellish Interior Passageways,"
    and "The First Noel" becomes "The Yuletide Occurrence Preceding
    All Others."
Would you rather have "Allow Crystalline Formations to Descend" or "Let
    It Snow," "The Vertically Challenged, Adolescent Percussionist" or
    "The Little Drummer Boy"?
It certainly brings out the various abilities of words;
    they can muddy and obscure, or clarify and enlighten.

Still, it seems that the more important something is to us,
    the more difficult it can be to render in words.
For instance, think of someone you love, someone you know very well.
Suppose I were to ask you to write a paragraph—a few hundred words—
    about that person.
What would you choose to say?
How long would it take to capture a person in a few hundred words?
Now, suppose I asked you to express the essence of that person
    in a sentence...in a phrase...in a word.

We are now in the realm of the poet, the artist.

Only poetry would attempt such a thing and be able to do it justice.

And that is what we have at the beginning of the Fourth Gospel:

> The work of a poet. A poet in love.

The writer chose to take a different approach in introducing us to Jesus of
> Nazareth from that of any other Gospel.

No Virgin Mary, no Joseph, no manger, no stable—

> no angels singing to shepherds out of the night sky—

> no star leading magi across a strange landscape.

John's Gospel starts out like Beethoven's Fifth: a bold chord.

It is like music. Listen to it:

> "In the beginning was the Word,
>> and the Word was with God,
>> and the Word was God.
>
> He was in the beginning with God.
>
> All things came to be through him,
>> and without him nothing came to be."

Hear the rhythm, hear the beat, hear the interplay of stressed and unstressed
> syllables?

It is fitting that the author of the Gospel of John is symbolized as an eagle.

John's Gospel soars, lifting us up on its wings,

> taking us back to the beginning of creation,

> when the world began with a word.

God spoke.

And the world began to be.

This word of God is a creative word that calls worlds into being.

This word called a people into being.

And after creation, God continued to speak.

God spoke out of the stillness to Abraham

> and two eighty-year-olds were chosen to parent a promise.

God spoke to Moses from a bush aflame, then in the event of the Exodus,
    and then in the words of Torah, and so began to woo the heart and
    soul of a new people.
God spoke through prophets like Isaiah and Jeremiah and Ezekiel and
    Amos and Hosea.
People would listen...for a while.
But then they would grow distracted or bored or tired of the message.
But God continued to speak in various ways, fragmentary and oblique,
    until God spoke most explicitly.
God said, "Jesus."

This Word came into darkness and darkness did not smother it.
This Word came and brought light.
It was a word that illumined and continues to illumine our world
    and our experience.
In the fullness of time, God spoke, and the Word became flesh.
And *we* have seen his glory.
Even in our own world of darkness, we have seen this glory.
In John's Gospel the glory of God is found in Jesus on the cross.
This is the hour of glory, of his being lifted up to draw all things to himself.
At that moment we saw and continue to see God's grace and truth.
The image of the invisible God is seen on the cross.
The truth of God and of us is seen on the cross,
    God who is love straight through,
    and we who wish to love God yet sometimes choose the darkness.
To us, God continues to say, "Jesus."
God continues to say this Word that can create a new world again and
    again, whenever that word truly takes on flesh, our flesh.

In a world in which a Chiapas happens and forty-five people, mostly
    women and children, are slaughtered, God says, "Jesus."
In the face of the memories brought back by the recent trial of Terry
    Nichols, making present once again the horror of that morning in
    Oklahoma City, God says, "Jesus."

In the face of children taking handguns into school
     and shooting down their classmates,
      God says, "Jesus."
In the face of a new racism aimed at the latest immigrants
     coming into the country,
      God says, "Jesus."
In the face of hatred, prejudice, and diminishment of all kinds that shrinks
     the souls of both victims and victimizers, God says, "Jesus."
Again and again and again, God says, "Jesus."
And the Word becomes flesh.
Here in this place, God says "Jesus" over the bread and wine that enters
     into our bodies.
And God breathes over us and with that breath God says "Jesus" over us.
And the Word once again and again and again becomes flesh—ours!

In the beginning was the Word.
And the word became flesh and dwelt among us, and we saw his glory.
And from his fullness we have all received grace in place of grace...
May we hear this word of love this day and in the days ahead.
May we make room for it to dwell in our hearts and fill us with its grace
     and truth.
Amen. Amen.

JAW

Questions for Reflection

1. When have you known the power of words? What are some ways words have had an impact on your life?

2. When God speaks "Jesus" to you and your life, what do you hear?

3. What grace and truth has Jesus brought to your life?

Other Directions for Preaching

1. The Christmas message is that God has sent glad tidings to us in the person of Jesus, the Son. Who are the messengers that continue to bring the good news of the Gospel to us?

2. What are some of the "partial and various ways" God has communicated with his people?

3. What is the world that does not know the Word? Where do we find this world in our own lives?

The Snowflake Family
THE HOLY FAMILY OF JESUS, MARY, AND JOSEPH

Readings:
Sirach 3:2–6, 12–14; Colossians 3:12–21;
Matthew 2:13–15, 19–23

The days around Christmas always abound in wondrous stories
    that warm even the coldest of hearts.
The Style sections of our newspapers tell of the Jewish community
    that volunteers to serve a Christmas meal at the homeless shelter
    so that the Christian volunteers can be with their families on
    Christmas day.
Or they tell the story of the little girl who gives her Tickle Me Elmo to a
    young boy she heard was very sick at Children's Hospital.

But the story that most fascinated me this Christmas was found in the
    Science section of *The Washington Post* two days before Christmas.
It was a report on the latest laboratory study made of snowflakes.
One of the reasons we make snowflake cutouts in school and feature them
    on Christmas cards
    is because a snowflake seems to be the perfect symbol of purity, sym-
    metry, and perfection.
The latest microscopic study conducted in Beltsville, Maryland, and
    Boulder, Colorado, used three-dimensional images of snowflakes, and
    what did it discover?

Only a few specimens of pure symmetry.
Most of the snowflakes are starkly imperfect crystals,
        many with riotous tufts of ice,
        patches of frozen carbuncles,
        or facets covered with ice zits.

The story of the most imperfect snowflakes
        lingers with me as I ponder this Feast of the Holy Family.
The images of the Holy Family are like our idealized image of the
        snowflake: pure, symmetrical, perfect, idyllic.
We remember the figures of Mary and Joseph from our childhood holy
        cards and of pictures that hung in our parish school rooms.
Mary was always weaving something, while Joseph held a lily in one hand
        and a carpenter's tool in the other.
These pictures always had the boy Jesus gazing at his holy parents,
        eagerly waiting to obey their next command.
The Waltons of Nazareth!

This idyllic portrait of the Holy Family was a favorite of parents and
        parochial school teachers.
It offered adults a ready-made moral lesson for children:
        "See, how peaceful and happy the Holy Family is!
        That's because Jesus, even though he was the Son of God,
        followed the fourth commandment: 'Honor thy father and mother!'"
Now there is no doubt that when Matthew and Luke wrote of the early life
        of Jesus, it was written as a story of idyllic obedience.
But is that the kind of perfect family that we all can aspire to?
Many a harried mother has reflected with a certain resentment
        that it would be great to raise one perfect child
        with the help of a perfect husband who was a model of chastity and
        hard work, gentleness and consideration of others.
And many a frustrated father, feeling defeated and tired,
        has looked upon this saccharine scene and found it unreal
        and even discouraging.

But when we begin to put the total Gospel record under a microscope,
> we get a more real and reassuring image
> of the Holy Family of Nazareth.

Matthew and Luke don't mask the fact that Jesus' illegitimacy was an early
> charge leveled at the Christian movement.

All of the Gospel writers, by their convenient silence, suggest Joseph's
> early death.

And in Jesus' public career, there wasn't a nuclear holy family
> but a whole village.

The evangelists portray a large, extended family, most of whom are unsym-
> pathetic and downright hostile to Jesus' vision.

Mark even writes that some of them thought that Jesus was crazy.

And Matthew's Gospel reading today does not portray a snowflake family,
> but a family constantly on the move for safety's sake.

We are not perfect snowflake families.

Even the family we revere today as most holy
> had its ups and downs.

The Holy Family lived through confusing moods and strange journeys,
> dealt with disgruntled cousins and people who just couldn't
> understand.

That is why this feast is not celebrated for the idealized family:
> a perfect mom, an honest dad, and an impeccable child.

This feast is for my aunt in Connecticut who was never blessed
> with children and
> who sits and brushes the hair of my eighty-eight-year-old uncle
> who is feeble and confused.

This feast is for a woman I met at Georgetown Hospital.

Her teenage son is about to have a bone-marrow transplant;
> she stays with him constantly while her husband simply cannot visit
> because of his fears.

This feast is for the lesbian couple whose adopted son is taught his prayers
> and alphabet with a commitment that puzzles their own parents.

This feast is for the single parent struggling to do the best she can to rear
    her children.
It is for the family whose father and mother are in a so-called irregular
    sacramental marriage
        but bring their children each Sunday for Eucharist.
This feast is for all of them and for all of us
        because we are "God's chosen ones, holy and beloved."
What we all have in common is the power of the Gospel and
        the pain of living close to or distant from those we love best.
At times it seems like an intolerable pain.
But in the end, there is nothing quite like a family, however it is composed.
Indeed, it is within our fragile families that we can begin to learn what the
    words
Holy Family mean.

RPW

Questions for Reflection

1. Has the ideal of the perfect family had any effect on my life? What does it mean to be a family in today's world?

2. Who are the *holy* families in your life that speak to you of how holiness can be found in the world?

3. Do you see the Church as a family? How so?

Other Directions for Preaching

1. Does the teaching and advice found in the reading from Sirach have anything to say to our lives today?

2. How is love the "bond of perfection"? If the longer reading is read, how do we reconcile the words directed to wives about being subordinate to their husbands with the rest of the exhortation in the Letter to the Colossians?

3. Consider how the holy family is ever attentive to the directives that come from God. Is this at the heart of what it means to be a *holy* family?

Seeing Through Mary's Eyes
Solemnity of the Blessed Virgin Mary, Mother of God

Readings:
Numbers 6:22–27: Galatians 4:4–7; Luke 2:16–21

It is interesting that on the day we begin a new year
    the Church celebrates the feast of Mary, the Mother of God.
This is the oldest title given to Mary.
As an official title, it goes back to the Council of Ephesus, held in 431.
Because Jesus is a person who is truly God and truly human
    and Mary is the mother of Jesus, she is recognized as
    the mother of God.
It is fitting to have a feast honoring her this way during the Christmas season.
It allows us to approach again this great mystery of the Incarnation from a
    different angle.
Today we focus on seeing through Mary's eyes.

Luke presents the brief scene of the shepherds suddenly showing up
    where Mary and Joseph were staying when the child Jesus was born.
Luke focuses our attention immediately on the child lying in the manger.
When the shepherds see the child, they began to tell Mary and Joseph
    what the angel had said to them earlier in the fields.
It is the heart of the Christmas proclamation earlier in Luke:
    "I proclaim to you good news of great joy that will be for
    all the people. For today in the city of David
    a savior has been born for you who is Messiah and Lord" (2:10–11).

39

This infant lying there, sleeping, is the one long awaited.

This baby, only a few hours old, who up until now has only cried, eaten, and slept

—this is the Savior, the Anointed One, the Messiah, the Lord, the Son of God.

Two responses follow from this message.

First is the response that all were amazed, astonished, "wiped out" in today's language.

No surprise there.

This is a fitting response to such a message applied to such an unexpected figure: a baby lying in a manger.

But then Luke moves Mary to the center of the picture.

Her response is an inner one: "Mary kept all these things."

Some translations say, "She treasured them."

Or, "she reflected on them—pondered them—in her heart."

Mary in her first hours after giving birth is brought a message that staggers all who hear.

And she quietly takes it in, to keep and ponder what it is all about.

Today it is most appropriate that as we consider this woman,

the Mother of God,

she is presented to us as one who began her unique role in this life

pondering what has just happened, pondering the meaning

not only of this life in her arms but also of her own life.

And she invites us to ponder what this child means for us.

By tradition, New Year's Day is a day to ponder.

It is a day when many of us once again make New Year's resolutions.

Sometimes these have to do with the physical side of life: weight loss, getting in shape.

But just as often our resolutions are more interior.

We might resolve to change how we act toward a particular person.

Or we might resolve to enter more deeply into a particular relationship, perhaps to get married, or to have a child.

Or we might resolve to take up a certain type of work or to change jobs.

This may be the year you decide what high school or college you will
    attend, the year to make a life decision about how to spend
    one's retirement.
All are important matters that demand resolve.

On this first day of the year, Mary is set before us pondering the meaning of
    her child.
And we are invited to do the same.
What does *he* mean for our lives?
The first response to hearing the angel's words about him was amazement.
But we have heard these words for so long that the wonder has worn off.
We cease to be amazed.
Can we stay still long enough to ponder this child—the treasure shared, the
    gift given—
    to recognize that, in this child who was born for us,
    and who wishes to be born in us,
    God has smiled upon us?

The words of the blessing we first heard this morning come true in this child.
The Lord does bless and keep us—in his Son Jesus.
The Lord does let his face shine upon us and is gracious to us—in his Son.
The Lord does look on us kindly and give us peace—in his Son.
These are the gifts this child brings to us as we begin a new year:
    Blessing, light, kindness, and peace.
So we can take a few moments and ponder the nativity scene in this church,
    and enter into the experience that Mary had.
We can ponder and treasure the words spoken by the angel:
"A Savior has been born *for you* who is Messiah and Lord" (Luke 2:11,
    emphasis added).

JAW

Questions for Reflection

1. Do we ponder the events of our lives as Mary did?

2. Do we see in Mary an image of the Church and hear the call to us as Church to ponder who we are in the world?

3. What do we see when we look upon the child in the manger?

Other Directions for Preaching

1. The book of Numbers invites us this New Year's Day to turn to God for the blessings we need as a world, nation, family.

2. Paul reminds us that the fullness of time has come. We live in the end time, and we as God's children have the Spirit of God in our hearts, who enables us to begin the year by calling on God as father.

3. On this day the Church celebrates the World Day of Prayer for Peace. The woman who gave birth to the Prince of Peace once more holds up her child for the world to see, calling us to resolve to do all that is possible to bring peace to our families, our Church, and to our world.

Epiphanies Come to Those Who Behold
THE EPIPHANY OF THE LORD

Readings:
Isaiah 60:1–6; Ephesians 3:2–3a, 5–6; Matthew 2:1–12

It's a wonderful story Matthew has given us: astrologers moving across a
night landscape, following a star, until they come to the place where
the child lay.
It is one of the two great Christmas stories—
the other being Luke's account of Jesus' birth, with its shepherds and
angelic chorus.
We hear this story of the Magi every year on the feast of the Epiphany,
a Greek word that means "a manifestation, a showing, a revelation."
In this story we see God revealing his Son to Magi, some call them astrologers,
those exotic figures who represent the pagan nations for whom Christ
came, to make Jew and Gentile into one people.
But it is more than a creative story that carries a theological message.
It reminds us of an ongoing reality: Our God is a God of Epiphany.

Have you had any epiphanies lately?
Something catches your eye.
You follow it, and it leads you on to something wonderful.
A photo in the paper—a person across the room—a star in the sky:
with such things, at times quite mundane, epiphanies begin.
Your journey may be several feet or several years.
At the end is wonder—joy—a precious gift.

But it begins with seeing something,
>   and it results in some sort of movement on our part,
>   until at last we arrive at the point we were destined for from the start.

Stars come in different shapes and at different times of the day.
Sometimes they simply shine from afar—
>   drawing us closer, or pointing us in a direction.
Sometimes they are quite close at hand.
I think of the beauty that so often surrounds me when I bother
>   to look about.
Sometimes it is found in a garden or a park, in a sunrise or the night sky,
>   sometimes in a visit to the zoo or one of the museums or galleries
>   nearby: Beauty that beckons.

Sometimes it is the words that move us along.
I thought it was interesting that the star by itself doesn't do all the work.
When the Magi get to Jerusalem, they need the help of the chief priests and
>   the scribes, and…help is given!
(Who would have thought the chief priests and the scribes would ever come
>   off well in Matthew's Gospel—a reminder that these were the people
>   who handed down the flame of faith in Israel for generations!)
And the chief priests and the scribes turn to the words of Scripture, words
>   that continue to guide us to Christ.
As do other words.
The words of a good spiritual writer—for some it is Merton,
>   for others Nouwen.
Among the living, I think of Kathleen Norris, Frederich Buechner, Anne
>   Lamott.
I enjoy listening to Garrison Keillor's words on public radio early in the
>   morning.
He usually sends me into the day not only knowing whose birthday it is,
>   but often he gives me some of their wise words, and always a poem
>   for the day.

His poems leave me laughing, pondering, even gazing over the edge at the
    Mystery that embraces all our lives, forever elusive, forever beckoning.
We need the help of words to bring us to the moment of epiphany.

And, of course, most often, it is the people that God puts in our lives.
When the Magi arrived, Mary and Joseph were there to pick up the child
    and place him in their arms.
We all have those people who help to put God into our arms.
Sometimes they are people that we only know from afar.
I am thinking of the impact that people like Cardinal Bernardin or Mother
    Teresa had on so many people while they were alive.
But sometimes they are just at our elbow, in the next room,
        around the next corner:
        the good friends who are there when you need them,
        or the stranger who passes through your life for only a short time.
Sometimes they have been with us forever, or stay with us forever through
    their words or the memories that continue to hold them for us,
        like what happens when a grandparent or favorite aunt or uncle or a
    teacher lives on in our memories.
Through their words or deeds or sometimes simply their presence,
    they have brought and continue to bring God to us.

One of the key words of Christmas is *Behold*.
"Behold, I proclaim to you good news of great joy," says the angel to the
    shepherds in Luke's Gospel (2:10).
And today Matthew tells us, "Behold, Magi came from the east...."
And then again a little later, after the meeting with Herod,
    "And behold, the star that they had seen...."
Often we do not behold what is before us and we miss the presence
    of the child.
Meister Eckhart once said, "The birth of Christ is always happening.
But what good is it if it is not happening in me. How can it help me?"*

---

*Quoted in David O'Neal, *Meister Eckhart: From Whom God Hid Nothing* (Boston: Shambhala, 1996), 45.

I think the same can be said of the Epiphany.

It too is always happening—God is at work,
     manifesting God's self through Christ
     and through those who belong to Christ—and that, of course, is all
     people and all creation.

But what good is it if I, if we, do not behold?

So this day, let us behold:

Behold the Body of Christ—in the bread of Eucharist.

Behold the Body of Christ—in the community gathered here.

Then, go forth and behold—Christ at work in our world.

The Mystery has been made known to all peoples.

For this we give not gold, frankincense, or myrrh but thankful hearts.

JAW

Questions for Reflection

1. The Magi needed both the star and the Word of God to arrive at their destination. God works through what speaks to our senses and what addresses our minds. What has served as your star or as guiding words on your journey to God?

2. People are often what draws us into the presence of God and helps connect us to him. Who have been some of the key people in your life who have revealed to you the face of God?

3. Consider the significance of the gifts the Magi brought: gold signified the royalty of the child, frankincense spoke to his holiness, and myrrh was used for burial.

Other Directions for Preaching

1. The feast of Epiphany speaks of God's plan that all peoples be saved. The role of Christ in God's salvific plan could be considered.

2. Isaiah speaks of the God who breaks through the darkness and the thick clouds that can cover God's people, the God who promises that we shall be radiant at what we see, and that our heart shall overflow at the riches that will be brought to us. What does this vision mean for us today?

3. The Magi continue on their journey, going back by a different way. What difference does it make for our lives once we have come into the presence of our Savior.

Watery Eyes
THE BAPTISM OF THE LORD

Readings:
Isaiah 42:1–4, 6–7; Acts 10:34–38; Matthew 3:13–17

He had that look in his eyes.
I could see him far off in the distance from where I was standing,
    hip-deep in the river.
It was that look that I rarely see here standing in the Jordan.
There are those who come who appear a bit curious.
Their faces search me, and then they search the cool waters.
Then there are the really needy ones.
They barely raise their eyes.
And then the defiant ones come, daring me to transform them,
    as if this baptism was about me.

But Jesus had another look altogether.
He knew why he was coming.
It was a look I recognized because it was also given to me,
a look that said he had a mission for his people.
It was a thirst for the living water
    that he himself was to bring to the people of Israel
    long after I departed the banks of the Jordan river, which had become
    my home.

I had almost given up, you know.
Voices crying in the wilderness become lonely after a while.

I began my days as somebody the city threw out, as refuse
    fit only for sand and wind
    and the wild things that grow in harsh terrain.
My message has always been repentance.
I could hear the prophets of Israel whispering in my ears at midnight.
Over the years, I saw that I was growing much larger.
The crowds grew too,
    but so did their hunger,
    and the sense of the nation.
Yes, I burned for the people of Israel the way Isaiah cried out for justice.
But how to reform a whole nation?
With water.

Once they even brought me a fake.
He had them convinced that *he* was the one
    who would bring his people into freedom.
He had been a big hit in Jerusalem, or so I gather.
But the tip-off came when we stood face to face
    and this one said that he didn't need any baptism.
His was a baptism of blood, he said.
It would come soon enough.
He said that he would eventually lead the people
    into victory over the Romans
    or anyone else who prevented Israel from becoming great.
He said he would bring about the destiny of God's people.
Many would die, but he would be a new king, he said.
We had a kind of face-off, at least for a while.
He eventually disappeared into the hills.
I heard that someone turned him into the authorities not too long ago.
Victory comes at a price even when it never comes.

But I knew Jesus was different not only by the way he looked
    but by what he asked for.
He wanted to be baptized!

This is the way the Messiah is going to come, I thought to myself.
The mark is not victory or the pretence of one, but humility.
Again, I heard the prophet say to me, as he said to so many before me:
"Here is my servant whom I uphold…,
Not crying out, not shouting,
       not making his voice heard in the street.
A bruised reed he shall not break,
       and a smoldering wick he shall not quench,
Until he establishes justice on the earth;
       the coastlands will wait for his teaching."
And so I waited for that teaching as well,
       shivering a bit in the early spring breeze.
Jesus told me again he needed to be baptized to fulfill all righteousness.
I was astounded.
It was *fulfillment* he was after.
It was the Law that he came to fulfill—a "covenant of the people"
       as the Lord told Isaiah.
It was all that important to him.
The people. The tradition. The covenant.

And so I plunged him down in the river.
Or rather, he had taken hold of the river itself by his own presence.
In hindsight, it seemed like such an isolated moment,
       but I forget that he deliberately wanted to be one of the many,
       a Messiah in flesh, just another of Israel's faithful sons,
       but God's truest witness.
When he came out of the water, he did not seem much changed,
       but there was a confidence there that, perhaps, I had missed before.
You know, it is not enough to just repent.
You have to trust that God is going to be there for you.
Jesus did not need to repent because he had no sin,
       but the righteousness that he showed us was that he trusted in God,
       deeply trusted in his Father.
When he came out of the water, he said very little.

He had watery eyes, all the while fixed on the sky.
I think I heard him say, "Thank you, Father."

There was, I think, another kind of righteousness fulfilled that day.
This was not the kind you find in the synagogues.
It is only born of water and the Spirit.
It happens because the Spirit of God has claimed
    the one who has been baptized in righteousness and faith.
I knew when Jesus came out of those waters
    that he meant to show me the meaning of what I was doing
    all those years in the desert;
    that those I was baptizing were also sons and daughters of God;
    that they had their natural parents,
    but this was a rebirth by adoption.
In a way, God was saying to *all* his children that moment
    when Jesus came out of the Jordan wet with the Spirit
    that we were all his beloved sons and daughters and that he was
    well pleased with all of us.
Jesus was our first and finest example.
God will never be pleased with any of us the way he was with his Son;
    he was the faithful witness beyond all others.
But he was the firstborn of the many who would come after him.
And we are all adopted because he came to sanctify the waters
    that I could only pour.

There is little for me to do here now at the Jordan.
I must become tiny.
My encounter with him has made all the difference,
    and yet I feel somehow empty.
What is my mission now?
I will continue to baptize those who come to me,
    but Jesus will take them into the kingdom that he alone holds
    as Son of God.
I know that something else awaits me.

I am told that danger awaits me in the city and the court of Herod.
So be it.
I fulfilled my part of righteousness too.
So far I have been baptizing in water,

> but perhaps I will be the first one to be baptized
> not in water,
> but fire.

GD

Questions for Reflection

1. An ancient hymn says that, "when Jesus comes to be baptized, he leaves the hidden world behind." That is to say, baptism engaged Jesus, and now the Christian community, in public ministry. To what extent have I claimed my role as a public witness to the Gospel?

2. Do I live as though I believe that "God shows no partiality?" How?

3. Righteousness is a key term in the Scriptures. What does it mean to be "righteous" in our contemporary world?

Other Directions for Preaching

1. In baptism God claims us as his adopted children—sons and daughters with responsibilities.

2. Proclamation is a dangerous practice in which more and more Christians should find themselves engaged.

3. Life is rooted in our covenant with God. What does this mean for our lives as a community, as individuals?

LENT

Passing the Test, Trusting the Spirit
First Sunday of Lent

Readings:
Genesis 2:7–9, 3:1–7; Romans 5:12–19; Matthew 4:1–11

Stephen Sondheim wrote a beautiful song for the musical *Sweeney Todd*.
It begins with these words:

> "Nothing's going to harm you, not while I'm around.
> Nothing's going to harm you, no sir—not while I'm around.
> Demons are prowling everywhere, nowadays.
> I'll send them howling—I don't care—I've got ways...."

It is a song that all parents would like not only to sing to their child,
    but to make a reality.
Every husband and wife, every true friend, would love to be able to fulfill
    these words.
But we know we can't.
We don't have control over harm, or over demons—in whatever shape
    they come.

Still it is comforting to take precautions, just in case.
A good friend of mine brought me back an amulet from Turkey to ward off
    the evil eye.
Some believe if you wear red or blue, these colors ward off evil spirits.

In Charleston, the porch ceilings were painted "haint" blue to keep
      the spirits out.

There is an age-old fear that evil spirits can take over a person or a family
      or a nation—and when one looks back to last fall, or even to the last
      century, that fear doesn't seem so far-fetched.

So we pay attention when two readings today feature evil spirits—the ser-
      pent and Satan.

But we do not see them taking possession so much as simply talking.

In the talking is the testing.

And so we listen, to catch something that might be meant for us.

The serpent comes to Eve and starts off quite innocently:
      "Did God really tell you not to eat from any trees in the garden?"

And Eve replies quite forthrightly: "It is only about the fruit of the tree in
      the middle of the garden that God said, 'you shall not eat it or even
      touch it, lest you die.'"

Score one for Eve.

But then the serpent plays his trump card (and you can almost hear him
      begin with "Aw, come on." He says,) "You certainly will not
      die!...[T]he moment you eat of it your eyes will be opened and you
      will be like gods who know what is good and what is bad."

And then he slithers off.

And Eve is left thinking and seeing that old piece of fruit in a different way,
      and before long it begins to look so good that she takes it and eats,
      and then, not to be left out, her partner Adam takes it and eats.

And they do come to know something—they discover they are naked,
      not just without clothes, but vulnerable, at risk.

When Satan comes to Jesus, he comes to test him, too.

But Jesus has been led to the wilderness by the Spirit.

Two things are important to keep in mind here, both from the past.

First, the wilderness was the place where Moses led the people of God
      and there they were tested.

Secondly, Jesus has just been baptized by John and the Spirit has come upon
   him, and he has heard a voice saying,
      "You are my beloved Son; with you I am well pleased" (Luke 3:22).
So Jesus is being tested as to whether he is truly God's beloved Son.
And the tests are the same ones that the people of Israel were given—
      Three tests but really about one subject: trust in God.
The first was about food: Would they trust God to provide it?
They didn't; they grumbled about not having any food,
      that God had led them out only to starve them.
The second was about God's presence: Would they trust God to take care
   of them?
They didn't; they kept saying that God had led them out there to die.
The third was whether God was really God, a God beyond their control.
And they rejected that possibility by setting up a golden calf and
      worshipping it.

Jesus is given the same tests.
The first has to do with food because he was famished: "Command that
      these stones become loaves of bread."
Jesus responds: "'One does not live by bread alone,
      but by every word that comes forth
      from the mouth of God.'"
      Jesus knew that God would feed him on a deeper level—with the
      words that come from God's mouth.
The second has to do with trusting God. And here Satan is very clever:
      He tells Jesus to throw himself from the pinnacle of the Temple, that
      God would send angels to rescue him, and that the crowds would be
      amazed and won over.
Jesus rejects him again, saying that he would not test God. God's plan
      would be carried out in God's time.
Finally—"Worship me," Satan says, promising all the Kingdoms of earth in
      return.
Again, Jesus rejects him: "'The Lord, your God, shall you worship
      and him alone shall you serve.'"

All these choices Jesus had to make, not just once, but throughout
    his ministry.
Would he do his Father's will, not manipulate either God or the people?
Would he trust God to be with him?
Would he choose the Father even though it meant the cross?
Look to Jesus to see what it means to be God's beloved child.
Look to Jesus to learn the lessons of survival in the wilderness.

The same test is given to us as individuals and as a community.
Where do we put our trust?
Do we trust God to feed us? To nourish us? To feed our deepest hungers?
Do we trust God to meet our basic needs or take care of us?
Do we really believe it when we pray the Our Father, which comes from
    Matthew 6 (9–13)? Do we really believe it when we pray, "Give us
    today our daily bread"?
And do we trust God to be with us—to be there in our dealings
    with others?
Or do we feel the need to manipulate, to dazzle them with our golden
    image?
Do we take it seriously when we pray, "Your will be done on earth as in
    heaven"?
Finally, do we trust God to be God? Or do we honor another god?
    Perhaps military might—a budget of $379 billion for defense this year.
And so much else gets slighted—from care of the poor, to care of the land,
    to care of the aging, to health care for all,
        to just treatment of prisoners, to….
Do we really pray, "And do not subject us to the final test, but deliver us
    from the evil one"?

God has claimed us at baptism.
We now have forty days to think about whether we recognize that claim.
And whether we want to renew our commitment to Jesus Christ.
Do we really want to be God's beloved sons and daughters?

In less than forty days we enter the Triduum, those three great days before
    Easter, and at the climax of these days, at the Easter Vigil or on Easter
    morning, we are asked:

Do you renounce Satan and all his works and ways?

Do you believe in the God who created heaven and earth, trusted you to
    care for it?

Do you believe in Jesus who suffered and died,
    who did not resort to the legions of angels the Father would have
    given him,
    who passed the test in the wilderness,
    who trusted in the Spirit at the last?

Do you believe in the Spirit who has been given to you and who wishes to
    work with, in, and through you?

We might say that the test goes on....
    demons are still prowling everywhere nowadays.
But God picks up the words of that song:

> "No one's going to hurt you, no one's gonna dare.
> Others may desert you—not to worry, whistle, I'll be there.
> Demons may charm you with a smile, for a while, but in time,
> Nothing will harm you, not while I'm around."

JAW

Questions for Reflection

1. When have you known the power of evil? When have you recognized its power to harm you and to work through you?

2. When have you known the power of the Spirit working in you to turn away the temptation to trust in yourself rather than in God?

3. How can you prepare this Lent to renew your baptismal promises at Easter?

Other Directions for Preaching

1. What is at the heart of the temptation in Genesis? Old Testament scholar Walter Brueggemann speaks of the basic choice that must be made between being an autonomous "I" or a covenantal "I."

2. What does it mean to speak of Jesus Christ as the New Adam? What difference does it make for our lives in the world today?

3. "Lead us not into temptation," we pray. How does that prayer gain urgency in our time, in our society, in our Church?

The "Vision Thing" of Lent
SECOND SUNDAY OF LENT

Readings:
Genesis 12:1–4a; 2 Timothy 1:8b–10; Matthew 17:1–9

The actress Demi Moore was in India the other day as a guest
    of a New Age guru.
She waxed philosophic in an interview in which she said,
    "We're all on a journey, and the journey is actually the destination."
While our Christian tradition would agree that we are all on a journey,
    it would part company with New Age religion
    that suggests that the journey is actually the destination.

Beginning with Abram and Sara, our ancestors in the faith,
    and with Jesus, our model in the faith,
    God calls each of us on a journey that has a destination
    beyond the journey:
    The destination is God's vision of where God wants us all to be.

Abram left his hometown with his wife Sara, relatives, and belongings
    and set out on a journey to a strange new land called Canaan
    because he heard a call from God.
God tells Abram and Sara that they were to become father and mother
    of a race of people
    as numerous as the stars.
Abram had every reason in the world to ignore that call;
    after all, he was seventy-five, and at this late age
    he and Sara had never produced one child.

How, then, could he become the father of a great nation?

The Gospel today also contains a call from God
> to Peter, James, and John on top of the mountain with Jesus.

"This is my beloved Son, with whom I am well pleased; listen to him," says
> the voice from the cloud.

Scholars argue over the significance and even the historical accuracy of this
> intense scene on the mountaintop.

It was a story, they say, that was meant to show the glory of the Risen Lord
> to the Christians in Matthew's time who were being persecuted for
> their beliefs.

It was, they argue, a kind of "hang in there" story designed to remind the
> Christians that there was an eternal destination to their journey
> of suffering.

Other biblical scholars have a different take on the transfiguration.

They say that it was an intense prayer experience
> that Jesus had with his favorite three disciples on the mountaintop.

Just as Abram had a vision that he held onto for the rest of his life
> despite his setbacks and sufferings, so, too, Peter, James, and John had
> experienced something heavenly on that mountaintop
> that sustained them through their difficult journey of faith.

I must confess that I find myself in the company of the second group of
> scholars.

Exactly a year ago next week, I was in Israel.

One day I went with a group of pilgrims to the top of Mount Tabor,
> where some have speculated the transfiguration took place.

There came a point where we had to get out of the tour bus and switch to
> taxis because the trek to the top of Mount Tabor is quite narrow and
> dangerous.

The taxi drivers who took us to the top were downright mischievous.

They whooped and laughed and drove quite fast, making all of us dizzy and
> the trip intoxicating.

When we got to the top of the mountain, we were told that some German
    pilgrims were occupying the church where we were supposed
      to celebrate Mass.
"Would you mind if you celebrated Mass outside?" the Franciscan sacristan
    asked.
"Mind? Are you kidding? We would love it!"

There on a rough-hewn altar of stone we celebrated the Eucharist,
    under a dazzling sun with clouds moving, overshadowing and envelop-
    ing our liturgy.
At one point, I stopped preaching and invited the people simply to look,
    feel, and breath this spectacular scene.
Coming down the mountain, we could now imagine the transfiguration.
In the midst of desert terrain, one could imagine how something like the
    transfiguration took place as an intense prayer experience
      on a high mountain, as a vision of things to come
      in the midst of adversity.
We can't all go to the Holy Land but we all need visions.
We are prone to despair without them.
Our men and women military in Bosnia, like all soldiers before them,
    carry a photo in their pocket of a loved one at home.
That photo is a reminder that their destination is not their muddy journey
    in Bosnia,
      but their reunion at home with their families.
Religious faith is something like those photos.
Abram and Jesus were able to stay on their journey of faith and convince
    others to do the same
      because they kept a vision in their pocket and took it out
      from time to time.

It's easy to get lost in the journey and forget our destination:
    For parents to forget who their children are and what they really need.
    For the elderly to become locked in their pains and not believe in
    God's promise.

For young people to view lifelike episodes from the *The Young and the Restless,*
without any sense of where God wants them to go.
For our country to dismiss the "vision thing" in an election year.
For our Church to forget its ultimate destination.

Lent is a time of almsgiving, fasting, and praying.
Not just saying our prayers but taking the vision out of our pockets.
Not so much talking to God but listening to what God has to say to us:
"This is my beloved Son...; listen to him."

Sorry, Demi Moore, you got it wrong.
There *is* a reason for our journey,
a goal of our life's struggles: God!

RPW

Questions for Reflection

1. Where has your journey brought you so far? Do you see the journey as the destination?

2. What has helped sustain your faith? Can you think of a mountaintop experience you have had in your life? Was anyone there with you, or did it occur in solitude?

3. What photos of faith do you carry in your pocket to help you hold onto the vision of faith?

Other Directions for Preaching

1. When God calls, blessings flow. Consider the case of Abraham. Consider where God's call has taken you, others around you, the community to whom you are preaching. Consider the blessings that have accompanied the call.

2. Consider the hardships we are called to bear for the sake of the Gospel and how Lent can help the community recognize the grace that has been bestowed to help us bear them.

3. We get a glimpse of glory at every Eucharist when not only the bread and wine are transformed but also all who receive them in faith.

Living Well
THIRD SUNDAY OF LENT

Readings:
Exodus 17:3–7; Romans 5:1–2, 5–8; John 4:5–42

A few years back I remember reading an article
    in the newspaper about a man who was in an accident in 1984
    and was just beginning to wake up from a semi-coma.
Incredible!
Like Rip Van Winkle, this young man was almost frozen in time
    and then woke up after a long period of sleep.
Consider, for a moment, what he awoke to:
    9/11 and its aftermath of terrorism;
    war-torn Baghdad;
    years of cloning, bombing, and Wall Street cheating.
At the same time, however, we would have to admit that the early 1980s
    were no paradise either.
In 1983, for instance, the U.S. Embassy was bombed in Beirut by terrorists;
    we invaded Granada;
    and there were years of cloning, bombing, and Wall Street cheating.
Little has changed.

No matter what the time, it seems, an unhealed wound,
    a kind of sinful restlessness, afflicts humanity.
Don Quixote searches in vain for his "impossible dream."
Millions of people appear to be looking for the ideal marriage partner,
    the perfect child, the utopian community.

Some disappear into a world of drugs, sex, or violence
>   in an attempt to calm their restlessness,
>   to satisfy a need that they cannot name.
Songwriter Bruce Springsteen characterizes the age
>   when he sings, "Everybody has a hungry heart."

This hunger, even at its most radically ugly,
>   might be called a search for God.
The contemporary theologian Father Ronald Rolheiser
>   terms this very quest for God a "spirituality."
For Rolheiser, it is impossible *not* to have a spirituality;
>   it is part of just being a person.
We know that human beings are capable of rational thought,
>   distinguishing right from wrong.
Yet the human subject also has a great longing—
>   what Rolheiser calls a "holy longing"—
>   an emptiness, that we fill with either good or evil.
In other words, there is a *lack* in the human heart, an empty space,
>   a hole that only God can both fulfill and sustain.
That is why St. Augustine tells God in the *Confessions* that:
>   "You were within me, but I was outside,
>   and it was there that I searched for you."
He speaks for us all.
Human history is a record of how people continue to search for God
>   in either ordered or disordered ways.
Sometimes they become mystics or prophets or Mother Theresas.
Other times they become terribly angry, addicted, or just plain bitter.

The Samaritan woman is one of us, isn't she?
This woman is all too human,
>   thirsting for water and looking for fulfillment that only Jesus can satisfy.
She says to him, "Give me this water, so that I may not be thirsty
>   or have to keep coming [back] here to draw water."
Clearly marginalized by her status as a woman and a Samaritan—

pretty low on the scales in first-century Jewish culture—
she articulates the ancient cry of all people.
Like Chaucer's "Wife of Bath," she has had five husbands;
     she is someone with a notorious, voracious appetite.
Ironically, this "outsider" and outcast in Jewish culture speaks
     for the long tradition of the Israelites in the desert.
The Israelites yearn for what no well can satisfy:
     "Why did you ever make us leave Egypt?
     Was it just to have us die here of thirst with our children
     and our livestock?"
She also echoes Nicodemus, a prominent Jewish teacher,
     whom she follows closely in John's Gospel,
     as one who needs living water in order to be born again from above.

Few of us have ever been thirsty for very long—
     trapped in thirst, as in a desert.
It is hard to imagine what the experience of water
     means to such a one who longs for water,
     where water is just out of reach.
In the marvelous film *The Miracle Worker,*
     Annie Sullivan faced a superhuman task of trying
     to teach her student, the young deaf and blind Helen Keller,
     how to understand the world around her.
They faced a tempestuous struggle of associations
     that just would not click.
Finally, there is a heart-wrenching moment in the movie
     when Helen puts her hands under a water spigot
     and gleefully shouts, "Wah-wah! Wah-wah!"
Everything had suddenly clicked.
It was as if Helen was learning about the most primal of elements.
Her teacher knew that, from then on, her student
     would begin to grasp the world around her;
     she found a meaning to created things and, like Adam,
     was able to name them.

It all began with water.

The thirst for living waters is especially poignant today, the Third Sunday
of Lent.

These texts are read precisely to remind the Church of the baptism we all
received and the waters that await our brothers and sisters
in the catechumenate.

These readings are wonderful examples to us of a universal hunger that,
perhaps, we have never fully identified for ourselves.

Many of us in this assembly were infants when we received those waters,
but all of us should know what it is like to yearn for them.

Indeed, our brothers and sisters waiting to be baptized are powerful witnesses to this Church community.

It is easy to treat those waters as a lukewarm, tepid stream
that we wade through absentmindedly.

Instead, these are powerful, living waters,
a mystic bath that gives everlasting life.

You, my friends in the catechumenate, are reminders of our holy longing.

These men and women before us are signs that turn our head directly
toward that moment when the risen Christ will lead us through the sea
with a pillar of fire.

We stand with you, beloved, in waiting, in anticipation of that great vigil
when water will flow from the Rock that is Christ Jesus.

Those waters are sanctified when the newly lighted paschal candle
is plunged into the baptismal font.

Christ sanctifies those waters so that no one will be thirsty ever again.

Sin is blotted out forever, and our hunger for holiness—for wholeness—
can be fulfilled.

We wait in hope and great rejoicing for that water that never ceases.

It is not water that is hidden in the ground,
but from God disclosed in Christ, present among us.
We send you forth, my dear friends,
but we will gather together at the river very soon.

GD

Questions for Reflection

1. Spirituality must begin with an acknowledgement of my basic desires. What do I want most?

2. How do I answer life's difficult and frustrating questions?

3. Where do I find myself thirsting, hungering for some meaning in my life? Do I allow those needs to touch my very core? Can I ask God for help?

Other Directions for Preaching

1. No one is excluded by Jesus—even those who are the most challenging and most marginalized. Who are the Samaritans today? How can we bring them living water?

2. Because of Christ's gift of redemption, the Spirit has gifted us with the grace to continue our prayer and works of mercy. Where is the Spirit leading this community?

3. The pilgrim people are always searching in the desert, but the only answer is utterly simple: living water—the love of God that has been poured into our hearts at baptism. How are we preparing to renew our baptismal promises at Easter?

Lent for the Baptized and the Elect
FOURTH SUNDAY OF LENT

Readings:
1 Samuel 16:1b, 6–7, 10–13a; Ephesians 5:8–14;
John 9:1–41

Each night on the evening news there is usually a report by some expert
    who tries to convince us of some new discovery
        that we never knew about.
One night we are told that scientists have discovered that salt and alcohol
    are bad for our health.
The next month, a new study shows that salt and alcohol are good
    for our health.

In our modern, enlightened age, we are bombarded by experts on all sides
    who are absolutely certain that what they know is true.
Peter Jennings, Dan Rather, and Tom Brokaw have all become experts on
    El Niño!
Our political pundits, our social and medical scientists, our congressional
    leaders and lawyers are just as dogmatic as any former member of the
    Inquisition or the Salem witch trials.
Infamous Rush Limbaugh announces each of his "shows" by referring to
    himself as "all-knowing."
There have been endless speculations about why the majority of Americans
    still support

President Clinton while most Americans hold the media pundits
in low esteem.
I have my own fairly simple analysis: most of us are turned off by the
so-called experts from both sides of the controversy,
who seem so sure that they have all the answers.

That is why I was mildly amused recently when one day a bunch
of know-it-all astronomers
announced that 1997XFII, a mile- to two-mile-big asteroid was going
to come within 30,000 miles of the earth
and might even (with a good wind) slam into earth in the year 2028.
The very next day, it was announced that the scientists had miscalculated
by a good 600,000 miles.
Who can doubt now that we need to beef up our math and science programs
in our American schools?

Today's reading about the blind man brought to enlightenment by Jesus
carries with it the strong theme of John's whole Gospel:
From darkness to light in Christ.
But it is also about knowing and not knowing.
The word "know" is found in seven of the story's verses.
Who knows and *how* one knows are central to the story.

At first the man tells the religious leaders that he doesn't even know where
Jesus is.
The only thing the man clings to is his experience:
"One thing I do know is that I was blind and now I see."
The man is on a journey of faith; he grows in knowledge of Jesus.
At first he calls Jesus a man, then a prophet, and finally, "Lord."
The religious leaders, the experts of the day, never make the journey
with Jesus.
They are so certain, so smug in what they think they know
that their very certainty prevents their openness to Jesus
and where his authority comes from.

The liturgy we celebrate today is about knowing who we are and who God
is in our lives.
This Fourth Sunday of Lent has ancient prayers and readings.
This same gospel story of the blind man was proclaimed and preached
about in the fourth century
by St. Augustine, who said in his homily:
"Now I am speaking, of course, to both faithful and catechumens.
What did I say of the spittle and mud? That the Word became flesh.
That is what the catechumens learn. But it is not enough for them to
have been anointed; let them hasten on to the font if they seek the
Light."*

Notice that Augustine addressed both the faithful and those who were
preparing for full communion in the Church.
Our Elect who were anointed today as a preparation for the Easter baptism
and our candidates who will enter full communion at the Easter Vigil
are wonderful reminders to us old-timers in the Church
about what our Christian lives are all about:
It is about growing, growing in the knowledge
that comes from communion with Christ.

We heard St. Paul tell us today that once we were in darkness, but now by
baptism we are in the light of the Lord.
But then he gives us an invitation: to live as children of the light.
Just because we are in the Church, we are Christians, we are Catholics,
does not mean that we are not prone to darkness, to sin,
to the foolishness of thinking we know it all.
The only guarantee our baptism gives us is that it gives us the possibility
and invitation to live as children of light, always knowing that we are
not there yet, that we need to learn, need to grow, need to change.

---

*Tractates 44.2.3

Lent is a time for all of us, both baptized and those preparing for baptism,
    to ponder
        both what we know and what we don't know about ourselves and
        about our God.
Frederick Buechner, a minister, poet, and novelist, once wrote about Lent as
    a time to ask ourselves important questions.
I invite you to reflect silently on some questions he offers:

> "If you had to bet everything you have on whether there is a God or
>   whether there isn't, which side would get your money and why?
> When you look at your face in the mirror, what do you see in it that
>   you most like and what do you see in it that you most deplore?
> If you had only one last message to leave to the handful of people who
>   are most important
> to you, what would it be in twenty-five words or less?
> Of all the things you have done in your life, which is the one you
>   would most like
> to undo? Which is the one that makes you happiest to remember?
> Is there any person in the world, or any cause, that, if circumstances
>   called for it, you would be willing to die for?
> If this were the last day of your life, what would you do with it?"*

To begin to listen to our own answers to such questions is to begin to know
    what the journey of Lent is all about, and to know what about our-
    selves and about our God that is most important.
It is to begin to know Amazing Grace, since I too "once was lost but now
    I'm found, was blind but now I see!"

                                                                        RPW

---

*Frederick Buechner, *Whistling in the Dark: An ABC Theologized* (San Francisco: Harper &
Row, 1988), 74–75.

Questions for Reflection

1. Have you had any experiences where what you were sure you *knew* prevented you from coming to wisdom?

2. Would you add any other questions that might help you to know yourself more during this season of Lent to the six that Frederick Buechner raises?

3. Can you look back and recognize times when you moved from the darkness to the light of Christ? Who was there to help you? Are there people you now can help?

Other Directions for Preaching

1. The story of the prophet Samuel is placed here with the story of the blind man, reminding us that even those anointed by God can be seers who do not see. The challenge is to ask for the grace to see beyond appearances, to see into the heart—this is a gift of God.

2. Paul's bold statement—"You once were darkness but now you are light in the Lord"—invites us to take seriously the responsibility of what it means to live as a baptized Catholic. How are we called to "expose the fruitless works of darkness" in our own time?

3. Coming to sight is a gradual occurrence for the man born blind. Is this more often the case with us—both as a community and as individuals?

A Death in the Family
FIFTH SUNDAY OF LENT

Readings:
Ezekiel 37:12–14; Romans 8:8–11; John 11:1–45

We have just heard a story of a death in the family.

It was a sudden death, and devastating to the surviving family members.

The grief of the two sisters of Lazarus cannot be avoided—

> nor their anger: "If you had been here, my brother would not have died."

The impact that a death in the family brings is worth thinking about.

We can experience this impact vicariously in two movies showing in our area.

> *In the Bedroom* deals with a murdered son whose death results in further destruction and desolation for almost everyone who has loved him, especially his parents.

The Italian film *The Son's Room,* however, while revealing the power of death to separate and isolate family members from one another in their grief, takes us in a different direction.

It holds out the possibility of grace to transform and transcend such a devastating loss.

What stays with you in both movies is the power of death to rend the lives of the living,

> to leave a gaping wound that might never be healed.

Jesus cries twice in Scripture that we know of—

> once over Jerusalem and here at Lazarus's death.

He cries in the face of a death in a family that he loved.

He cries because he has lost his friend,

But perhaps there is another reason he cries,

     having less to do with the dead man than with those around him.

Jesus is moved to tears because he sees the power of death over the living,

     and how it effects their relationship with him.

In this story the power of death blocks everyone from coming to full faith

     in Jesus.

This conclusion might come as a surprise, since Martha is often held up

     as *the* example of faith in Jesus—but consider the story again.

Jesus hears that Lazarus is sick, but from the outset he says,

     "This illness is not to end in death, but is for the glory of God,

     that the Son of God may be glorified through it."

From the beginning Jesus says that Lazarus will not be conquered

     by death's power.

He knows that what is happening to Lazarus is for God's glory, and that

     death is not the end.

Then he waits two more days before suddenly deciding to return to Judea.

The disciples oppose his decision:

     "The Jews were just trying to stone you, and you want to go back

     there?"Jesus replies, "Lazarus is asleep, but I am going to awaken

     him."

And when they press him on this, he finally says, "Lazarus has died.

     And I am glad for you that I was not there, that you may believe."

The purpose of this event is to lead to faith, but the disciples

     do not understand.

We see this in Thomas' response: "Let us also go to die with him."

From the very beginning, then, the focus of those who surround Jesus is on

     death—not on coming to belief, but on death embracing all of them.

When Jesus gets there, Martha comes out.

Traditionally, this conversation is seen as a great expression of faith.

But Johannine scholar Francis Moloney argues that it is no such thing.

No one in this story comes to full belief, and especially not Martha.

Martha's conversation with Jesus starts with a rebuke,
> "If you had been here, my brother would not have died."

She is looking to Jesus as a miracle worker, one who cures sickness.

When Jesus says, "Your brother will rise," she replies, "I know he will rise,
> in the resurrection on the last day."

Then Jesus, the Word of God, says:
> "I am the resurrection and the life; whoever believes in me, even if he
> dies, will live,
>
> and everyone who lives and believes in me will never die.
>
> Do you believe this?"

And Martha responds, "Yes, Lord. I have believed that you are the Christ,
> the son of God, the one who is coming into the world."

But Martha does not express belief in Jesus as the resurrection and the life.

She says what she *has* believed about Jesus for some time, that is,
> her long-held beliefs.

She expresses belief in Jesus in the terms used at that time for the Messiah.

These are expressions used by others who do not have full faith.

So, too, with Martha; it is not full faith she expresses,
> but only a partial one.

This is confirmed when they get to the tomb and she responds to Jesus'
> command to roll away the stone by saying, "Lord, by now there will
> be a stench; he has been dead for four days."

And Jesus rebukes her:

"Did I not tell you that if you believe, you will see the glory of God?"

Martha has only been able to go so far on the way to faith.

Mary goes further.

When Martha tells her, "The teacher [a minor title] is here,"
> she responds immediately and goes to him.

She kneels at his feet and repeats part of what Martha says:
> "If you had been here, my brother would not have died,"
> but she does not ask that Jesus be a miracle worker.

It looks like Mary has it right—she trusts in Jesus.

But then she is pulled back in the grief of the moment; she goes back to
     weeping.
And the Jews with her are weeping.
And they express their stance: "Could not the one who opened
     the eyes of the blind man have done something
     so that this man would not have died?"
For them, Jesus is no more than a miracle worker.

Here we see the power of death over the living.
There is not one person who is not taken up in grief.
There is no one who trusts in Jesus as the resurrection and the life.
Not the disciples, not Martha, not Mary, not the Jews…no one.
The power of death overwhelms them all.
Death has conquered their hearts. Death has swallowed them up.
Then Jesus prays, "Father, I thank you for having heard me. I know that
     you always hear me;
     but because of the crowd here I have said this, that they may believe
     that you sent me."
And finally comes the cry: "Lazarus, come out."
And then the dead man came forth, hands and feet bound, face covered,
     swaddled in the bonds of death and lurching out from the darkness of
     the grave.
The tears of Jesus at the failure of all present to put their trust in him
     gives way to a word of liberation: "Untie him and let him go [free]."

Death continues to be the greatest threat to faith—to *our* trusting God.
The power of death is omnipresent in our own day:
     the endless series of deaths in Israel and the West Bank and Gaza—
     an escalating spiral of vicious bloodletting;
     the power of death in our own country, as we turn more and more to
     military power
     and defense spending to bring peace to the world, with a defense
     budget more than that of the next sixteen countries combined.

The power of death has come into our Church in the wake of the tragic
  occurrences of pedophilia and the death of trust between hierarchy
  and laity.
The power of death crushes life, not only the life of those who die,
  but of those who surround them.
In the face of death, Jesus continues to proclaim: "I am the resurrection and
  the life."
And then to ask us who gather around the table, "Do *you* believe this?"

Lent is a season that allows us to linger at the various graves that life has
  set before us: the death that ends a life, that severs a relationship, that
  strangles a spirit.
Lent calls us to look at death and then to look into the face
  of the One who says,
    "I am the resurrection and the life."
At the end of Lent we are invited to answer his question, "Do you believe
  this?" to profess our faith in the risen, crucified Lord,
    who broke death's chains and walked from the grave
    into the dawn of a new day.
And in the meantime, we continue to do our Lenten preparation:
  to fast, to pray, and to reach out in generosity and care toward those
  in need.
To this end, on this day, we receive the bread of life and the cup
  of salvation—to renew our life in Christ,
    to continue our transformation into a community of resurrection and
    new life.

JAW

Questions for Reflection

1. Have you felt the pain of a death in the family?

2. How do you answer Jesus' words of promise and challenge: "I am the resurrection and the life. Whoever believes in me, even if he dies will live, and everyone who lives and believes in me will never die. Do you believe this?"

3. Jesus is more than a wonder-worker, more than the long-awaited Messiah; how does Jesus who is the resurrection and the life make a difference in how you live your life?

Other Directions for Preaching

1. Death comes not only for individuals but for the community, for the body and for the spirit. Death can take many shapes. Ezekiel witnesses to the death that came to Israel through exile and he proclaims the promise of God to "put the spirit in you that you may live."

2. Paul's contrast between the flesh and the spirit calls for understanding: "You are not in the flesh; on the contrary, you are in the spirit, if only the Spirit of God dwells in you." This text witnesses to the promise of baptism that rings out for both the elect and all those renewing their baptismal promises.

3. God is a God of the living, not of the dead. God has the power to give life, to restore life, and to renew life. Lent calls us to a new springtime in our personal lives and our lives as members of the Church and of our country.

A Piece of Palm and a Passion
Palm Sunday of
the Lord's Passion

Readings:
Matthew 21:1–11; Isaiah 50:4–7; Philippians 2:6–11;
Matthew 26:14—27:66

A piece of palm and a passion—
>that is what makes today different from all other Sundays.

Each is important in itself.

But neither can be separated from the other.

First the palm.

A slender thing, really.

We used to call it a sacramental when I was growing up
>because it was blessed.

And what do you do with it?

Take it home and tuck it behind a crucifix or a holy picture,
>or put it on the dresser for a few days, until it blends
>into the surroundings.

Some of it will be burned next Ash Wednesday and made into ashes.

Its importance is in its symbolic power:
>a reminder of that day when Jesus entered Jerusalem to waving palms
>and whooping cries of "Blessed is he who comes in the name of the
>Lord."

Today we remember that day, but, more than that,

to take up the palm is to take up that cry:
"Blessed is he who comes in the name of the Lord."

Then, there is the Passion—Matthew's this year.
Why hear this story of Jesus' suffering and death every year?
Because suffering and death are the test of one's deepest values,
    the crucible we all have to face.
The passion of Jesus tells us how Jesus faced death
    and the sufferings of death.
The passion is, literally, crucial for the Christian life.
Matthew's passion shows us Jesus overwhelmed with suffering,
    dying in pain.
Matthew's passion needs to be looked at squarely;
    first of all because it has fueled anti-Semitism in our history.
This was not the intent of Matthew, nor can this ever be justified.
When we hear Matthew's passion, we can look at the attitudes, actions, and
    reactions of each character to see how light is shed on our own lives,
    to see how they might reveal something of our own response to Christ.

In Matthew's passion we find various portrayals.
There are the disciples:
    throughout the Gospel they are presented as having "little faith"
    (which is a step up from Mark's Gospel where they have no faith).
In the darkest hour, they bail out.
Consider both Judas and Peter—both caved in when the chips were down.
Judas has proved more intriguing to our age; musicals have been built
    around him.
But perhaps Peter may be more easily identified with by most of us—
    good intentions but not so good in following through.
Still Peter gives us all hope.
While Judas went out and hung himself, Peter went out and wept,
    and became the rock on which the early community was built.

As for the others, the final image we have of them here is one of flight,
>   but that too will be transformed to one of reconciliation and renewal
>   on Easter.
Failure can give way to fidelity.

The opposition is found among the chief priests and elders, the leaders.
They plot in secret, turn one of his own against Jesus,
>   set up false witnesses at the trial before the Sanhedrin,
>   taunt and abuse Jesus, persuade Pilate to condemn him,
>   turn the crowd against Jesus, and mock him on the cross.
But remember, they serve to remind us how we, too, can be closed off to
>   him and his message
>   and fail to respond to the grace the Gospel offers us.
The opponents of Jesus invite us to examine our values as a nation,
>   our tendency to resort to violence to solve our problems,
>   whether it is crime at home or fear of hostility abroad.

It is often the unexpected ones who respond with courage and generosity,
>   like the women who followed him from Galilee: Mary Magdalene,
>   and Mary the mother of James and Joseph, and the mother of the sons
>   of Zebedee.
Two of them show up at the cross, at the burial, and at the empty tomb;
>   they are sent to proclaim the good news of his resurrection.
(Jewish tradition demanded two witnesses to important events.)
There are also the centurion and the soldiers with him who move from fear
>   to faith: professing, "Truly, this was the Son of God."
There is the wife of Pilate, whose nightmare sent her running through the
>   governor's mansion to her husband's side:
>   "Have nothing to do with that righteous man."
Did she see just her husband's career or their whole world
>   coming to an end?
Or was it simply another instance of an outsider responding to the
>   movement of grace?

Finally, there was Joseph of Arimathea, the rich man who summoned
     courage to face up
          to fickle Pilate and to lay Jesus' body in his own new tomb.

All of Matthew's people have something to say to us,
     if we stop and spend time with them.
The passion was written for all who would hear the Gospel,
     calling us to examine ourselves in relation to the characters of the
     Gospel and to the ways in which we are invited to respond to the call
     of grace in our lives.

But at the center of the passion is Matthew's Jesus,
     the obedient son, faithful to the Father until death.
Matthew's passion is a story of fidelity
     Jesus as the faithful Son whose blood will be shed for the sake
     of the kingdom.
In the garden, Jesus prays that the Father's will be done;
     that is what matters.
When arrested, Jesus refuses violence so that the Scriptures will be fulfilled.
He stands before the Sanhedrin and accepts his role as Christ and
     Son of God.
He stands silent before Pilate and the people as they condemn him.
He ends his life with the words of Psalm 22, the prayer of the Just One
     who holds onto trust in God, despite the assaults of his enemies.
In Matthew, Jesus is presented as fulfilling Sacred Scripture; he is the Son of
     God, royal Messiah.
He is *the* Israelite, remaining true to God, the longed-for redeemer of Israel
     and the ultimate expression of God's will for his people.
In Matthew Jesus is put to death, but this death is foreseen and accepted.
Jesus is the servant, his mission finding completion in the cross that frees
     people from sin and death.
At his last meal Jesus proclaims how his blood is to be poured out for many
     for the forgiveness of sins.

Jesus is the servant of Isaiah who gave his back to those who beat him,
     who did not shield his face from buffets and spitting.
At his death we see this freedom in the signs that Matthew records:
     The earth is split and the tombs broken open, liberating the dead.
Jesus is the one whose death brings salvation.
In his suffering and dying, Jesus is the dawn of a new age.
He fulfills the words he spoke to the Sanhedrin:
     "You will see the 'Son of Man seated at the right hand of Power.'"
For greatness is not to be found in oppressive power.
The powerful of this earth are revealed to be bankrupt, impotent.
They cannot contain him in the place of death.

Jesus' death ushers in a new age—the age of sin and death has given way
     to an age of forgiveness and new life.
Jesus, whose obedience reveals God's will for the world....
Jesus, whose service signals the inbreaking of the kingdom of God into our
     world....
Jesus, who suffers and dies for the ransom of many—
     From this death comes new life and new hope.

Those who pick up the palm are called to listen attentively to the passion.
Those who take home the palm are to live lives of obedience,
     sons and daughters who listen to hear God's will for them,
     who follow him by lives of service, walking the way of justice and
     peace, finding life by giving life.
Those who pick up the palm are to live as children of the new age,
     living in hope and commitment.
Taking this slight piece of greenery carries with it a proclamation to the
     world.
It proclaims who you are and who you will declare yourself to be on Easter:
     a disciple of Jesus, risen and crucified Lord, the Son of God.

JAW

Questions for Reflection

1. How does the palm call me to express my commitment to Jesus, Son of God?

2. Which of the characters in the passion speaks most to me at this time of my life?

3. Is there a particular moment in the passion that invites me to stand before it and contemplate its importance.

Other Directions for Preaching

1. The prophet Isaiah offers one of the songs of the Suffering Servant, who knows how to speak to the weary a word that will rouse them because he has heard God's word, has trusted in God as his help, and will not be put to shame. These are all gifts from God.

2. Paul uses a hymn in the reading from Philippians to speak of the downward-upward movement of Jesus' life, his humiliation and exaltation, his self-emptying and fulfillment in doing the Father's will. The arrogance and disobedience of the first Adam are replaced by the humility and obedience of the second Adam. How do these tensions continue to challenge and shape the life of the community of faith?

3. Jesus was seen as a threat to Roman Empire. How should the followers of Jesus continue to threaten those structures that oppress and control in the name of peace and security?

EASTER

Where Is Easter in *USA Today?*
EASTER SUNDAY

Readings:
Acts 10:34a, 37–43; 1 Corinthians 5:6b–8;
John 20:1–9

About two weeks ago I got a phone call from a reporter from *USA Today*
  who wanted an interview.
Since the story was not about this parish, I decided to go ahead with the
  interview.
The reporter was working on a story about
what preachers say in their sermons on Easter Sunday.
I thought: at last, a serious story about the central act of faith in the
  Church!

But the Passover of Jesus is not an easy story to cover.
The media demand images: something we can see and feel and touch.
But what is there to report or to see of Easter?
Today's Gospel reminds us that the story of the resurrection begins with an
  empty tomb, with Mary Magdalene who weeps not just because Jesus
  has died, but because she believes someone has taken his body from
  the tomb.
That is why the story of Easter is presented in the media
  with Easter-egg hunts, wide-rimmed flowered hats,
  and an occasional shot of the Pope washing feet, carrying a cross,
  or giving his Easter greetings to the world.

According to the reporter, some ministers said that what they try to do in
    their Easter sermons
        is to explain or prove the resurrection of Jesus.
Some preachers told her that it would take at least thirty minutes to do this.
At that point, I then referred the reporter to the Scripture readings we pro-
    claim on Easter Sunday.
After all, the first reading from Acts is one of the earliest Easter sermons
    recorded.
Those preachers who think they have to explain or prove the resurrection in
    thirty minutes
        could certainly take a clue from St. Peter.
It took Peter just one minute to give the *kerygma*, a Greek word which
    means "the kernel,"
        the kernel of what it means to be a Christian and to believe in the
        Risen Lord.

In the sparse and economical language favored by *USA Today,*
Peter reports what the early Christians believed:
        that Jesus, filled with the Holy Spirit and power, preached, did good
        things, and healed those gripped by the devil.
Then his enemies killed him by hanging him on a cross, but after three days
God raised him up, and he was seen by his followers who now must give
        witness to Jesus in whose name we have forgiveness of sins.
Notice how Peter does not try to prove the resurrection or explain it.
Peter doesn't even refer to what Jesus taught but to what he did and what
        God did for him:
God transformed the scandalous death of Jesus on a tree
        to a glorious resurrection in which all of his followers share
        the same power of transformation.
The resurrection is about Christ and it is about us!

What do you tell a reporter about what to preach on Easter Sunday?
I referred her to our second reading today from Paul's Letter to the
    Corinthians.

Again, Paul is speaking about the resurrection of Christ but also about our
own transformation.

He speaks these lovely words about Christ's Passover in the context of an
ugly pastoral problem.

In the Corinthian community there was a man who was living
with his stepmother.

Imagine that!

The Corinthians didn't seem to mind this scandal; they even seemed to be
proud of the novelty.

Paul uses the image of the old yeast that has the potential to ruin the whole
batch of bread
to advise the Corinthians to put aside their sinful ways
and celebrate with the fresh unleavened bread of Christ.

Once again, the resurrection is about Christ but also about us!

Finally, I referred the reporter to today's Gospel where there are no
explanations or proofs given of the resurrection, simply a story of the
beloved disciple who had the guts to enter the empty tomb,
and who saw and believed.

Again, the resurrection is about what God has done for Jesus, but it is also
about what God has done for us.

The beloved disciple represents all of us who even in the midst of death
are sensitive to the presence of the risen Jesus in faith and love.

It's a pity that Mary Magdalene does get shortchanged in the lectionary
reading today.

If we read further on in John, she stays there at the empty tomb and is the
first person
to see the Risen Lord and is the first Christian to actually preach:
"I have seen the Lord!" (20:18).

Now what do those who believe women shouldn't preach do with a text
like that?

I didn't dare point this out to the reporter.

On Friday morning, I put two quarters into a newspaper stand
  to get the weekend edition of *USA Today*.
But guess what?
The story about what to preach on Easter Sunday never appeared.
What happened?
Did I give the reporter too much material to fit into the abbreviated style of
  USA Today?
Did the reporter's story get bumped because it wasn't jazzy with trivial
  images of Easter bunnies and hats?
Or did the reporter finally learn that the resurrection is not something we
  explain or prove?

The resurrection is something we celebrate, and the best place to do that is
  at the Lord's table.
There we confess our broken infidelity, and then, with eyes of faith,
  we name the grace evident in our common lives, and share his Body
  and Blood,
  which is given as a source of our own transformation to new life.
The resurrection of Christ is not just about the glorious event of the past
  but about seemingly impossible transformations that occur in the
  present because of Christ's power and the Holy Spirit,
  like the transformation begun in Northern Ireland on this
  Good Friday,
  like the transformations taking place in our own searching lives.
There may not have been a story of resurrection in *USA Today*
  but indeed Christ is risen today!

RPW

Questions for Reflection

1. What would you tell a reporter if he or she called you and asked what you believed about the resurrection?

2. Have you experienced the transforming power of the resurrection in your life?

3. What is the "old yeast" that Easter calls you to throw out "so that you may become a fresh batch of dough"?

Other Directions for Preaching

1. Pope Paul VI wrote that "modern man [sic] listens far more willingly to witnesses than to teachers, and if he does listen to teachers, it is because they are witnesses" (On Evangelization in the Modern World). The preaching of Peter in Acts today offers one of the earliest witnesses to who Jesus was and the significance of his saving death.

2. In the alternative second reading (Col 3:1–4), the author calls on his listeners to "seek what is above." The reason given is that "you have died and your life is hidden with Christ in God." What does that mean for today's listeners?

3. The responsorial psalm today proclaims, "The right hand of the Lord has struck with power, the right hand of the Lord is exalted." Our response is to "give thanks to the Lord, for he is good, for his mercy endures forever." Sound the note of Easter joy boldly this first day of the Easter season.

The Easter Agenda: Pipe Dream or Dream Come True?
SECOND SUNDAY OF EASTER

Readings:
Acts 2:42–47; 1 Peter 1:3–9; John 20:19–31

A revival of one of the great American plays opened this week up in
New York—Eugene O'Neil's *The Iceman Cometh*.
It makes an interesting contrast with the Gospel we just heard.
All four hours of the play take place in a single room—a barroom,
a barroom of losers—almost all are men and all are alcoholics.
They have names like Harry Hope and Jimmy Tomorrow—
which could sound corny, but it captures the sadness of lives unlived,
lives fueled only by the fantasy of a successful past,
and the futile hope that this fantasy could be resurrected as a future
reality.
Into this scene comes Theodore Hickman ("Hickey") who has been off the
scene for awhile.
Hickey is everyone's favorite, the life of the party, a string of fireworks
exploding.
But you notice after a short time that he is not drinking.
More than that, he is spreading a new gospel:
about finding inner peace by shedding your illusions,
inner peace through stripping away the happy lies we cling to.
At the end of four hours, Hickey is expelled and everyone makes a joyful
return to their cherished illusions, their pipe dreams.

Some say O'Neil is claiming that the ultimate illusion is to think you can
    live without illusions?

Today's Gospel takes us to another room, an upper room,
    a room of stale air and the stink of sweating bodies—the smell of fear.

A man comes into this room and offers inner peace and joy.

"Peace be with you," he says.

The first gift of the risen Lord is peace.

"The disciples rejoiced when they saw the Lord"—that's the second gift:
    the joy of the risen Lord.

This is God's dream for our world: peace and joy.

Then the risen Lord gives the gift that makes both of these possible:
    "Receive the Holy Spirit. Whose sins you forgive are forgiven them,
    and whose sins you retain are retained."

A man comes into a room and offers a world of forgiveness and reconcilia-
    tion with God.

Jesus comes with the Easter agenda for transforming the world.

But, you might ask, "Is it just another illusion, the ultimate illusion, God's
    pipe dream?"

This is the gift of resurrection that Jesus offers: a new creation.

Note that it is on the first day of the week—the first day is always the day
    of creation.

Every year we hear this story on the Sunday after Easter.

It is a great story of one of the appearances that took place following Jesus'
    brutal death.

And it might sound like an appealing tall tale but totally irrelevant for our
    world today.

Peace? Joy? Reconciliation? In our world?

The past decades have brought us Bosnia, Somalia, Rwanda, Timor, Kosovo
    —to name but a few of the more horror-filled spots on our earth.

The agenda for the future is more likely what it has always been:
    nationalistic bloodbaths.

And that's why we need to hear the story of Thomas each year.

Tradition has reduced Thomas to "*doubting* Thomas"—as if the rest of
them did not also doubt who Jesus was when he first appeared.
But take another look at Thomas.
He lays down his conditions for accepting that Jesus has been raised:
"Unless I see the marks of the nails in his hands and put my finger
into the nailmarks and put my hand into his side, I will not believe."
He wanted a touchable Master.
He got more: when Jesus did appear and offered him his body to touch,
Thomas was given the gift of speaking the great proclamation of faith:
"My Lord and my God."
Thomas stands for all of us who now and then wonder if anything good is
still possible,
in light of the blows life can deal,
in light of the horrors we can inflict on each other,
in light of the questionable values we find accepted
and accept ourselves.

A newly hired professor of bioethics at Princeton holds the opinion that
under certain conditions,
like being a hemophiliac or severely disabled,
an infant could be killed at birth.
The primary criterion is quality of life rather than sanctity of life.
In this brave new world, the Easter agenda of peace, joy, and forgiveness
can seem like a beautiful illusion.
But that evening long ago those people in the upper room did not cast out
the risen Jesus.
They took him at his word and they went forth.
And a dream took root, one that needs to be reaffirmed
and recommitted to.
And so last week we were asked:
Do you believe in God, in Jesus, God's only Son,
and in the Holy Spirit?
Do you accept God's dream as a reality to be achieved through our
working under the power of the Holy Spirit?

Here today we are in a room—only here it is bread and wine
    that fuel our future,
        transformed bread and wine that are truly a gift of the Spirit.
In eating the Body of Christ, we grow into the Body of Christ.
We are the Easter people, sent to bring about God's dream for our world:
    peace, joy, reconciliation.
The First Letter to Peter tells us that in God's great mercy we have been given
    "a new birth to a living hope through the resurrection of Jesus Christ
    from the dead."
Our future is not one of dreams deferred but "an inheritance that is
    imperishable, undefiled, and unfading."
And so we say, "Alleluia, alleluia, alleluia."
Let us praise God from whom all blessings flow.
Let us praise the Father, Son, and Holy Spirit.

JAW

Questions for Reflection

1. When you come together in the room where the community gathers on Sunday, do you find there a place where the risen Lord comes to bring peace, joy, and reconciliation?

2. Where are you sent to bring the gifts of the risen Lord at this time?

3. Which of these gifts do you, your family, community, city need most at this time?

Other Directions for Preaching

1. What are some of the reasons that draw us to doubt rather than to believe?

2. Can the community described in today's readings from Acts help to shape the community to which you belong?

3. What is meant by "seeing" in First Peter and in John? Is it really possible to love and believe without "seeing"?

A Journey into Joy
Third Sunday of Easter

Readings:
Acts 2:14, 22–33; 1 Peter 1:17–21; Luke 24:13–35

Have you noticed that most of the Easter stories have one thing
    in common?
They do not start out very happily.
You have the story of the women going to the tomb to anoint the dead
    body of Jesus,
      or the apostles cowering behind locked doors in fear,
      or Mary Magdalene weeping at the tomb;
      Thomas clinging to his doubts,
      two depressed disciples walking down a road.

Of course, they did not have the benefit of Dr. Joyce Brothers in those days.
A few weeks ago in *Parade*, an article by Dr. Joyce Brothers appeared
    entitled, "When a Dream Doesn't Come True."
It was about what to do when disappointment comes into your life.
How does a person like Michelle Kwan, Al Gore, or Kristin Hawkins (who
    lost the National Spelling Bee last May) avoid being devastated
    by disappointment?
Some of Dr. Brother's suggestions were:
    —Rate expectations on a scale of 1–10, so everything isn't a ten.
    —Lighten up and learn to laugh.
    —Get rid of a sense of entitlement, as in "Whatever you hope for,
    I deserve."

   —Know that control has limits; the people you are disappointed in
   are free.
   —Have something in the mail; don't make this the one thing
   in your life.
Now these are practical guidelines, good for many occasions in life.
But they are not for an Easter people in regard to the most important things
   in life.
Easter people are told to have great expectations—
       to not give up on their dreams,
       but to dream mightily, bravely, courageously,
       because there is a power at hand
       that can bring life out of death, hope out of despair,
       light out of darkness.

In the stories of the appearances of the risen Lord,
       Jesus turns the downside back up.
When Jesus comes onto the scene in this story,
       the two disciples do not recognize him.
"Their eyes were prevented from recogonizing him," we hear.
(It is interesting to note that some reputable scholars think this is a couple
       because–
       —Mary, the wife of Clopas, is mentioned in The Fourth Gospel as
       standing at the cross.
       —It is likely that a couple would invite Jesus to stay with them
       for a meal.
       —There were missionary couples in the early Church.)
Whoever they were, they do not recognize him.
This is to God's purpose.

And Jesus does three things.
First, he asks about them and listens to them: "What are you discussing?"
They respond with the longest speech in the New Testament, other than
       those of Jesus.
Second, he then interprets Sacred Scripture for them.

After a less-than-pastoral start (the equivalent of "Dumb, dumb, dumb"),
    he turns to the Scriptures to help them understand he *had* to die for
    our redemption.

Finally, he takes, blesses, and breaks bread with them.

And their eyes are opened.

That is the goal of the risen Lord in all the appearances: opening eyes.

He wants people to see—with eyes of faith.

He wants his followers to see him as risen Lord and to see life differently.

And when they do, they are moved to act.

They get back on the road, return to the place of death, only to find it a
    place of new life.

"[He] has appeared to Simon," the apostles shout out as they come through
    the door.

Easter life is about coming to see beyond the darkness, about returning to
    hope.

We are all on the road; again and again we go from Jerusalem to Emmaus.

We leave the pain of broken dreams behind us, and just keep walking.

But that is not enough.

No matter what the brokenness—this is not God's plan.

God has destined us for life—and to bring life.

We belong to a Church that is suffering a terrible blow: our children have
    been abused.

And decisions were made at the top that protected the abusers.

This was a terrible thing, and we must recognize it as such.

But we are not meant to stay here, but to move beyond hurt to healing,
    as much as that is humanly possible, trusting in God to care for what
    we cannot do.

We are not abandoned by God, by Jesus, by the Spirit of new life.

New life is possible. We have to see and work for new possibilities.

Every week we have an Emmaus experience when we come here:
We start by calling to mind what's happening—what is the sadness, the
     crushed hopes,
          the things we have messed up that prevent us from seeing.
Then God speaks to us of Jesus through the Scriptures and the preaching.
Then Jesus becomes present in the breaking of the bread, and our eyes are
     opened to respond to the words: Behold the Lamb of God.
Then we, too, are sent on our way back into life, to see with the eyes of
     Easter faith.

This happens again and again in different ways.
The mother of one of my closest friends was recently near death.
No one thought she would come back from the edge, but she did.
"These days, she sees the beauty of everyone," he tells me.
She has Easter eyes.

Thomas Merton has written about this experience of seeing
     with Easter eyes.
He was on a street in downtown Louisville, he writes,
     watching people pass by:

> "Then it was as if I suddenly saw the secret beauty of their hearts, the
> depths of their hearts where neither sin nor self-knowledge can reach,
> the core of their reality, the person that each one is in God's eyes. If
> only they could see themselves as they really are. If only we could see
> each other that way all the time, there would be no more war, no
> more hatred, no more cruelty, no more greed. I suppose the big prob-
> lem is that we would fall down and worship each other."*

The gift of the risen Lord is the gift of faith, of recognizing his presence.
And when he comes, he brings peace and hope and joy.
Perhaps you recall some of your own moments of Easter vision.

---

*Thomas Merton, *Conjectures of a Guilty Bystander* (New York: Doubleday/Image, 1968),
158.

Often they come barely noticed:

a sudden appreciation for another person,

an impulse to do "the right thing" for another,

being filled with a sense of inner peace and joy at the beginning or end
of a day.

We are an Easter people continuing on our journey;

but we do not walk alone.

JAW

Questions for Reflection

1. Have you had moments of Easter vision recently? Have you known the journey from darkness to light, from death to life? What is a moment or image of one such journey that you have known?

2. Where do you turn to know and understand the risen Lord? Have you turned to the Scriptures and let them reveal who he is to you?

3. What is the gift you most feel in need of from the risen Lord?

Other Directions for Preaching

1. Peter proclaims in Acts 14 that the eschatological age of fulfillment has been inaugurated in the saving death and resurrection of Jesus Christ. What does that mean for your listeners?

2. First Peter invites preachers to reflect on what it means to call God father and what are the responsibilities of those who call themselves children of God.

3. Luke begins his account by noting that it is the first day of the week, evoking the first day of creation, here a new creation. How does Easter draw us into the joy of a new creation?

A Shepherd To Be Trusted
Fourth Sunday of Easter
(First Holy Communion)

Readings:
Acts 2:14a, 36–41; 1 Peter 2:20b–25; John 10:1–10

Today is a very special day in our parish.

Six of our young people will come up with their families to receive
their first communion.

Today we rejoice with Luke, Erin, Michael, Kara, Elena, and Nicole.

This is a wonderful day for a first communion celebration because it is also
Good Shepherd Sunday.

Now that can sound like something very strange if you have grown up
in a city.

We don't see too many shepherds around these days.

And probably most of us here have never met a shepherd in our lives.

But two of the readings help us to understand how important shepherds
were in Jesus' time.

Not all shepherds were good shepherds.

Some were careless and didn't watch carefully over their sheep.

They would let them wander off and get lost.

One of the things a good shepherd would do is have a special call for his
sheep, and he would have a special name for each of them.

So at night, he would take the sheep into a big pen, or sheepfold, through a
gate and there would be someone to guard them during the night.

Now the sheep would be put into this pen with sheep that belonged
to other people.

And when the shepherd wanted to take them out, he would come and call
them, using that special cry and calling them each by name,
then lead them out to a place where there were green pastures to feed
on and cool water to drink.

And if any of the sheep wandered off, the good shepherd would go out right
away and find them.

It was important that he find them right away because when a sheep got
lost, it would just drop down and start bleating, and if the shepherd
didn't get to it first, a wolf might and, well, "Good-bye sheep."

I have a little statue at home of a good shepherd, carrying a sheep that has
gotten lost.

He put it on his shoulders and he has this big smile on his face.

So you can see why Jesus picked a shepherd, a *good* shepherd, to talk about
himself, because he is our shepherd and we are the sheep of his flock.

At our baptisms we were given a name by Jesus, each of us has a special
name, but we also share a name that marks us as part of his flock.

We are called Christians.

And Jesus walks with us all the time as our friend.

He is close to us and wants us to be safe.

He wants us to be careful, of course, and never go off with anyone
we don't know.

But he promises that he will always be with us, no matter what.

And best of all, Jesus feeds us with a special food, the sacrament
of the Eucharist.

He feeds us with the sacrament of his Body and Blood.

I remember when I was growing up there was an ad for a bread we called
Wonder Bread.

The commercial would say, "Wonder Bread builds strong bodies
in seven ways."

I can't remember what the seven ways were, but we can think of the
sacrament of the Eucharist as "wonder bread."

It builds us up by making us strong in different ways.

It makes us strong in faith in Jesus.

Before we receive communion, the host is held up in front of us and someone will say, "Body of Christ," and then someone will hold up the chalice in front of us and say, "Blood of Christ," and each time we say, "Amen."

Amen means "Yes! That is true! I believe!"

Each time we make an act of faith that this is truly the Body and Blood of Christ, our faith grows stronger.

And each time we receive communion, we are reminded that we can trust Jesus always, and so the sacrament makes us full of hope, hope in what he has promised us, that we are made to live with God forever.

And this sacrament makes us grow in love, because it is a sign of God's love for us.

God loves us so much that he gives us his Son Jesus in this sacrament.

And God holds us all close together as God's family.

We can see the difference it makes when Jesus is in our life when we look at St. Peter.

In today's first reading, St. Peter is preaching about Jesus.

This is Peter's first sermon and he is doing it with great courage.

This is the sermon he gave on Pentecost after the Holy Spirit came upon him and upon the others who were waiting in the room where Jesus had told them to wait.

Remember that Peter had really failed Jesus on the night Jesus was arrested.

Peter must have been frightened, and he said he didn't know Jesus.

He denied knowing Jesus three times.

He wasn't strong but weak.

But Jesus forgave him, and when he rose from the dead, he sought Peter out, and three times he asked Peter if he loved him, and three times Peter said, "Yes."

And then Jesus told Peter, "Feed my lambs….Feed my sheep" (John 21:15–17).

Jesus trusted Peter to take care of his followers, to be their leader, and on
    Pentecost, after the Holy Spirit came upon all of them,
        it was Peter who gave a speech talking about his faith in Jesus and his
        hope in Jesus and his love for Jesus.

Now this same Holy Spirit comes down upon the bread and wine
    and changes them into the Body and Blood of Christ.
When we eat and drink them today, God begins to change us
    over the days and months and years ahead into the Body of Christ.
Jesus comes to us as food, as a gift from God, a gift changed by the Holy
    Spirit, and as with all gifts, we open our hands to receive it.
And we are sent out of Church to tell others that we believe in Jesus as our
    Good Shepherd.

Sometimes the world is very sad.
These days we have been hearing about what is happening in Kosovo,
    about what has happened in the high school in Littleton, Colorado.
God is very sad at these events when people hurt each other.
And so he asks us to make the world a better place by taking care
    of each other.
He asks us to join him in being good shepherds, in taking care
    of each other.
Just as the Good Shepherd watches over us and feeds us,
    we are invited to look out for each other and to do things
    for each other.
So when you receive first communion today, and when we all join you,
    we want to remember that Jesus comes for all of us because he loves
    all of us, and he wants us to bring this love into our world.

JAW

Questions for Reflection

1. Do you know Jesus as a good shepherd who knows you by name, searches you out when you are lost, and who feeds you in the Eucharist?

2. Have you experienced in your life the power of the Holy Spirit to transform you more fully into the Body of Christ?

3. How do you find yourself called to share in the work of the Good Shepherd?

Other Directions for Preaching

1. Jesus is both *Lord* (the Hebrew name for God) and *Christ* (the long-awaited Messiah). Baptism into him is an ongoing call to renewal and reform as individuals and as a people.

2. Christ is the shepherd who laid down his life as an example so that all who were dead to sin could live in accord with God's will.

3. It is important that leadership in the Church be modeled on the good shepherd who knows the sheep, protects, and guides them.

Divine Hospitality
FIFTH SUNDAY OF EASTER

Readings:
Acts 6:1–7; 1 Peter 2:4–9; John 14:1–12

Our readings this day deeply implicate us in the mystery of the resurrection.
The Acts of the Apostles that we hear so much of during this Easter season
    is a kind of autobiography of the early Church.
But it could be our record as well,
    if we are living in the shadow of the risen Jesus.
Those acts of the early Church are like a fabulous slide show of testimonials:
    the curing of the lame man at the Beautiful Gate,
    Peter's speech in Solomon's Portico,
    the stoning of Stephen.

Stephen's call to martyrdom began with service to others.
For the Lord continued to reveal himself to his disciples
    in mysterious ways long after the resurrection,
    particularly as a servant to the community he died for.
The seminal act of washing the disciples' feet is found in John 13:14—
    "If I, therefore, the master and teacher, have washed your feet,
    you ought to wash one another's feet."
There was reason aplenty for service in the young Christian community,
    especially in Jerusalem.
For one thing, the Greek-speaking Jews (or Hellenists) were
    complaining that their widows were being neglected.

And there is a long tradition in the Scriptures of providing for
      the widow, the orphan, and the sojourner.
So the response came through the community
      and through the laying on of hands by the apostles.
The apostolic link further underlines
      the connection of service already established by Jesus
      and his mandate to his followers to do the same.
What a marvelous flexibility of Spirit the early Church
      witnessed in responding to the needs of their brothers and sisters.
What could have been a cause of division—
      complaints of one group against another—
      became instead a source of great strength.

The call to serve the Church can take many forms,
      perhaps even heroic ones.
My Benedictine community at St. Meinrad
      had a small priory and seminary in Huaraz, Peru,
      together with a parish in the capital city of Lima.
Father Bede Jameson was part of the small group of monks who were mis-
      sionaries and was named their prior.
In the early 1970s, there was a terrible earthquake in Peru.
Some of the folks in the parish took refuge in a nearby building.
At some point, we are not quite sure when,
      a wall began to collapse on top of a woman and her child.
Father Bede acted quickly and shielded them with his own body.
As a result, he was killed,
      crushed from the weight of the building,
      but the woman and her daughter lived.

Although we never met, I think of Father Bede
      whenever I encounter the mysterious, haunting phrase in 1 Peter,
      "living stone."

That is one of the virtues of being in a monastic community:
>> we are converted by the personal witness of those who have gone
>> before us.

What a marvelous image 1 Peter gives to the people of God,
>> the community of the Church,
>> who are called to be servants of one another.

To serve my brothers and sisters, even sacrificially,
>> means to protect and shelter them with the living stone
>> that is Christ Jesus.

To see Christ as a living stone means apprehending him as a cornerstone,
>> yet so mightily alive that he can lead us to the Truth
>> that he alone shares with the Father.

The invitation to know Christ as the way, the truth, and the life
>> comes from Jesus himself;
>> it is a call for intimacy and a welcoming into God's hospitality.

Jesus told his disciples that he was going to prepare a place for them.

We often think that we should be receiving the Lord in the guest
>> or in the widow, the orphan, and the sojourner, and rightly so.

But here Jesus himself lays claim to the role of guest master,
>> welcoming his disciples into his own home.

When the great servant of God Dorothy Day died, a number of her colleagues at the Catholic Worker
>> were worried that she would be reduced to a kind of folksy old lady
>> who ran a soup kitchen for poor people down on their luck.

Dorothy Day was so much more than that.

She got down on her knees and served the poor tirelessly.

She wrote page after page of articles reminding everyone
>> of their responsibility to service,
>> welcoming what may appear to be the lowliest of human beings.

She was a pacifist who would not compromise her vision
>> and was thus harshly criticized by some Church officials.

Unlike Blessed Mother Teresa of Calcutta,
>> whom she preceded in extraordinary works of mercy,

Day could not separate her work with the poor
from the politics that oppressed them.
She always faced difficult situations with superhuman courage
when few people rose to the occasion to do so.
She welcomed her difficulties like a guest at her table.
For Dorothy Day, the Lord was especially visible in the poor.
The table she served was not limited even to the numerous shelters
she helped to establish in every major city.
From the time of the Great Depression in the 1930s until the present day,
The Catholic Worker movement became a kind of "living stone,"
a home for so many during hard times.

We may not be called to sacrifice our lives completely in heroic self-service,
like Mother Teresa or Dorothy Day,
but all of us are invited to respond to Jesus' invitation
to follow him along the way.
We might have to change our image of him in order to serve better—
and to change our attitude about the people around us as well.
Somewhere along the line we grabbed hold of a way of thinking
about Jesus.
But he is much more than what we imagine him to be.
Offering us divine hospitality, he is opening the door to something in this
Gospel that wants to shake us up a little—or maybe, a lot.
What about the doors that we keep pretty well locked?
After having experienced personally the risen Lord,
we should want to be servants of one another,
to shelter one another.
Paul, after all, was converted by the risen Lord.
On the road to Damascus Jesus asked him why he was persecuting *him*.
This is no abstraction, but the real thing.
There it is again:
the encounter is radically personal, the truth so intimate.
Changing ourselves from the stone idols we have made will be
like walking out of the darkness of a silent tomb

into the music of God's wonderful light—a blinding, life-changing
light.

That light can only lead to an open door where all are welcome.

He welcomes all of us now to this altar

where he is host, servant, and real food.

GD

Questions for Reflection

1. Do I welcome guests into my house readily? Does my hospitality extend to strangers?

2. How do I treat others when I am welcomed into their home?

3. What is my sense of the liturgy as a sacred space of welcome? Am I radically open to receive the Word?

Other Directions for Preaching

1. Service to the Lord and others may require reimaging myself.

2. Divine hospitality is radical, more than we can know.

3. Faith is a cornerstone upon which all we do is built.

Waiting for God
SIXTH SUNDAY OF EASTER

Readings:
Acts 8:5–8, 14–17; 1 Peter 3:15–18; John 14:15–21

"Hurry up!…Don't be late!…Order now!"
Those refrains have become as familiar as night and day in our culture.
They are the hallmark of the impatient society,
> tired of waiting in line, sick of being just a number
> at a government office, or just bored with standing still.
Yet the liturgical year has taught the Christian community otherwise:
> we know how to keep vigil for the big feasts.
Advent encourages us to long for the coming of Christ
> who will set his people free.
Think of those readings in which Isaiah implored us to prepare a path,
> or when the Baptist carved a way for the coming Messiah
> by his own vigil of locusts and honey in the desert.
Easter is anticipated by Lent, of course,
> and the mother of all vigils, on Holy Saturday.
We get used to the fasting and repenting and waiting for forty days and
> forty nights until, at long last, the Triduum begins on Holy Thursday,
> taking us through the glorious passion, death, and resurrection
> of the Lord.
Wasn't it worth it?
At the end, there was the angel,
> some pale, scattered linen, and an empty tomb.
He is risen, as he said.

But the vigil that we keep in anticipation for the great feast of Pentecost is
      like no other.
Let's face it: Advent and Lent are a deprivation;
      they have a built-in character of waiting;
      they are seasons that deliberately move us from darkness to light,
      from the desert to the ocean of God's mercy.
But our vigil for Pentecost is something altogether strange.
This vigil occurs in the middle of rejoicing;
      we are in the season of Easter! Alleluia! Alleluia!!
We have already experienced the risen Lord,
      already been covered by the saving waters of baptism.
We may find ourselves, then, a bit like the folks in Samaria that we find in
      Acts: we have experienced Jesus but long for the Spirit to fall on us
      so that we can carry that presence to others.

Many of us have already kept this vigil,
      believe it or not, over a period of years.
If we were baptized as infants,
      we typically had to wait a long period
      before we were confirmed in the Spirit.
Those years are hardly something that remind us of a waiting,
      since most of us were too young to know what it meant to long for
      the Spirit.
I was in fifth grade when I received my confirmation.
And my preparation was not a vigil,
      but a multiple-choice test of fifty very direct and objective questions,
      such as, "What are the twelve fruits of the Holy Spirit?"
Almost every day Miss Tossi would line us up
      and we'd have a "confirmation bee"—everyone had to answer
      a question.
If you were wrong, you sat down.
If you were right, you stood there.
If you were *always* right, you were the only one left in line.
Then you were the champion.

This was our preparation for the Spirit.

I am not sure what you had to get to pass the test and be confirmed.

But there was certainly a failing grade.

From my adult perspective,

      I have wondered on and off how anyone could fail confirmation.

Ironically, when I attended a class reunion of my grammar school a few

      years back,

      I realized that some of those kids who were victorious

      in the confirmation bee have not seen the inside of a church in years.

The Spirit will fall when he wills;

      that makes this Vigil of Pentecost all the more dynamic.

I believe that God wants us to long for the Spirit,

      even in the midst of great rejoicing.

The character of the Vigil for Pentecost is closer

      to riding on a roller coaster than taking a test.

Even if we are not especially into amusement parks,

      we can sense the excitement and anticipation on peoples' faces.

"Hold on!," the kids say. "Here it comes!"

Those are not impatient cries of complaints of people on a line,

      but the anticipation of what is yet to come.

It is a rush upon a rush.

Waiting for Pentecost during the Easter season can be likened only

      to something we can hardly imagine,

      what Paul calls, "transformed...from glory to glory" (2 Cor 3:18).

Pentecost is a descant on an already gorgeous melody that awaits us.

It is the high, unimaginable voice of the Spirit guiding us,

      leading the Church, probing an even more mysterious harmony.

This waiting for Pentecost holds a special place, I think,

      for those of us who border on being what I call "flat Christians."

Now we know what flat characters are in novels and movies.

The critic and novelist E. M. Forster first used the term
>   to describe characters that really don't have a life of their own;
>   they are predictable.

Nothing gets them too excited either.
They do what we expect them to do.
Well, Christians can be flat, too.
We can act in very predictable ways.
But even more sad: we often live as if there is nothing exciting awaiting us.
No surprises.
And so the real question for this Vigil of Pentecost is this:
>   what is going to push us over the edge
>   so that the Spirit falls upon us kicking
>   and screaming for joy.

For some of us, the joy of the Spirit will not come by vigil
>   but by crisis.

It seems that sometimes the Spirit has to act forcefully first
>   before we begin to acknowledge its joyful claims on us.

We might say that although we are preparing to receive the Spirit,
the whole idea of expectation has to be qualified .
We *beg* the Spirit to come down.
We *implore* the Spirit to give us new life,
>   just as we ask the Spirit to come upon the bread and wine
>   at the Eucharist.

"Let your Spirit come upon these gifts."
The Spirit will move according to God's plan, not ours.
And that may mean surprising us
>   right smack in the middle of our vigil—
>   where we least expect it.

Charles Dickens' *Oliver Twist*, a novel about an orphan's search for his true
>   home and the struggles he meets along the way,
>   speaks to a lot of people about a crisis they themselves
>   have experienced one way or the other:
>   loneliness, abandonment, poverty.

Oliver is orphaned as a young child,
    is sent to a workhouse in London, and eventually
    winds up taken in by a band of thieves, professional pickpockets.
They are really the only family that Oliver has ever known.
There is a moment in the novel when the young boy has to face
    a difficult situation, a disillusionment, a rejection by those he loved.
Yet the collapse of the young boy's world would ultimately unite him
    with the grandfather he never knew.
Ultimately, God decides the length of our vigils.

These few days before Pentecost urge us
    to remember the promise that Christ himself will not leave us orphans,
    but that he will send the Spirit to us,
    the Spirit that will come upon us flaming out like burning candles.
Let us come together—for that is where we find the Spirit
    most at work, in the community of love—
    and bring our candles, and be ready to be set ablaze
    by the fire of divine heat.
He will not disappoint those who are so eager to be with him.

GD

Questions for Reflection

1. Have I ever sat in a room alone with the lights off and waited to receive the Spirit? Try it.

2. What was something you waited for more than anything else in your life? What were those feelings like as you waited?

3. If you consider yourself a happy person, what would make your joy complete? If you are sad or depressed at the present time, what would make your joy complete?

Other Directions for Preaching

1. Remembering Jesus' love commands are the key to our relationship with him.

2. The First Letter of Peter speaks of ready explanations for hope. Explore reasons for hope today.

3. Trusting Jesus as one who keeps his promises—no matter what—is a gift of the Spirit.

The Loss That Is Gain
THE ASCENSION OF THE LORD

Readings:
Acts 1:1–11; Ephesians 1:17–23; Matthew 28:16–20

There was a play a few years ago called *Mass Appeal*.

There were only two characters in it: the pastor of a parish, Tim Farley,
and the young seminarian assigned to work with him, Mark Dolson.

At one point the seminarian, talking about the parish he grew up in, says:
"When I was a teenager, the church was a circus. Everyone sang top
forty tunes at Mass.

I remember once on Ascension Thursday…the hip hymn committee
selected 'Leaving on a Jet Plane' [as the opening hymn]."

The line got a laugh.

Most liturgists would throw up their hands in horror at the very idea of this
song (and rightly so).

But I remember feeling at the time that, if the laugh was rooted in reality
(and I suspected it was), still in some way, I could understand someone
picking that song for this feast.

It has a melancholy refrain, referring to certain departure and uncertain
reunion.

When I imagine the scene of the ascension with the apostles standing there,
staring up into the sky, feeling lost and at a loss over their departed
Master, a certain sadness colors the moment, and that song, apart
from its anachronistic image, does not seem far off the mark in terms
of the mood of the moment.

The image of the ascension I have had since childhood is what artists have
frequently portrayed: Jesus floating up, up, and away, entering into glory,
and leaving the disciples to go on with the mission entrusted to them.
In some churches in Europe, artists depict the event simply by showing the
bottoms of Jesus' feet with the rest of him swallowed up by heaven.
The image is one of Jesus leaving and returning to the glory of the Father,
where he sits at the Father's right hand, interceding for us.
It is one of the glorious mysteries, marking the return of the Son to his
rightful place.
It is a happy event, but there is also that other note of his no longer being
with us *as he had been.*

For the apostles, this is the last time in this life that they are with their
friend, the Jesus they had known and walked with in the flesh and
encountered as risen Lord.
The stories of the risen Christ present him as a risen but also very much
embodied Lord.
He is always inviting them to touch him, even put their finger into his
wounds; and he eats with them, in one scene nibbling on a piece of
fish, in another fixing breakfast for them on the shore of the sea of
Galilee, and in yet another breaking bread after walking from
Jerusalem to Emmaus.
But this moment of the ascension brings all that to an end.
And so I have always found this scene carries with it a sense of loss,
 a feeling of something wonderful ending, at least in this lifetime.

Spiritual writer Ronald Rolheiser captures this same reality when he writes
about what Mary Magdalene might have thought after the risen Lord
told her not to cling to him:

"I want to cling, despite your protest,
cling to your body,
cling to your, and my, clingable humanity,
cling to what we had, our past.

But I know that...if I cling,
you cannot ascend
and I will be left clinging to your former self
...unable to receive your present spirit."*

Part of this feast is about loss, surrendering, allowing Jesus to become the
    glorified Lord.
It calls us to let go of the old so that the new can enter.
The ascension reminds us that there are two kinds of death—terminal and
    paschal.
Terminal death brings loss of life and spirit; of all the joys of this world;
    paschal death means a dying so that there can be *new* life
    and *new* spirit.
The ascension speaks of opening ourselves to the fullness that comes as a
    gift of the Spirit.

So, "Don't cling" can be translated into our personal and communal lives:
Don't cling to old dreams, old ideas, old desires, old hurts, old agendas.
Don't cling to any "certain" idea of God.
God is greater than any single human idea or image.
Don't cling to the Jesus you knew as a child, a young adult, a middle-aged
    adult, a senior.
Only Jesus, the image of the invisible God, reveals God to us,
We continue to understand who both Jesus and God are for us as a gift of
    the Spirit.
But don't put the Spirit in a box either, limiting, containing, what can not
    be confined.

Perhaps we are asked to let go of other things, too—set ideas, attitudes,
    certainties.

---

*Ronald Rolheiser, *The Holy Longing: The Search for a Christian Spirituality* (New York:
Doubleday, 1999), 166. I am indebted to Father Rolheiser's wonderful treatment of the ascension
in this book for the main ideas in this homily.

No longer can we cling to the idea of the Church as perfect,
>   run by people who do not make mistakes;
>   but, rather, we must face the fact
>   that they have failed grievously at times,
>   and some have done great, irreversible harm.

The innocent have been sinned against, and that must be acknowledged and addressed.

But we also go into the future as God's people,
>   who have known suffering and death
>   but also who know that God is true to God's promises,
>   and that God is first and last a God of life and love.

In Luke's Gospel the account of the ascension offers a detail that is quite comforting.

As Jesus is ascending, he raises his hands in blessing.

This is the last thing the apostles see, not the bottom of his feet,
>   but the blessing of his hands.

And today in Matthew's account, the last thing we hear is his words:
>   "Go, therefore, and make disciples of all nations,
>   baptizing them in the name of the Father, and of the Son,
>   and of the Holy Spirit, teaching them to observe all that I have
>   commanded you. And behold, I am with you always,
>   until the end of the age."

But let those angels in today's first reading, who came after Jesus departed,
>   have the last word, in essence saying,
>   "Why are you standing here? Why are you pining for what was?
>   New things are about to happen. You are not alone. Get moving!"

The ascension calls us to open our hearts to the new ways Jesus can be present to us, to the surprising ways the Spirit can work, even in the most tragic of circumstances.

Suffering and death will not cease in our days,
>   but neither will the power of resurrection and new life.

Go forth from this place in peace and in love.

He walks with us all our days.
Amen. Alleluia.

JAW

Questions for Reflection

1. What do you find yourself clinging to? What might Christ be asking you to let go of?

2. Have you experienced moments when—suddenly—you sense that God is near, that all is well, that one can rest in the peace of Christ's presence?

3. Do you trust that Jesus is with the Father, interceding for us, that we are not alone and on our own?

Other Directions for Preaching

1. Matthew's Gospel says that, after the eleven disciples went to Galilee, "when they saw him, they worshiped, but some doubted." It was to such as these, disciples who worship yet still doubt, that Jesus gave the mission to spread the Gospel, to make disciples of all nations by baptizing and teaching.

2. The mission of the disciples in Matthew's Gospel to make disciples by baptizing and teaching is rooted in the final proclamation that Jesus speaks to them: "All power on heaven and on earth has been given to me....And behold, I am with you always, until the end of the age."

3. Ephesians tells what the Spirit will bring from the Father to those who are in Christ: knowledge of the hope that belongs to his call, the inheritance of glory we can expect, and the surpassing greatness of his power for those who believe.

A Church in Fear
SEVENTH SUNDAY OF EASTER

Readings:
Acts 1:12–14; 1 Peter 4:13–16; John 17:1–11a

This day of the Easter season has been called, by some, "Waiting Sunday":
> Waiting Sunday because we recall those days between the ascension of
> Jesus into heaven
> and the sending of the Spirit on the day of Pentecost.

The first two readings show the early Church using this time of waiting as a
> kind of retreat.

They gather in the upper room to pause, reflect, and pray over the mar-
> velous events of the resurrection they have experienced the last few
> weeks.

There is a rich and wonderful tradition in our Church
> of God's people deliberately putting time aside to go on retreat
> in order to reorient themselves to what really matters in life,
> in order to find God in a fresh new way in their lives.

I look forward to my own Sulpician retreat that begins next Saturday
> at the Oblate Retreat Center in San Antonio.

The retreat master will be Bishop Moreau, who has a great reputation not
> only for being a retreat master but for being a poet.

Would that more bishops could be poets!

As I pack my bag for the retreat, I am haunted by a line that either Thomas
> Merton or Henri Nouwen once wrote:

"You can always tell what kind of retreat you are going to make by
what you pack in your suitcase!"
What will it be? Chocolate bars or the Bible? Dewars or
a spiritual autobiography?

Since I am planning to write an article this summer on the fears of today's
youth, I do plan to take some reading material on that subject.
Not only to read about it, but to pray over it,
because I am convinced there is a new kind of fear
that young people are feeling these days,
which has great consequences not only for our Church
but for our world.

Listen to some surprising statistics:
A recent study of the Nickelodeon/Yankelovich Youth Monitor shows that
the top fears of nine-to-seventeen-year-olds include not doing well in
school (65 percent), not having enough money (59 percent) and—here
is the one that really got my attention—52 percent of these young people are afraid of getting cancer.
A recent congressional report indicates that 71 percent of grade-school students are afraid that they will be either stabbed or shot while attend-
ing school.

There are serious implications to these fears.
Children often reflect the fears of their parents and teachers.
And so parents and teachers are fearful their children will not do well in
school.
They also fear there won't be enough money to support them as they want
to support them.
They also fear the sickness that's surrounded by so much ignorance: cancer.
And everyday parents smile and kiss their kids goodbye for school,
but always with the haunting images of Columbine in mind.

There seems to be a loss of hope in the future.

I sometimes hear that kind of "lost hope" talk

> from priests who mourn the passing of the kind of Church
>
> they once knew and loved and served.

They realize that our seminaries and convents are becoming like those old

> dilapidated motels we spot along Route 1 where the neon sign forever
>
> blinks "Vacancy."

Priests says that their greatest fear is wondering who will follow after them

> in leading
>
> God's people in Word and worship.

In a recent study of lay people in the Archdiocese of Seattle,

> they listed their greatest fear about the "new" Church:
>
> How will they be able to pass on our Catholic tradition
>
> to their children?

It is with these real fears and concerns that we gather as a community of

> faith this morning and listen to God's Word.

What is most striking about this last farewell speech and prayer of Jesus

> before he leaves is not just his trust in his Father,
>
> but also his trust in his disciples.

Jesus believes that these eleven really do belong to the Father,

> and that through these "earthen vessels" his work will carry on.

Jesus prays for his disciples because he believes like the poet that the "best

> is yet to be."

The prayer of Jesus from the Bible is like the Bible itself.

It is never a closed book of past events,

> but a book that is open toward the future and not open in fear;
>
> it is a book about God's promises.

Today's reading from Acts is the last time we will hear of the historical

> Mary in the Bible.

This last portrait that Luke paints of Mary is like the first portrait
   he painted of her in his Gospel.
She is the disciple who is not paralyzed but who is waiting, praying,
   expecting that great things are going to happen.
That is why we call her the "Mother of the Church."

The God of the Bible is acutely aware of our fears and takes them seriously,
   but our God also invites us to live in the present and hope in the
   future.
Our God is something like those TV announcements constantly telling us
   to "stay tuned, there is more to follow."
Let us pray in this Eucharist in the spirit of the prayer of Jesus:
   with faith not only in our God but in those people and events God
   will send us.

RPW

Questions for Reflection

1. What are your greatest fears? Do you know what those you love fear?

2. Do you believe that Jesus sits at the right hand of the Father and intercedes for us?

3. What are your greatest hopes for yourself, your family, your Church, your country, the world?

Other Directions for Preaching

1. The reading from Acts presents us with an image of the Church at prayer. A worthy topic is the importance of prayer and the kinds of prayer that can best serve the needs of the community you are addressing. Consider the Eucharist as our greatest prayer.

2. First Peter speaks of sharing in the sufferings of Christ. Consider the role of suffering in the life of a disciple.

3. In the high-priestly prayer of Jesus, he prays for himself and those the Father has given him. He speaks of eternal life as knowing God and the one God sent. This notion of eternal life in the Fourth Gospel speaks to us today as something that has already begun.

The Rainbow Lady
of Pentecost
PENTECOST SUNDAY

Readings:
Acts 2:1–11; 1 Corinthians 12:3b–7, 12–13;
John 20:19–23

Have you ever met someone filled with the Holy Spirit?
Have you ever met someone like the disciples in our first reading from Acts,
    who spoke boldly and powerfully about God in a language
    that you really could understand?
Have you ever met someone who seemed to have a bright flame crackling
    out of the top of his head,
        you know, like the pictures of saints on the holy cards we received at
        confirmation?
Have you ever met someone like that in your whole life?
I did once.

A few years ago, I was on vacation with a friend,
    driving through a deep redwood forest in California.
It was about two in the afternoon and we hadn't had any lunch.
The forest was wildly captivating but lacking in eating establishments.
But suddenly, thank God, a stone building appeared with a welcome sign:
    "Food and Drinks."
It was a tiny German restaurant filled with beer steins,
    overgrown philodendrons, and old cuckoo clocks.

The place was drenched with age and the smells of tempting Bavarian
    dishes.
The restaurant was empty except for three elderly women who were seated
    next to us.
Because there was no Muzak and because they spoke quite loudly,
    we couldn't help but hear their conversation.
One of the women was moving far away in retirement with her husband.
The lunch was a farewell given by her two best friends.

After they finished their meal, they gave their friend some gifts,
    and then one of the women began to pray.
The leader of the prayer was about eighty years old.
She was dressed in the most colorful clothes I had ever seen:
    bright greens, shocking pinks, bold oranges.
She wore flowers in her hat—real flowers.
One of her sneakers was green, the other orange.
She carried a cane entwined with multicolored ribbons.
In my mind, I named her "the Rainbow Lady."

Now I have been a priest for many years and have heard many prayers,
    but never had I heard a person pray like the Rainbow Lady.
She prayed for her friend and husband, a beautiful prayer for their safety,
    their happiness, their new home.
She prayed for the wonders of the friendship the three women had enjoyed
    for many years.
She prayed for everything: for the earth, the seasons, the forces of nature.
She prayed with feeling.
At one point, she held her hands over her friend
    and prayed for the Holy Spirit's power to come over her.
"Are you feeling anything yet?" she asked.
"Nothing," her friend responded.
"That's OK. Sometimes it takes a long time."
The Rainbow Lady would not take no for an answer.

She believed and felt God's Spirit so powerfully
 that nothing would dampen her enthusiasm.

When we got back on the road,
 my friend and I talked about how the whole scene in the restaurant
 was like something out of an old *Twilight Zone* show.
But the more we thought about the Rainbow Lady,
 the more we agreed that she was not some California kook
 but a woman of authentic faith
 who really believed her body was a temple of the Holy Spirit
 and so she dressed the part.

The Rainbow lady really believed that she had received the gifts of the Spirit
 and that the only way to live life was to share those gifts with others.

That's the kind of people who are represented in today's story of Pentecost
 in our reading from Acts.
The Jews were celebrating the Pentecost that was the feast of the covenant
 between God and God's people at Mt. Sinai.
The disciples of Jesus were also celebrating a new Pentecost,
 fifty days after the Passover Feast.
Just as on Mt. Sinai, the people experienced God's presence through wind
 and fire, so in the new covenant, the disciples felt God's presence in
 wind and fire.
They were dramatically filled with the Holy Spirit.
It charged through their bodies,
 and they were given instant courage, clarity, and eloquence
 to reach across all barriers of language, culture, and even prejudice
 with the good news about the new covenant of Jesus Christ.

But we would be making a huge mistake if we thought that, from Pentecost
 on, the disciples of Jesus didn't have to struggle in giving birth to the
 Church.
We must not view this scene of Pentecost as if it were a magical event.

All we need to do is read the rest of the stories in the book of Acts
    that follow this Pentecost story
    to realize that the Church had to struggle, to pray,
    to discern just where the Holy Spirit was leading them.
Even the Rainbow Lady knew that:
    "Sometimes it takes a long time."

The other story about God's Holy Spirit that we heard this morning is not
    as dramatic
    as the Pentecost story in Acts.
John's Gospel story is not filled with a mighty wind
    but a gentle breath of Jesus upon his disciples, and he tells them to
    receive the Holy Spirit so that they can forgive sins,
    reconcile people in conflict, and bring peace to those who are anxious.

These two stories about God's Holy Spirit,
    the mighty one from Acts and the quiet one from John's Gospel,
    are not contradictory stories.
They show both sides of the coin.
Sometimes, we do experience God's Spirit in our life and in our world in a
    dramatic way as the disciples witnessed on that first Pentecost,
    as we sometimes experience in our own lives when we encounter some
    turning point,
    some critical test and conversion,
    some powerful witness of the Holy Spirit like the Rainbow Lady.
When these precious moments do appear, only an "Alleluia" will do as our
    response.

But mostly our Christian lives are spent struggling to find and discern just
    where and what God is calling us toward.
We're not so much burning with the Holy Spirit,
    but burnt-out by the demands of our times.
We're like the disciples locked in our rooms of fear and depression.

We are waiting to hear the gentle whisper of Jesus greeting us with his peace
and with his power to forgive and be reconciled.

In the play *Waiting for Godot*, Vladimir asks Pozzo, "Where are you
going?"

Pozzo answers, "On."

Pentecost reminds us of the power and possibilities of the Holy Spirit in our
lives and in our world, and gives us the only true Christian answer to
the question, "Where are we going?"

With God's Holy Spirit, we are going on.

RPW

Questions for Reflection

1. Have you ever met someone "filled with the Holy Spirit"? Was the encounter like one of meeting fire or wind or a gentle breath?

2. Where is the Spirit moving you this day? Where is the Spirit moving your community? Have you called on the Spirit to come upon you like the Spirit came on Pentecost?

3. Have you given thanks for the gift of the Spirit, first given at baptism, and who continues to "blow where it will."

Other Directions for Preaching

1. The Spirit affects our communication with others, drawing together strangers into one community, reversing the story of the tower of Babel when the languages of people were made diverse.

2. Paul speaks in First Corinthians of the different kinds of gifts, services, and workings that come from the one Spirit and that all these gifts are given for the common good. Consider the sequence for the feast and the various ways it names the gifts of the Spirit.

3. The first gift of the risen Lord is the gift of the Spirit, a Spirit of peace and reconciliation. Our world hungers for a peace that is built on forgiveness.

ORDINARY TIME

The Baptism of the Lord
FIRST SUNDAY
IN ORDINARY TIME

Readings:
Isaiah 42:1–4, 6–7; Acts 10:34–38; Matthew 3:13–17

The First Sunday in Ordinary Time is also the last Sunday of the Christmas season. See "Watery Eyes," page 48.

"Here I Am"
Second Sunday
in Ordinary Time

Readings:
Isaiah 49:3, 5–6; 1 Corinthians 1:1–3; John 1:29–34

There is nothing ordinary about "Ordinary Time."
Think of it:
We just celebrated the Baptism of the Lord last Sunday.
We vigorously renewed our own promises as sons and daughters
    of the living God.
And now we are asked to reflect on what it means to be in a deep,
    abiding relationship with the One who has called us out of darkness
    into a marvelous light.
That is hardly ordinary!
    We are to consider what Paul names as the invitation to be "sanctified
    in Christ Jesus."
That's us: "called to be holy, with all those everywhere who call upon the
    name of our Lord Jesus Christ, their Lord and ours."

Nobody puts this call to holiness better than the psalmist who says, "Here
    am I, Lord; I come to do your will."
And there really is no better disposition for cultivating a relationship with
    God than good, old-fashioned waiting.
The prophet Isaiah knew that as well.
From the moment he was called, Isaiah doted on God's Word
    and its power to transform him.

Having seen an ecstatic vision of the Lord seated on a lofty throne,
>   Isaiah experiences a seraphim touching his mouth with a burning coal,
>   cleansing him for a mission that begins with, "Here I am...; send me!"
>   (6:8).
And Isaiah is not alone among those who say, "Here I am."
Even as a boy, another prophet, Samuel, responded to God's call, confound-
>   ing his elders.
To the voice that had called him three times, Samuel finally responded:
"Speak, LORD, for your servant is listening" (1 Sam 3:9).

The apostle Paul clearly sees himself as part of a succession of those
>   who have waited for God.
Paul tells the Corinthians that he is "an apostle of Christ Jesus
>   by the will of God."
Paul understands his own vocation as a person disposed
>   to the weight of divine wisdom;
>   it would transport him from vicious, Church-persecuting zealot to
>   apostolic witness.
The defining moment for Paul appears when God's will becomes manifest
>   in the person of Christ Jesus.
Tradition reckons Paul as an Apostle—with a capital A,
>   not because he was present to the earthly Jesus,
>   but because the risen Lord transformed him.
This is the same Lord who now calls everyone to holiness.
Paul derives all his graced encounters from Christ himself.
Jesus is the faithful witness who says with the psalmist,
>   "Here I am, Lord; I come to do your will."
That Jesus has come to be "a prophet to the nations" is obvious
>   in the Gospel's account of his meeting John the Baptist.
I like to think of the meeting of John and Jesus in John's Gospel as a recog-
>   nition scene, that has a kind of mystical and literary parallel, an echo
>   of a similar meeting in Luke.
We might recall that the first fateful meeting between John and Jesus
>   occurred before either of them was born.

Elizabeth, pregnant with John, announced to Mary that "the infant in my
   womb leaped for joy" (Luke 1:44).
John's preaching that the Lamb of God would come began even then!

This relationship between John and Jesus cannot be overestimated.
In the almost magical meeting between John and Jesus in today's Gospel,
   we can see the link between the prophetic tradition in the Hebrew
   Scriptures—represented by John—and the new covenant brought
   by Christ himself.
The temporal gives way to the eternal,
   as Jesus comes to baptize not with water but with the Holy Spirit.
Like Paul after him, John recognizes Jesus and is transformed, leaping and
   testifying that this Holy One is the Son of God.
"Here I am" becomes "He is the one."

Our graced skill to say, "Here I am" to the Lord depends crucially
   on the recognition of the Holy.
The graced skill to notice the workings of the Lord within us—and within
   others—determines our openness to receive the fullness of the Spirit.
And so, we wait with our brothers and sisters together in community.
We never discover God in complete isolation.
A couple of years before the famous Trappist Thomas Merton entered
   Our Lady of Gethsemani Abbey in 1941, he went on a short trip to
   Cuba.
As he watched from the back of a church, he heard some children shout
   just at the moment of Consecration, *Creo en Dios!* ("I believe in
   God!").
The first thing that Merton could think of at that point was: "Heaven is
   right here."
We need a John the Baptist, a faith community, some shouting children,
   pointing out to us and saying, "Look! There is the Lamb of God!"

In Denys Arcand's marvelous film *Jesus of Montreal,*
   a young actor's life is about to be transformed;

no longer will he be a performer playing the part of Jesus in a passion play in Quebec,

but he will actually be sharing in the death and resurrection of Christ.

Early on in the film, a well-known actor is surrounded by adoring fans,

but he points to the young Daniel, somewhat isolated in a crowd, and says, "Look, there is a real actor!"

By a strange series of circumstances, Daniel will become a real actor— God's actor.

Daniel plays Christ in a passion play and literally dies on the cross.

His heart is then donated to someone else.

Daniel's transformation in Christ begins here:

with recognition, with a frank acknowledgement, that God is writing the story.

Our response is at its best when we can say, "Here I am."

Behold the Lamb of God present at this Eucharist: Here we are, Lord!

GD

Questions for Reflection

1. How busy am I these days? Too much to notice the Lord working in my midst?

2. What has God's grace done in me? In the overall pattern of my life? Recently? In the world around me?

3. "Here I am" is a dangerous statement. What is at stake for me personally when I make this my prayer?

Other Directions for Preaching

1. God asks everything from us.

2. We recognize the Holy in the mysterious way God chooses to disclose it.

3. We have a mission to become a light of the nations.

How To Broaden
Your Horizons
THIRD SUNDAY
IN ORDINARY TIME

Readings:
Isaiah 8:23–9:3; 1 Corinthians 1:10–13, 17;
Matthew 4:12–23

A few years ago I made a pilgrimage to the Holy Land.
During most of my stay in that ancient part of the world I was
      in the company of other pilgrims
      or "tourists" as some call themselves.
But there was one trek I took solo.
It was to the town of Capernaum, which is the important city highlighted in
      today's Gospel.

The group I was with was not scheduled to go to Capernaum, but I was
      intent on doing so.
At the small hotel where I was staying by the sea of Galilee, a receptionist
      had written out
      in modern Hebrew the name Kaphar-na-um.
I was to give it to the local bus driver who would drop me off at the town
      where Jesus began his public ministry.
I was the only non-native on the bus, which was packed with Israeli soldiers
      with their rifles in hand, young mothers nursing their kids, people on
      their way back home after a long day at work.

I was told the trip was not going to take long.
But the bus driver apparently forgot my note and never stopped at
     Capernaum.
I realized something was dreadfully wrong when I was one of
     the few people left on the bus.

The bus driver told me to get off and wait for a bus to take me back
     to my hotel.
I waited for over an hour.
It began to get dark and cold and I wondered where in the world I was.
Then a young man came out of the blue.
He was hitchhiking his way back to Galilee.
He told me he was from Bethesda...Maryland!
He had decided to leave his family back home and live on a kibbutz in
     Israel for a while in order to broaden his horizons.
When I asked him where we were standing at that moment, he said,
     "See that mountain range over there.
     Over those mountains is Lebanon."
My bus driver not only forgot to let me out at Capernaum,
     he dropped me off by the Golan Heights.

When I prayed over today's Gospel, all those emotions of feeling lost
     in a strange yet beautiful land came back to me.
The adventure of it all!
     —Which, after all, is what life is all about: an adventure.
It isn't just narrative fluff for Matthew to say that when John the Baptist
     was arrested, Jesus left his hometown of Nazareth and went to live in
     Capernaum by the sea.
Jesus' move is very important for Matthew's story.
Now that John has been "handed over," it is time for Jesus to take over.
The new order has begun.

And just as the young man left Bethesda, Maryland, to go to Israel to
     "broaden his horizons,"

Jesus leaves his close-knit family and friends of his hometown
of Nazareth,
and travels to the larger, busier town of Capernaum
by the Sea of Galilee.
Jesus' mission of teaching, proclaiming the Gospel of the kingdom, and curing illness is not merely for his family, the people he knows and feels
comfortable with.
He begins his mission in the long-troubled, racially mixed region where
Isaiah had foretold
a light would shine in the midst of gloom.
Jesus' mission is not just for the Jews but for the "District of the Gentiles."

In today's Gospel, Jesus not only broadens his horizons, he calls others to
do so as well.
Notice how Matthew emphasizes the family relationships of the people
involved in this story.
Peter and Andrew are specified as brothers, as are James and John.
Matthew is so eager to note the brotherly relationship of Peter and Andrew,
he mentions it twice in the same sentence.
He does the same for James and John and underscores the fact that they
leave their father
and their boat in order to follow Jesus.
I am wondering this morning about the people in our country
who constantly chant, "Family values, family values."
Are they bothered by this Gospel this morning?
Jesus is telling us that to be his disciples we sometimes have to question the
values of our families, indeed, even sometimes to leave our families.
Remember the bumper sticker: "Hate is not a family value."

After all, even at this 9:00 a.m. wonderful family Mass at Holy Trinity,
researchers tell us that one in every five families suffers some form of
domestic violence.
And even in some families who pray together and stay together,
in the name of love there can be a lot of control and at times too

much smothering love,

so that children are not allowed to follow their own destiny,

to broaden their horizons, to be who God wants them to be.

Even Jesus' family tried to restrain him from his ministry.

In Mark's Gospel, they were beginning to believe the neighbors who said

that Jesus was insane.

They tried to bring him back home.

Jesus knew how powerful families are in our lives,

whether they are working well or not at all,

whether they communicate or are utter strangers to one another.

I think he knew how easy it is to be so consumed by them that we forget

who we are apart from them.

The Gospel today speaks loud and clear to us a message that is perhaps

hard for us to hear,

but hear we must.

The Gospel tells us that the kingdom of heaven doesn't exist to serve the

family; the family exists to serve the kingdom of heaven.

Jesus is always calling us even from what is most secure,

more sacred, most safe in our lives,

to something and someone higher.

You are parent, child, spouse, aunt, uncle, sister, brother, grandparent—yes.

But you are first of all a Christian, a child of God.

That is your true identity.

That is who you most truly are and where your real peace and security lie.

Once you get that into your heart and head, chances are you can survive

even a broken family

and go on to choose a better one from the strange people God sends

your way.

When Matthew first told this story about leaving family and boats and all

familiar ways to follow Jesus,

it didn't frighten his congregation.

After all, there were many sitting in his congregation
    who had already been kicked out of their families
    for believing in Jesus.
When Matthew first told this story, it didn't frighten people;
    it comforted them.

Let us also hear this Gospel as a story of comfort and reassurance.
In this Eucharist, in the partaking of his Body and Blood,
    may Jesus give all of us the strength and the courage
    to broaden our horizons.

RPW

Questions for Reflection

1. Have you ever felt the need to "broaden your horizons"? What did you do?

2. Does your family serve the kingdom of God or do you try to make the kingdom of God serve your family?

3. Who is your family? What are your family values? How does your identity as God's child fit in with this?

Other Directions for Preaching

1. The prophet Isaiah spoke of a people who walked in darkness seeing a great light. Matthew picks up on this quotation to introduce the ministry of Jesus. How does the ministry of the Church lead to bringing light into the darkness?

2. Paul speaks of divisions in the church at Corinth, asking "Is Christ divided?" The Church continues to know inner divisions, and the words of Paul continue to speak of the will of the Lord that "there be no divisions among you."

3. The apostles respond immediately to the call of Jesus to follow. Consider the differences between a job, a career, and a vocation.

The Other Side of the Gospel
FOURTH SUNDAY
IN ORDINARY TIME

Readings:
Zephaniah 2:3, 3:12–13; 1 Corinthians 1:26–31;
Matthew 5:1–12a

One of the more intriguing features of our secular television age
　　is the success of some religious figures on the screen.
Mother Angelica comes to mind.
While I admire her chutzpah for getting into the competitive and influential
　　world of television,
I'm often dismayed when I hear her present only one side
　　of what the Church officially teaches.
Like a lot of us, she presents the one side she likes and is familiar with.
You will never hear her or any of the preachers and teachers on her network
　　talk about the current welfare stalemate,
　　　　nuclear arsenals,
　　　　domestic violence,
　　　　discrimination against immigrants, gay people, and people of color.
Mother Angelica debunked the Women's Conference in Beijing as demonic,
　　even though the Vatican was represented at the Conference
　　and concurred with all the major points of its final statement.
Her program is literally draped in Catholicism from habits to statues and
　　yet one hears
　　only one side of Catholic teaching.

You never hear talk about the tough social gospel teachings of the Second
Vatican Council,
Pope John Paul II, and the American Catholic Bishops.
You never hear a Catholic teaching on capital punishment.

That's why I'm sure Sister Helen Prejean will never be an invited guest on
Eternal Word Television Network.
Sister Helen is a nun who ministers to prisoners on death row at Louisiana
State Penitentiary.
Her life story is right now up there on the big screen in the haunting movie
Dead Man Walking.
The film haunts you about the issue of capital punishment more powerfully
and eloquently
than any encyclical from Rome
or document from the Catholic Bishops' Conference.
Sister Helen argues statistics and Catholic teaching.
Of the 24,000 homicides in the United States last year,
only a few dozen killers will be executed.
Most of these will be black or Latino; most will also be poor.
The people with the power, money, and resources will never face
the death penalty.
And from statistics, nobody can make a convincing argument that the death
penalty deters homicide or is less expensive for the state.
Now some people have accused Sister Helen of also preaching only one side
of the Gospel.
Her tough and loving ministry to killers shocked a lot of good Christian
people, even though she always made it clear to everybody, including
the killers, that she does not condone murder.
Once in a clemency hearing, the father of one of the victims
confronted Sister Helen when she was pleading for the killer's life.
"Why didn't you come to us?" he asked the nun.
Sister Helen told the father she had been afraid that they would demand
her support

for the killer's death as proof of her compassion
for their pain and loss.

Sister Helen discovered from that encounter the other side of the Gospel.
She realized that so many people leave the families of victims alone.
They don't know what to say, especially months after the crime when the
   deep grief sets in.
In a recent interview, Sister Helen said she was wrong.
She said, the Roman Catholic Church "has to be on both sides
   of the issue."

Our readings from Scripture today challenge us to look at the other side of
   the Gospel.
The Beatitudes are not a nine-step program for ethical perfection.
The Beatitudes don't contain everything you have to do to get to heaven.
The Beatitudes are Jesus' way of having us see
   the other side of the Gospel,
   the side that we would rather not see or deal with.
From his vantage point on the mountain, Jesus saw people
   that even the pious of his day overlooked:
   many who were poor;
   some who were homeless;
   others who were still feeling that terrible ache in the pit
   of the stomach because they
   had lost the one person dearest to them in all the world;
   others who refused to give into the rat race of greed and hatred,
   but were bewildered because those who did seemed to be doing
   quite well.
He saw the odd ones and the deformed ones,
   those who had committed sexual sins but still were poor in heart.
He looked at all of them and called them by a name nobody had ever called
   them, a name that they never would have dreamed
   of calling themselves.
He called them blessed!

The first Beatitude is "Blessed are the poor in spirit;
> for theirs is the kingdom of heaven."

The New English Bible translates that first Beatitude this way:
> "How blest are they who know their need of God, the kingdom of
> heaven is theirs."

Jesus could call them blessed because even in their sorry plight
> they recognized their need for God.

There is a lot of talk these days of listening to the new Moral Majority.

They are the people who are absolutely convinced that God
> is in their corner only.

While they talk the religious talk,
> if you listen closely, you'll hear that they boast not in the Lord
> but in themselves
> and their one-sided agenda..

Our Scriptures today remind us that the Bible knows nothing
> of a Moral Majority.

The Bible always insists that a prophetic minority has more to say
> to a nation
> than any majority, silent or moral.

In fact, majorities in the Bible generally end up stoning and killing the
> prophets.

Today's prophet Zephaniah speaks not of a majority but a minority.

He calls them *anawim*, which means
> a remnant, the leftovers,
> a tiny band of God's poor and forgotten who would always survive
> to teach us not to be arrogant or boastful about our religion
> and not to see only one side of the Gospel.

Let us give thanks to God that remnant is still with us teaching us to be
> humble, teaching us to see both sides of the Gospel.

RPW

Questions for Reflection

1. Have you ever found yourself on what others around you considered "the wrong side"? What impact did it make on your life? Did you stay there or move? Why?

2 Can you find some areas in your life where God might be asking you to look at the "other side" of the argument? Is there an invitation being given now to see "both sides of the Gospel"?

3. Which of the Beatitudes speaks most to you at the present? Which comforts you? Which challenges you?

Other Directions for Preaching

1. The prophet Zephaniah today called for reform and renewal. There is no renewal without reform, and the Church is called to a life of ongoing reformation in light of the Gospel. Both are gifts from our God who shelters and protects us.

2. Emily Dickinson begins one of her poems (#288) with the lines, "I'm nobody. Who are you? Are you nobody, too? Good—there's a pair of us." The excerpt from the Letter to the Corinthians reminds us of the special role of "nobodies' in the divine plan.

3. The Beatitudes speak of God's kingdom as a world where things are reversed from how we often experience them here. Such a reversal can bring freedom now and new life.

How To Be Salty
Fifth Sunday
in Ordinary Time

Readings:
Isaiah 58:7–10; 1 Corinthians 2:1–5; Matthew 5:13–16

While on my exercise bike I frequently find myself watching TV programs I
    ordinarily wouldn't have time for nor even be interested in.
A few weeks ago while peddling away, I watched a Jewish cooking show,
    which I found both informative and entertaining.

One Jewish mother, who demonstrated how to make vegetarian
    chopped livers,
        convinced me that what my kitchen desperately needed
        was kosher salt.
I found a box on a Safeway shelf—a large box, large enough
    to last me forever.
But what really surprised me was how inexpensive salt is—even kosher salt.

That's why the image that Jesus uses in today's Gospel of Matthew needs
    some updating.
In Jesus' time, salt was a precious and expensive commodity.
It was one of the most important necessities of human life,
    used for everything from preserving and seasoning food to making
    covenants.
It was used in some cultures as money itself.

But even though the price of salt has changed, one aspect of it hasn't.
Salt in Jesus' time and in our own is useless on its own.
You can't do anything with just salt.
In a time of famine, you cannot eat it.
In a time of drought, you cannot drink it.
That would make things only worse.
Salt by itself is no good.
It makes the fields infertile and kills life.
It is heavy. It is useless.
Salt, as Jesus, tells us is useful only when it is mixed up with other things.
Salt by itself is unbearable and deadly.

There is a always a danger that we think we can live our Christian lives
    only for ourselves without getting mixed up like salt.
Some contemporary sociologists have told us that our American "habits of
    the heart" are highly individualistic.
That is why the social encyclicals, the pastoral letters of the U.S. bishops
    on economy and peace, and the preaching of John Paul II about the
    poor and disenfranchised have yet to make a major impact on the way
    we preach and worship.
Our individualism keeps us from being salt,
    from getting mixed up with the world and its needs and concerns.

This past October, I lectured at a major theological school in America.
While there, I attended the daily Mass at the seminary.
I was astounded that during communion, a number of the seminarians
    not only did not sing the communion hymn but had their heads buried
    in their hands in what seemed like contemplative prayer
    until the closing prayer.
I couldn't help but wonder about their eucharistic theology.
Why wasn't it based on our Catholic Body of Christ theology,
    rather than a "Jesus and me" individualistic piety?
Some recently ordained priests from the diocese over the bridge have told
    sacristans and eucharistic ministers not to touch "their" chalice.

Again, where does this dangerous individualistic kind of eucharistic
	theology and spirituality come from?

Have they not read John Paul II's encyclical on the Eucharist in which he
	writes:

> All of us who take part in the Eucharist are called to discover, through
> this sacrament, the profound meaning of our actions in the world in
> favor of development and peace, and to receive from it the strength to
> commit ourselves ever more generously following the example of
> Christ who in this sacrament lays down his life for his friends.*

But now comes the tricky part, just exactly how are we to be salt to the
	earth, light to the world?

Jesus is big on the concept but silent on the "how to."

Like St. Paul in today's reading, I as preacher have no specific blueprint,
	because like him I, too, come to you in weakness and much trembling.

All I know is that during my lifetime I have been most called to get out of
	my own shell of individualism and become salt and light
		when I have met salty and 100-watt Christians along the way.

Last Sunday, *Washington Post* columnist Mary McGrory wrote a splendid
	piece on the occasion
		of the death of her dear friend Gertrude Cleary.

I actually used the article in my preaching class as an example
		off what a funeral homily could be.

It was a wonderful story of a salty Christian who maybe didn't change the
	whole world
		but brought light to the people of her world because of her faith.

Mary writes:

> She was the most religious person I know. Daily mass and communion,
> good works and Bible study at Blessed Sacrament Church, and yet
> never a whisper of self-righteousness from her. She lived St. Paul's

---

*Sollicitudo Rei Socialis, § 49.

epistle on charity: believed all things, hoped all things, endured all things. She was a small person with a great soul....You probably haven't seen many eighty-five-year-olds who are laid out in a pine box wearing a pink feather boa. That was totally appropriate for Gertrude, though....[She] understood the importance of austerity for those who seek God. But she was also a party girl to the souls of her feet....

Gertrude was a hospitable hostess and a spectacular guest. She was nice to everyone, respectful and attentive to boors and boars. It wasn't because she thought an angel lurked somewhere with them— she was too earthy for Pollyanna piety. I think she felt that if God could love such creatures, she could at least take a stab at it....For years she opened her home...to some fourteen or fifteen homeless children who needed love and peanut butter sandwiches and batteries for their toys. She loved the invasion, ignored the wear and tear on her furniture....She hung in there. She beamed through her bruises, which had turned purple and green....

[Once] there was a nine-year-old boy, who was so startled at seeing his hostess at eye level when she opened the door, that he blurted out, "You an elf?" ....Gertrude loved the world and almost everybody in it, but it was beginning to look less and less like a place for a genuine Christian who never did complain and never, for a second, thought that she was better than anybody else."*

This week whenever I am tempted to lose my saltiness and hide my light
    under a bushel basket, I will try to remember Gertrude and the many
    examples of people who lived what Jesus spoke about in today's
    Gospel.
I pray that you will, too, so that the people of our world
    can see our good deeds and glorify our God.

RPW

---

*Washington Post, January 28, 2001.

Questions for Reflection

1. How am I being salt for my world? What is God mixing me up with? How am I helping to preserve life in our world?

2. While in no way disparaging devotion and prayer before the Blessed Sacrament, it is good to ask: Where does my view of the Eucharist lead me—to a "Jesus-and-me" approach to the celebration of the Eucharist or to a greater recognition of the sacrament as food for the Body of Christ, present here and now in the living members of the community.

3. Is there a Gertrude in your life who has been salt and light for you?

Other Directions for Preaching

1. The words of Pope John Paul II are an echo of what prophets like Isaiah have been reminding us: that darkness will be dispelled when we let our light shine by feeding the hungry, sheltering the oppressed and homeless, clothing the naked, and taking care of our own.

2. This week's reversal: God's wisdom and power are revealed in the crucified Jesus. Like Paul we are invited to "resolve to know nothing but Christ Jesus and him crucified."

3. The light that shines from us is not simply for our own benefit or to win the gratitude of others, but for all in the house so others may see our good deeds and glorify God.

Somewhere Is Here, Now
SIXTH SUNDAY
IN ORDINARY TIME

Readings:
Sirach 15:15–20; 1 Corinthians 2:6–10; Matthew 5:17–37

Happy Valentine's Day! A day for all who love and all who have ever been
    loved.

But have you ever noticed how so many great love stories are about
    thwarted love?

There's Will and Viola of this year's highest-nominated Academy Award
    movie, *Shakespeare in Love.*

There's Jack and Rose of last year's *Titanic,* and *The English Patient* and his
    beloved from the year before.

And think of the popular movies of the past: for every Elizabeth and Darcy,
    there are at least three with Scarlett and Rhett, Heathcliff and Cathy,
    and even Bonnie and Clyde.

Yet we know we are made to love and to find our fulfillment in loving.

We know that most of our efforts to love are imperfect, but most of us
    keep trying.

We live in the hope that someday, somewhere, our efforts
    will find completion.

Remember the beautiful song from *West Side Story* (yet another sad
    love story):

"There's a place for us, somewhere a place for us…."

It was a song of longing for a place where two people could love each other
    and find peace and rest:
    "Someday, somewhere, we'll find a new way of living.
    We'll find a way of forgiving, somewhere."
That place is what Jesus is talking about today.
We are made to live now in love, now and forever.
We are called to choose today the ultimate Love in creation: God.

We can hear it marked out for us this morning in the readings.
Wisdom calls us to choose life, reminding us that life and death are set
    before us.
The choice is up to us.
God has given us both freedom and responsibility.
The wise person chooses life.

Paul casts this choice in terms of choosing either human wisdom
    or God's wisdom.
And if we choose God's wisdom—
    "What eye has not seen, and ear has not heard,
        and what has not entered the human heart,
        what God has prepared for those who love him."
God's wisdom is revealed to us in Jesus through the Spirit.
And that is who we hear today in the Gospel: Jesus, the teacher of wisdom,
    Jesus on the mount, the new Moses, the lawgiver of a new covenant,
    giving the blueprint of what it means to live the life of the kingdom,
    laying out what it looks like when the kingdom of God draws near.
It's a law that fulfills the old one, not abolishes it, bringing it to completion.
In the spirit of Valentine's Day, the law Jesus sets before us gets to the heart
    of things.
Jesus looks at three areas, three areas of choices:

First, there is the choice to be a person of peace or a person of violence.
Jesus points out that murder is the eruption of the volcano.
Violence begins with an angry heart, a heart festering with hurt.

Violence begins within, deep within.

To be a person of peace means being a person of forgiveness.

Unless you forgive, anger builds—

    it might take years, but it will blow, scalding everyone.

This is so important for bringing about the kingdom that, even if a person is

    at worship

and remembers that a brother or sister has anything against him or her,

we are told to leave and make peace.

That is when the kingdom comes on earth.

The choice is to be part of a community of forgiveness.

When we make that choice, there is a place for us;

"somewhere" is here and now.

Then, there is the choice to live our relationships in fidelity.

The text is complicated here, and scholars debate what is meant by the

    Greek *porneia*

It's not simply a matter of not committing adultery;

    it's a matter of honoring our own commitments and those of others

    from the heart out.

In Jesus' day, adultery was only committed between a man and another's

    wife—the violation was against the husband of the woman; the wife

    belonged to the husband.

When another took her, the husband's property rights were violated.

Jesus calls for wholeness in relationships between men and women,

    not treating another as an object.

And that starts in the heart.

Furthermore, for Jesus, marriage was part of the plan of God,

    mirroring God's fidelity to the chosen people.

The marriage relationship is to be a place of safety, nurture, and honor,

    not danger, dishonesty, or destructiveness.

By forbidding divorce Jesus was calling for

    a reconciled relationship between husband and wife.

In the culture at that time, the wife was often abandoned for the flimsiest of

    reasons.

Most commentators note that this is not about keeping together what is
    irretrievably broken, but at bringing about reconciliation when it is at
    all possible.

Finally, there was a custom in Jesus' time of making oaths.
    and calling on God to stand by one's word.
But Jesus is saying there should be no need for this,
    because we should be speakers of truth all the time.
There should be no need to call on God to uphold what you say.
The mark of those who live in the new law is truthfulness,
    speaking the truth in simplicity.

Now these three areas can send many people off on a guilt trip,
    especially the calls to forgiveness and fidelity.
(Not that guilt is always a bad thing! It can get us moving
    in the right direction.)
What is important is to understand the root values Jesus is calling us to:
    To have a heart that is forgiving, faithful, and truthful.
This is the wisdom of God, that comes as a gift of God.
Behind these statements is a God who wills that human society be just and
    merciful, that human life be nourished, and relationships restored.
God's will lies at the heart of the law.
The wisdom that is God's wisdom is a gift of the Spirit.
It is not mere human wisdom, as Paul reminds us.
And the power to live it is also a gift of the Spirit.
We don't earn it or work our way to it.
The Spirit gives wisdom in the Spirit's own time to those able to understand.
In bringing the law of God to completion, Jesus calls us to live in love,
    a love that completes us and makes us whole, because it is God's love.

Jesus calls us to a radical way of living,
    to bring about that *Somewhere* that is marked by the face of divine love,
        a face that calls us to forgiveness, faithfulness, truthfulness.

There is a place for us—it is the kingdom and it has begun now
  when we live as a people of the covenant.
Eucharist commits us to the search for that *Somewhere*
  and strengthens us in our efforts to make it a permanent dwelling
  place.

JAW

Questions for Reflection

1. How does Valentine's Day call you to celebrate the relationships in your life?

2. Is there somewhere you have known forgiveness, faithfulness, truthfulness?

3. How does the life you live witness to God's wisdom?

Other Directions for Preaching

1. God is all-seeing and his eyes are on all those who fear him. God has set before us "fire and water," life and death, good and evil. We are to make a choice, which God will take seriously.

2. There is a wisdom of this age and God's wisdom is revealed in Jesus Christ and through the Holy Spirit. How does this wisdom shed light on our lives?

3. Jesus came not to abolish but to fulfill the law. What does it mean to be a people of the law Jesus fulfilled?

Doing the Impossible
SEVENTH SUNDAY
IN ORDINARY TIME

Readings:
Leviticus 19:1–2, 17–18; 1 Corinthians 3:16–23;
Matthew 5:38–48

I felt sorry for my students this past week.
They preached their first homily in class and their homilies were based on
      the readings we just heard proclaimed.
I'm sure they thought, "Why don't the lectionary readings for today have a
      neat miracle story, a simple proverb, a mighty story of God's love?
That's something we can get our homiletic teeth into!
Instead, we're stuck with these readings that tell us
      what we're supposed to do."

First, there's that strange book of Leviticus designed specifically to tell Jews
      what to do in order to be separated from the unholy so that they
      might be holy like God.
Then there's St. Paul telling us that we are holy
      because we are God's temple.
And worst of all there's Jesus in Matthew's Gospel still preaching his
      Sermon on the Mount
        sitting up there telling the people that they have to do
        ridiculous, demanding, impossible things
        like turning the other cheek, handing over our coat when someone

wants our shirt,

and worst, worst of all, loving our enemies.

"Good God," my students must have thought, "anything but this for my
first homily."

I mean, let's face it, who wants to be told what to do these days?

Whether young people, old people, people in between,
conservatives, liberals, and people in between—
who wants to be told what to do, especially being told
to do the impossible,
especially being told that we are to be perfect as our Heavenly Father
is perfect?

Who wants to be told that we are supposed to be like God?

I listened and watched as my students valiantly tried to make some sense
out of the impossible commands of these scripture readings.

At least one student didn't sentimentalize the commands of Jesus.

His name is Luke and he is an associate pastor at a southeast DC parish
in a low income neighborhood
infested with drugs, poverty, and violence.

Luke spoke of a project he is involved with where he gives classes to young
kids on anger and violence prevention.

He told us that one day he noticed two boys arguing with each other on the
playground at school.

From about twenty yards away, Luke yelled to one of them, "Walk away,
Dennis!"

And he did and Luke was gratified.

But as Dennis turned away, the other boy hit him on the back of his neck.

He reached them in time to prevent a serious fight.

Luke realized that he had asked an awful lot from Dennis.

Jesus also asks an awful lot from us in our Gospel today.

It's interesting to note, however, that he doesn't ask us to turn our back to
violence, he asks us to turn the other cheek.

But what, exactly does that mean?

The ancient law that Jesus spoke about, "An eye for an eye and a tooth for
     a tooth" was actually a pretty good law for the time.
If someone stole your lamb, that didn't mean you had the right to steal his
     spouse or his children.
If someone broke your tooth in a brawl,
          that didn't mean you had the right to knock out all his teeth.
This law was designed to restrict the spiral of violence and put some
     measure of proportion to it.

But Jesus realized that the law didn't work.
There is something dark about human nature, that when we finally take
     revenge and take out one eye or one tooth, we want to continue, and
     the violence spirals.
That is what domestic violence is all about.
A husband hits his wife or children perhaps to get even with the violence
     he experienced
          from *his* father or mother.
But one slap isn't enough.
One slap leads to another and then to another.
An eye for an eye and a tooth for a tooth simply doesn't work.

That is why Jesus proposed a new way of responding to violence.
We can find out what he meant by the way he responded
     when someone slapped *him* on the cheek.
We read in John's Gospel that a guard slapped Jesus
     because he dared to answer back the high priest.
What did Jesus do?
He looked his enemy straight in the eye and challenged him,
     "If what I say was wrong, tell me. If I am right, why did you hit me?"

Turning the other cheek doesn't mean we become a doormat when anyone
     seeks to degrade us.
It means, as Jesus told us and as he showed us,
     that we must not return evil with evil.

We must not become part of the problem by giving into the spiral
of violence and hatred.

Sometimes we think we are too civilized and sophisticated to have the kind
of enemies that we hear about so often in the Scriptures.
But maybe the reason we don't have enemies is because we're less honest,
open, and brave.

Most of us tend to avoid confrontations.
We're afraid of what our fiery outbursts will set off.
And so we often smolder instead.
If people hurt us or cheat us or stand for things we abominate,
we don't bear arms against them—we bear grudges.
We not only turn the other cheek, we stay out of the way.
When we do declare war, it is mostly submarine warfare.
And since our attacks are beneath the surface, it may be years before we
know how terrible the damage we have either given or sustained.
Jesus looked his enemies in the eye and saw not only judgment and
meanness but fear and frustration.
He looked in their eyes and saw not only darkness but their hurt
and vulnerability.
Which is why, when his hour came, he was honestly able to pray:
"Father, forgive them for they know not what they do" (Luke 23:34).

In the end, it may be far easier to love and pray for the enemies
we look in the eye
and confront with truth,
than the ones we choose not to look at, at all.
Maybe that's what Jesus meant by being perfect as our God is perfect.

RPW

Questions for Reflection

1. Have you ever been the recipient of a violent act, physical or verbal? How has it affected your life?

2. Do you ever find yourself practicing "submarine warfare"?

3. Is there a need to speak the truth to anyone or to any higher authority (government, church, or workplace)?

Other Directions for Preaching

1. We say in the Creed "We believe in one, holy, catholic, and apostolic church." How is this holiness found in today's Church?

2. Examine the implications of Paul's proclamation that we are the temple of God and that the Spirit of God dwells in us.

3. Consider some ways as a society we can respond to the call to generosity and perfection heard in today's Gospel?

God's Future
Eighth Sunday
in Ordinary Time

Readings:
Isaiah 49:14–15; 1 Corinthians 4:1–5; Matthew 6:24–34

We have come to think of the modern age as the age of doubt.
"There is a crisis in faith," we hear over and over again.
If only we believed more fervently, more intensely,
> things might actually get better.
Now maybe they are right and I am wrong.
It may very well be that we are a faithless generation,
> but I wonder if what we really lack is not faith so much as hope.

Hope is a building block for faith itself and, indeed, for happiness.
There is certainly a lot of unhappiness going around.
Common sense tells us that there is no future without hope.
A culture that has lost hope numbs itself from the future.
And there are a great deal of folks who seem to have lost a sense
> of a future.
Far from faithless, ours is really closer to an age of despair,
> with the signs of a society that has evacuated hope all around us.
There has been an enormous increase in clinical depression over the last several years,
> and the apathy, the cynicism, and the irony
> that seem to grip contemporary society are quite remarkable.

171

We see that hopelessness time and time again in the extraordinary number
　　　of suicides, especially among the young;
　　　　the drugs for recreation or for escape or "just to take the edge off";
　　　　the cycle of poverty that gets deeper and deeper;
　　　　the lack of justice, especially in capital crimes;
　　　　the racist immigration laws.
We could go on forever until we wind up in complete despair.

"The LORD has forsaken me;
　　　my Lord has forgotten me."
Those words could have been written yesterday.
This is the language of despair and hopelessness and loneliness.
How poignant that these words of abandonment would echo down
　　　the corridors of history
　　　　and slam against our own front door,
　　　　where so many families are broken by infidelity
　　　　and where children are left to fend for themselves in a loveless world.
In a world of unwanted children,
　　　it seems that even the worst fears of the prophet Isaiah have come true,
　　　that a mother would forget her infant and be without tenderness
　　　for the child in her womb.
No wonder that many have lost a sense of trust and deep hope.

The loss of hope in God is a universal phenomenon.
Sensing the anxiety present in the early Christian community,
　　　Paul uses a very telling and useful metaphor to remind
　　　　the Corinthians not to lose hope and to remember God's
　　　　steadfast love: stewardship.
For Paul, the most important quality for a steward is that he or she
　　　be trustworthy.
It is that sense of trust that God owns completely.
For the Lord will bring to light what is hidden in darkness
　　　and will manifest the motives of the heart.

God has stewardship over creation and refuses to let it go.

This stewardship of creation is part of God's very self.

As one of the Prefaces for Sunday reminds us, "even when we lost our
    friendship with

    God, we were not abandoned."

Remember? After Adam and Eve mistook a rotten piece of fruit for a gift,
    Yahweh sewed for them little aprons to brave the world
    as they were exiting the Garden of Eden.

Even after God sends the Great Flood, he repents with a rainbow.

There is in God an unbreakable bond, a covenant with the whole earth.

Paul continually saw that endless rainbow
    that God painted for Noah and us.

Paul senses that all creation is groaning for fulfillment,
    for freedom when God will make all things new;
    it is a stewardship that lasts forever.

As the psalmist says to the Lord, "nor will you suffer your holy one
    to see corruption" (Acts 2:27).

Surely, this is a hope-filled ratification
    of the God who is the steward of all creation.

It is true that some may lack hope entirely and with good reason.

Yet, that despair and dread cannot be gleaned from God's record.

It is, however, our own.

We are the ones who betray,
    who flee the world of love and commitment,
    who kill the hopes and dreams of our children.

The roughest part of our journey is brought about not by God
    but by ourselves.

When Martin Luther described sin,
    he thought of it as the human subject collapsing into a kind of heap.

By some standards, that is also the look of despair.

By contrast, the psalmist rests completely trustful and hopeful in God.
So did Jesus.
Utterly.
This is what Our Lord is trying to get the disciples to realize.
"Look at the birds of the sky; they do not sow or reap,
> they gather nothing into barns, yet your heavenly Father feeds them."
There is the trust that even the creatures of the earth know,
> perhaps because they have long known God's own stewardship and
> care for them.

We don't know how many of Jesus' disciples heard his teaching
> that morning when he preached what we now call
> the Sermon on the Mount.
Yet for many saints throughout the ages,
> this particular passage became a formidable invitation
> to leave everything and follow the Lord.
They relied totally on God for their needs.
St. Francis comes to mind most obviously here.
Francis gave away all his fancy clothes and went naked in the streets—
> a big embarrassment for the family!
But that action is meant to convict all of us
> who may laugh in the face of radical trust and hope.
Voluntary poverty is, after all is said and done, not about rejoicing in desti-
> tution; simplicity of life celebrates trust in God clothed in vulnerable
> humanity.

Professor Thomas Long tells the story of a group of children
> in a Sunday worship service
> who were expected to memorize Paul's famous passage
> in the Letter to the Romans in which he asks the question:
> "What will separate us from the love of Christ?" (Rom 8:35).
As it happens, one of these children, Rachel, had Down syndrome.
So anticipation ran pretty high when the question was posed to the children
> and then, finally, came to Rachel.

Long said that when she was asked the question,
> the young girl flashed that big, familiar smile
> and then, full of confidence said, "Nothing!"

What better illustration could we ask for as an example
> of hope that abides—
> a hope that never grasps for anything
> but is content to live with open hands and an open heart,
> pointing us only to the kingdom of God.

Such a hope lives on the edge of that kingdom,
> seeking it above all.

It is the kind of hope that joins faith and love together in perfect harmony.

For Jesus, the end of all seeking is the kingdom of God
> and its righteousness.

That is hope enough for a lifetime—and an eternity.

GD

Questions for Reflection

1. Where do I place my trust? Do the people in whom I place my trust lead me to celebrate my life as a gift from God?

2. What are my limitations in trusting others, specifically? Have I allowed past hurts or betrayals to cast a shadow on a future of possibilities?

3. Do I live simply?

Other Directions for Preaching

1. It is possible to leave behind our past misfortunes if we trust in God's care for us.

2. God is the steward of creation in life and also in death.

3. Anxiety about our lives is symptomatic of the age in which we live, but God calls us into a future based on our redemption in Christ.

The Rest Is Silence
Ninth Sunday
in Ordinary Time

Readings:
Deuteronomy 11:18, 26–28; Romans 3:21–25, 28;
Matthew 7:21–27

A young man reaches for his cell phone while having lunch with friends.
Yet another talk show host blathers on about the latest neurosis,
    with the guests to prove it.
One more commercial about getting your teeth whiter than white.
The latest sound bite from the Washington spin doctors.
More information on information radio.
Talk, talk, talk.

The old expression that "words are cheap" was never more applicable than
    today.
We live out of our mouths.
Just try going to a restaurant and finding one person in the room
    who does not feel the need to talk on the cell pone during the meal.
I guess real multitasking is managing to answer your e-mail, while talking
    on the phone, while watching the morning news, as you listen to the
    kids' plans for the school day.

All this influx of useless verbiage impacts the Christian community
    when we attempt to deepen our relationships with God and one
    another.

The mere multiplication of words—
    even the most precious of them, "Lord, Lord"—
    seemingly accounts for very little in Jesus' reckoning.
Words become what Moses calls "a blessing and a curse,"
    if they are not rooted in the immaculate, pristine rendering of God's
    commands.
Jesus even says that good works and prophecy are of little value
    without the right motive.
What matters is purity of intention, humility of heart, simplicity of soul.

In his *Rule* for monks, Chapter 20, St. Benedict says that
    prayer should be "short and pure."
Obviously, God is not persuaded by human rhetoric.
But there is even more.
With language comes stratification,
    classification of human beings according to their position in society.
Experts tell us that they can identify a person's education
    within seconds after a given individual opens his or her mouth.
This taxonomy was, of course, Henry Higgins' profession,
    wonderfully burlesqued in George Bernard Shaw's *Pygmalion* and
    Lerner and Lowe's *My Fair Lady.*
Language separates the Eliza Doolittles of the world from their "betters."

But Jesus is no respecter of human divisions, and the Sermon on the Mount,
    of which this Gospel passage is a part,
    is the great blueprint for the kingdom of God
    where no caste system exists.
"Blessed are the poor" (Matt 5:3),
    for those who cannot speak, are uneducated, or infirm:
    their hearts are what matters.
Paul underlines this grace that is given to all when he tells the Romans that
    they are justified by faith, and not by the manipulation
    or activities of language—
    that is, the practice of law.

"The righteousness of God has been manifested apart from the law...

for there is no distinction;

all have sinned and are deprived of the glory of God.

They are justified freely by his grace through the redemption in Christ."

Grace is the great leveler, isn't it?

You cannot talk your way into the kingdom.

Only the Word himself has the authority to remind us

of the failures of our own words, ineffectual as they are without a

pure heart.

The rest, of course, is silence.

In a certain sense, Jesus is recommending building

a place of solitude, a quiet house in the country, to keep us

from the endless avalanche of junk mail,

useless words that befall us day after day.

A funny thing about silence: not only does it create a space for our prayer,

but the absence of language reminds us later that

we do not have to live from mouth to mouth,

enjoying the latest little tidbit of gossip or meaningless piece

of information.

Monks may be known for the silence they keep in the cloister,

but such an atmosphere is deployed

so that they might be better listeners than talkers.

It is interesting that in addition to silence,

Benedict is very insistent about hospitality as well.

Guests should be treated as Christ.

They are welcomed with love, not a lot of talking.

By all accounts Moses had a difficult time with words.

He complained to God at their first meeting on Mount Horeb that

he did not have a facile tongue.

Oddly, not only did he defeat Pharaoh, but he received a set of words vital

to Israel, the Law.

Nevertheless, one of his chief problems continued to be words,
    particularly the murmuring of the people as they crossed through the
    desert: The complaints. The griping. You can just hear them.
Here again, language can be used to tear down and destroy.
St. Benedict is so strict about silence that
    he advises that even talking about good things
    should be refrained from.
The monk lives in a world of grace, as we all do,
    building a house on a foundation of stone.
The true listener of Jesus' words dwells in a house of interior silence
    and peace.
On the other hand, the one who fails to listen deeply
    constructs a house built on sand.
That sand is something like words—so numerous, so ephemeral.
The tiny grains blow this way and that.
A storm alone could wipe out anything made of sand
    or change the configuration forever.
Such a house made of sand collapses like a child's fortress on a beach,
    made for an afternoon in the sun but gone by nightfall with the tide.

What is the condition of our house?
A little shaky?
Purity of heart is the architecture of the Beatitudes.
We might consider relocating on rock, with a firm foundation of silence.
While we are repositioning ourselves,
    perhaps we might also take a look at our interior space, with humility
    of heart.
We can only assess this if we are honest about our interior lives.
It is well for us to invite the Lord into our houses.
He himself says that he will come with the Father
    and make his dwelling there.
And as St. Ambrose says, though he can enter,
    he does not want to force his way in.

Many of the furnishings of our house have already been provided by the
    Church.
And so with faith and love we come to the eucharistic altar,
which has been placed before us by Christ himself, the true host
    of this meal.
There is little for us to do but live in faith.
What can works do in the face of such a free gift?
Wisdom has set her table and mixed his fragrant, bloody wine.

GD

Questions for Reflection

1. What does it mean to speak to God from the heart?

2. How often am I really silent? Do I welcome people by my reception
of them as a sacred guest in my life?

3. The psalmist says, "Your word is a lamp for my steps and a light for
my path." Do I welcome the Word of God into my midst? If so, then what
kind of space does the Word find?

Other Directions for Preaching

1. The heart contains our true intentions and these motives may surprise
us—can we face them?

2. We may think that we are holy because we multiply religious practice
and language, but God cares little for such empty praise.

3. We spend a lot of time talking but not as much on proclaiming.

All of Me
TENTH SUNDAY
IN ORDINARY TIME

Readings:
Hosea 6:3–6; Romans 4:18–25; Matthew 9:9–13

God loves sinners.
Three little words.
Let's think about them
     and about the kind of Lord
     who has gathered us around this altar today.
This is God, who is not interested in perfection,
     but who sent His Son to rescue us
     after the human race made its mortal mistake in the Garden of Eden.
This is Yahweh, who appeared to Moses, the outlaw of Egypt
     in the burning bush on Mount Horeb, not to ask for special offerings,
     but because he heard the cry of people being tortured in Egypt.
This is Jesus, who did not relate to the ultrarespectable,
     but made his apostles out of poor, dull fishermen,
     his friends from sinners,
     his disciples from tax collectors.

And so if we were going to convict God of loving sinners,
     the Gospel for today is Exhibit A.
"He saw a man named Matthew sitting at the customs post.
He said to him, 'Follow me.'"

Now we know that in first-century Palestine,
    tax collectors were the lowest of the low,
    despised collaborators with the Roman government,
    who would typically skim money off the top of the revenue
    they collected from their own townspeople.
To associate with such as these would have brought
    disrespect immediately upon Jesus as a teacher,
    who was expected to gather a more pious cohort of students
    around him.
No chance.
Yet in his very choice of apostle, Jesus tips his hand as to his real interest.
He is not interested in people who just look holy.
He is not interested in people who just pretend to do the right thing.
He does not care about the outward appearances of obligations.
And our Lord tells us as much, when he says,
    "Go and learn the meaning of the words,
    'I desire mercy, not sacrifice.'
    I did not come to call the righteous but sinners."
We have to find God guilty of loving sinners.

That should be good news for us,
    if we are willing to let God love us even in our sin.
After all, the kind of table that Jesus found himself eating around
    in today's Gospel—full of sinners—
    is not so terribly different from the one he gathers us
    around at this eucharistic celebration.
All of us are sinners and we admitted as much when we began this liturgy:
    Lord, have mercy!
That is the catch: it is not just a matter of following,
    but of recognizing our self on the road.
The first movement in our relationship with Jesus is
    knowing that we are all tax collectors, so to speak.
We all make mistakes and need forgiveness
    from a God who accepts us for who we are and where we are.

That acknowledgement should make us grateful,
>   happy, speechless, ecstatic, and a little crazy
>   because we do not have to be perfect.

Some people who have no real insights about religion think
>   that people of faith are mindless conformists,
>   that people of faith follow a God or a Church that puts them
>   through a lot of useless sacrifices.

Quite the contrary.

Contemporary culture is the instrument that does not forgive,
>   that forces people to become something they are not,
>   that holds us up to unrealistic ideals.

Over the last several decades, for example, the plastic surgery industry
>   has mushroomed and expanded into a multibillion dollar industry.

A great deal of that business has been fueled by young teen-age women
>   who are unhappy with who they are,
>   and who have an unquenchable desire to be someone else.

This culture places ruthless demands on everyone,
>   especially those who are impressionable and vulnerable.

How sad that much of the world has not only failed to hear the voice of
>   Christ, but never really grasped the meaning of the God of mercy,
>   who never asks us to be anything other than who we are:
>   human beings who make mistakes, admit our faults, and start over.

Our life in Christ, then, must be built on faith,
>   on a relationship with God who knows us intimately.

When Paul talks about Abraham, he reckons his righteousness
>   on one thing alone: faith.
>>   "[Abraham] did not doubt God's promise in unbelief; rather, he was
>>   empowered by faith and gave glory to God and was fully convinced
>>   that what [God] had promised he was also able to do. That is why 'it
>>   was credited to him as righteousness.'"

This faith, then, was a continual call to hope, to believe, to convert.

It is significant that Abraham was an old man and still associated with faith.

Why?

Because faith is not a one-time conversion experience,
>   but is brought about by continual openness to humility
>   and conversion.
Certainly, baptism brought us into the unfailing light of Christ,
>   but that defining moment must be ratified over and over again.
Like Abraham, we are called to be fruitful,
>   even when we think the well has gone dry.
Just when we believe that we have run out of hope,
>   God will send us light.
We can be sure that all our outward religious practices,
>   good as they may be,
>   are often severely tested when we have to face an incident
>   that cuts us to the bone.

Some years ago, there was a terrible accident involving a young man
>   who eventually died of his injuries suffered in a car crash.
There is no accounting for such a tragedy, and
>   God's merciful heart must have certainly cracked
>   at the promise of a young life cut so short.
Yet in the course of his hospital stay,
>   hundreds of the teenager's classmates from a Catholic high school,
>   together with two priests from the diocese, came to visit him
>   and his family.
A mysterious hope of another kind is present there.

Stories like that are out there but we don't hear enough of them:
>   hope built on faith, an abiding trust that even in the midst of tragedy
>   and loss,
>   the Christian community will drop everything and open its arms wide.
There is God's mercy.
We can all be that sign of God's presence for one another,
>   if we hear the call to follow Jesus more deeply.

As we gather around this altar,
> we dine with Jesus who welcomes everyone,
> even as he died for all.

We come together to accept one another
> as we all have received, so graciously, over and over,
> an invitation to his banquet: "Follow me."

GD

Questions for Reflection

1. That God loves "all of me" means that every inch of me has been redeemed. Is there a corner of my life that I secretly believe God wants no part of?

2. When was the last time I showed this kind of mercy: I know something potentially damaging about a person I dislike but I said nothing?

3. Are there limits on my forgiveness?

Other Directions for Preaching

1. "I slew them by the words of my mouth" makes a good case for the power of God's Word to change our lives, now.

2. God's saving power is not only shown in the upright, but in the sinner.

3. The vocation to follow Jesus is occasionally weakened by pressures that chip away at our confidence in what God has done for us and in God's mercy.

Summoned and Sent
ELEVENTH SUNDAY
IN ORDINARY TIME

Readings:
Exodus 19:2–6a; Romans 5:6–11; Matthew 9:36—10:8

These days have been difficult ones for just about everybody in the Church.
People are reeling from the disclosures of sexual abuse of children
    by priests.
People are equally if not even more taken back by the actions of bishops
    who moved some of these priests to other places
    and put other children at risk.
In the midst of all this, we hear a Gospel about the mission of the followers
    of Jesus.
I believe this Gospel is most appropriate at this time.
It calls us to move from feeling like victims to becoming active participants
    in our world.

Matthew presents Jesus as a teacher like Moses.
Because Moses was believed to have written the first five books of the Bible,
    Matthew gives Jesus five major discourses.
The first one, of course, is the Sermon on the Mount, offering a vision of
    what marks the lives of believers when God truly reigns over our
    hearts and minds.
Today we have heard the beginning of the second great discourse,
    where Jesus addresses his followers about their role in his mission.

Like a concerto, this Gospel has three movements: first, Jesus surveys the
   scene, then Jesus summons the twelve, then he sends them out to their
   work.
We will consider each movement.

First, the scene.
Jesus is on the road, going through the towns and villages of Galilee.
He has been teaching in synagogues,
   curing sickness and disease, and preaching the good news of God's
   being near.
Suddenly he stops and looks at the crowd.
And his response is a telling one.
He sees a people troubled, dejected, harassed, depressed.
"[His] heart was moved with pity," Matthew tells us,
   "because they were…like sheep without a shepherd."
For us, compassion is an abstract word—but not for the Hebrews and the
   Greeks.
The root of the word is the same as the word for *womb,*
   the place where life begins to unfold.
Being moved with compassion has to do with the deepest,
   innermost feelings.
And out of this deep womblike well of feeling, Jesus speaks:
   "The harvest is abundant but the laborers are few."

A similar mood seems present today: a people dejected, discouraged,
   depressed at what has come to light;
   a people in need of the healing words and gentle touch
   of God's presence.
But good workers are needed to bring this word and this touch.
So Jesus' first words seem very much to the point for us here and now:
   "Ask the master of the harvest to send out laborers for his harvest."
Then Jesus summons.
He summons the Twelve to do what he was doing:
   liberate from evil spirits and lift the burdens of pain.

The Twelve build on Matthew's presentation of Jesus as the new Moses
> with the Twelve representing the twelve tribes of a new Exodus,
> moving from slavery to freedom.

The first ones Jesus called were certainly a mixed lot:
> four fishermen,
> a tax collector (and therefore a collaborator with Roman oppression),
> a Zealot (and therefore a member of a political party that hated
> Rome)—those two must have had some interesting exchanges on the
> road—a cousin, and the rest fairly anonymous.

One would betray him, one deny him, one doubt him.

It is obvious that Jesus wasn't going for the top draft picks.

But most would die violent deaths on his account.

And all would be remembered because he had summoned them and they
> had answered.

Most of us probably do not have many experiences of being the first choice,
> whether for the team, or the prom, or the lead in the school play.

But we, too, have been summoned in our day and for our time.

After the summons comes the sending.

Jesus tells them:
> Go to those who are lost.
> Tell them God is near.
> Do all that you can to lift the burdens that oppress them, physically or
> spiritually.

The same holds today.

People need to hear good news, and so we say at the end of every Mass,
> "Go in peace to love God and serve one another."

The first work of the Church is to bring the Gospel
> and then to bring healing and liberation from all that imprisons.

We are summoned by baptism to do what he did:
> help, heal, herald the good news.

Pope John Paul II in his 2001 message for World Day of Prayer for
> Vocations wrote:

"Within the Christian community, each person must rediscover his or her own personal vocation and respond to it with generosity. Every life is a vocation and every believer is invited to cooperate in building up the church."

The Pope calls us to be a community of healing, reconciliation, forgiveness, compassion.

What does that mean today?
Here things become more difficult.
The decisions of this past week at the bishops' gathering in Dallas are momentous ones.
We pray they are the beginning of healing.
We have only begun to walk a very long road to restore trust,
     to bring healing,
          to see that such terrible abuse of power does not happen again,
     to our children, to our communities.
But this is something that must engage us all.
How can all of us help good leadership to arise from our midst,
     leadership that is not self-serving, nor destructively protective?
"Ask the master of the harvest to send out laborers for his harvest."
Let us pray for that this morning as we join in this Eucharist,
     and let us pray that the power of the Holy Spirit will continue to transform the Church
     as that same Spirit transforms the bread and wine into the Body and Blood of Christ.

JAW

Questions for Reflection

1. How would you describe the people of the world in our own day?

2. Do you see yourself as summoned and sent out to the world to bring peace and healing?

3. Where do you find there is most need to bring healing and liberation from evil?

Other Directions for Preaching

1. Consider the Church's calling to be "a kingdom of priests, a holy nation."

2. The reconciling power of God's love revealed in Jesus Christ continues to call the Church to ongoing reform.

3. How does the mission of the Church today continue at a time when the value of other religions is both recognized and valued?

Where's Your Lawn Chair?
TWELFTH SUNDAY
IN ORDINARY TIME

Readings:
Jeremiah 20:10–13; Romans 5:12–15; Matthew 10:26–33

It's become somewhat fashionable now for some bishops to sell
    their mansions.
But the Diocese of Saginaw is way ahead of the game here.
The first act Bishop Ken Untener performed
    when he became bishop of Saginaw
    was to sell the bishop's mansion.
When asked why he did so, Bishop Untener replied,
    "The house had seven bathrooms and I only needed one!"

Actually, the bishop has no permanent home.
He travels from parish to parish, living in a rectory for a couple of months.
He then packs up his belongings, gives away what he has accumulated and
    doesn't need anymore, and then takes off for another rectory.
Ken Untener has two priorities as bishop of his diocese:
    1) consider how every diocesan decision will affect the poor;
    2) improve the quality of the Sunday homily.
Before becoming a bishop, he taught homiletics.
Now, as bishop, he meets each week with the preachers of his diocese to
    help improve the quality of their preaching.
Now you know why he's a favorite of mine, and now you know why he is
    probably the last homiletics' professor to become a bishop!

A few years ago, Bishop Untener gave our Sulpician retreat.
I will never forget one story he told us.
He talked about a nun who was the principal of a Catholic school
        who had been undergoing a rough time in her ministry.
The bishop invited her and another sister to take some time off
        and spend a relaxing day at a lakeshore property the diocese owned.

On this property, high on a hill, is a parish church and rectory.
When the bishop and the two sisters arrived, the first thing they did was to
        take three lawn chairs out of the garage and place them on the lawn
        where they could relax
        and enjoy a lovely summer day.
But just as they did so, they heard the pastor shouting down
        from his rectory window:
        "Put the lawn chairs back in the garage.
        The lawn chairs are not to be put on the lawn!"

The irony of the story:
The pastor had allowed himself to be paralyzed by one tremendous fear—
        that someone would put the lawn chairs on the lawn.
In his anxiety he had forgotten that the very essence of a lawn chair
        is that it is destined for a lawn.

The pastor's fear seems so small when one listens to the kind of fears
        that Jesus prepares his followers to get ready for.
In this section of Matthew's Gospel, Jesus tells them that because of him,
        they will face persecution, suffering, death.
It is hard for us modern North Americans to fear that our following Christ
        will ever get us into that kind of trouble.
Not that it never happens:
        the high school senior at Columbine who was asked whether she
        believed in God while a
        gun was shoved in her face
        courageously acknowledged Christ before her executors.

Christians in China this very night are suffering horrible torture
     because of their love of the Church.
But these sufferings, these sacrifices, these fears seem so distant from our
     own.

That's why, I believe, we can relate more to the stupid, tiny, unwarranted
     fears of the pastor in Saginaw with his fear that
     someone will place lawn chairs on his lawn.
Because after all, we all have our lawn chairs.
We all have allowed something insignificant to get in the way of
     our relationship with God and with the people in our lives.

Even people who are faced with the most daunting challenges in life like a
     cancer diagnosis can allow petty fears to block peace and healing.
And I can say that from experience.
Oncologists have told me that the two things people ask when they are
     diagnosed are
     1) how long do I have to live? and 2) will I lose my hair?
And sometimes the two are not asked in that order!
It is hard for someone facing chemotherapy to hear Jesus say:
     "Even all the hairs of your head are counted. So do not be afraid."

Yes, we are sometimes dealing with big fears, the kind Jesus speaks about
     today.
But mostly we allow ourselves to be paralyzed by the small, petty fears
     like lawn chairs, hair falling out, fear of being accepted,
     fear of never making a mistake.
This is why Richard Carlson had made a bundle from his book
     Don't Sweat the Small Stuff—and it's all small stuff.

We come as a community of believers who struggle with the small stuff,
     the petty fears that keep us from becoming a true community of
     believers.
We hear God tell us not to be afraid.

But the shocking good news we hear tonight is that we should fear God:
"Be afraid of the one who can destroy both soul and body in
Gehenna."
When we fear God, we do not fear God
as we do a dentist about to perform a root canal
or a police officer who pulls us over for speeding.
No, that is a foolish, childish notion of the fear of God.

The biblical notion of the fear of God is much more positive.
It always involves a deep sense of God's otherness and ultimate meaning
and leads us to wonder and awe and respect for a God who loves us
and believes we are worth more than many sparrows.
May this Eucharist help each of us to have such a fear of God:
a fear that leads to wonder and awe,
a fear that puts all the small stuff we sweat each day into perspective.
This is why we pray together to the Lord not only to keep us from sin
but to protect us from all anxiety
so that we can keep waiting in joyful hope
for the coming of our Savior Jesus Christ.

RPW

Questions for Reflection

1. Can you recognize any "lawn chair" in your life that gets in way of your being at peace?

2. Can you think of any "small stuff" that we as a community, as a Church, as a country are "sweating"?

3. Do you have a healthy "fear of the Lord"?

Other Directions for Preaching

1. Jeremiah speaks of God as "a mighty champion" who "rescues the life of the poor from the power of the wicked." How does this fit with the reality we find in our world today?

2. Today's Letter to the Romans presents Paul's contrast between the old Adam and the New Adam. At the heart of this passage is the proclamation of the overflowing and abundant grace of God.

3. Paul VI wrote in his apostolic letter *On Evangelization in the Modern World* that the modern person listens far more willingly to witnesses than to teachers, and if he or she does listen to teachers, it is because they are witnesses. The Gospel ends with a call to witness to Christ before others.

Waters That Kill
THIRTEENTH SUNDAY
IN ORDINARY TIME

Readings:
2 Kings 4:8–11, 14–16a; Romans 6:3–4, 8–11;
Matthew 10:37–42

Let's think about getting back to basics for a moment.
For Christians, it doesn't get any more fundamental than baptism.
The Greek word *baptizein* literally means to immerse or to bury.
The connection between death and baptism is obvious.
In the early Church, the neophyte would be baptized, fully immersed
     in a large pool, certainly in waters deep enough to drown.
And the associations between baptism and death did not stop there.
The early church fathers read Moses' crossing of the Red Sea
     and the defeat of Pharaoh as a prefiguring of Christian baptism.
Just as the waters covered Pharaoh and his charioteers,
     so do the waters of baptism kill the old self with its sin and decay.

Paul reminds the Romans of the claim of baptism
     on the Christian community when he says,
     "Brothers and sisters: Are you unaware
     that we who were baptized into Christ Jesus were baptized
     into his death?"
Certainly, Paul could have said that we were baptized into Christ's *life*,
     but he refuses to do so for a very good reason:

196

Baptism conforms the Christian to a pattern
    already lived out by Christ.
The physical and historical death and resurrection of Christ
    is reproduced in Christian baptism.
For Paul, there has got to be a death for there to be a new life.
He goes on to say that, "we were indeed buried with him
    through baptism into death,
        so that, just as Christ was raised from the dead by the glory of the
        Father, we too might live in newness of life."
And so after the immersion into death, we are liberated from sin.
Sin has been conquered.
We are literally a "new creation."
And in the baptismal rite, the one who comes from the waters of baptism
    is clothed in a white garment,
        signaling the literal re-creation of another person,
        a new creature, born again from the womb of the Church in baptism.

When seen through the mystical waters of baptism,
Jesus' words in the Gospel today make infinite sense.
"Whoever does not take up his [or her] cross and follow after me is not
    worthy of me"; not worthy because that person is
    not yet conformed to the difficult, personal task
    of imitating Christ's own life, death, and rising.
If the price of baptism is a death to sin,
    then the cost of discipleship is a recognition
    that the old self is dead and that we are alive in Christ.
I am no longer driven by self-interest,
    but focused on Christ, we say.
I am no longer an ego-centered person,
    but compelled by love for others, we proclaim.
Indeed, it is no longer I who live, but Christ who lives in me.
This is the work of Christ,
    accomplished for all of us in baptism that makes us truly alive.

And after all, being truly alive means living for others,
      for my family, my friends, the stranger, the guest—for God alone.
All this is wonderfully echoed in the fourth Eucharistic Prayer,
      which says, "so that we might no longer live for ourselves
      but for him, he sent the Holy Spirit from you, Father,
      as his first gift to those who believe,
      to complete his work on earth and to give us the fullness of grace."
Some fires burn brighter than others.
All originate when we accept the new life of the paschal candle,
      God's burning love for us at the cool waters of salvation.

Cooperating with the life-giving grace of baptism
      enables us to pick up our cross
      and rise to things we never thought possible.
If the old self has died, we live to the call to service.
How else can we explain the supernatural dying
      and rising that enabled God's holy ones to live out
      their baptismal commitment so completely.
Damian the Leper was a Belgian priest who found himself
      compelled to live in and minister to leper colonies
      in the islands of Hawaii
      and who finally caught the dreadful disease himself.
Dorothy Day founded the Catholic Worker movement
      and ministered to thousands in soup kitchens in New York City and
      elsewhere.
Blessed Mother Teresa of Calcutta worked with the dying
      of every religious persuasion in India.
These superhuman actions were animated by one thing and one thing only:
      God's sanctifying, ever-living grace working in us.
That is why the fervent prayer at every baptism is
      that the new life in Christ may be kept
      brightly burning for all to see.

The life of every Christian is marked by a sign of the cross for a reason.
We sign ourselves without thinking,
> but it recalls the cross that was traced
> on our foreheads by the priest or deacon, parents, and godparents
> so long ago.
That cross calls us to live our baptismal
> promises each day in serving one another.
Loving service allows God's work
> to come to fulfillment, even perfection.
When St. Francis was at the end of his time on earth
> he had already lived a life of self-sacrifice,
> compassion and dedication to the human family.
There is a moving scene in Roberto Rosellini's film of St. Francis
> in which the saint embraces the leper and then,
> after the man departs, the saint just
> collapses in a heap, weeping in a barren field
> as the wounded man looks on from a distance.
St. Francis earned his stigmata at the end of his life as an echo
> of the cross on his forehead on the day of his baptism.
St. Francis's baptismal promises came to life fully in him.
And surely very few people conformed their lives so profoundly
> to the crucified and risen Lord.
And yet St. Francis, like all of us,
> simply allowed his own baptism to unfold within him and take root.
The signs of God's redemption for us in Christ are covering us even now.
Surely, this week we can rise from our sins,
> face whatever challenges await us,
> like a swimmer emerging from vibrant waters into the sunny air,
> and bring that burning, crucified love to all we meet.

GD

Questions for Reflection

1. Can we trace the cross in our lives? Where has it been made manifest?

2. Practically speaking, how do I die to myself in day-to-day life?

3. Some people believe that they have died to their self-interests but never become fully alive. What does it mean for me to "put on Christ" and *really* live?

Other Directions for Preaching

1. God's fruitfulness is shown in prophetic witness and brings hope to what was once barren.

2. Renouncing the things that keep us from seeking God begin at baptism and continue throughout our lives.

3. We become sharers in divine life by taking up the specific cross that God has given each of us as individuals.

A Children's King
FOURTEENTH SUNDAY IN ORDINARY TIME

Readings:
Zechariah 9:9–10; Romans 8:9, 11–13;
Matthew 11:25–30

I was once visiting a rectory and the guest bedroom
    had a familiar picture of Jesus surrounded by children.
I had seen this print so often in other places,
    yet I had never stopped to see the signature of the artist.
That did not seem too important, I guess.
This time, for some reason, I was struck with the traces
    of real hunger that the children revealed—all of different races—
    as they approached Jesus.
There they were, a kind of juvenile version of the United Nations,
    circling in on the Lord.
"What were all these kids doing off on their own?" I thought.
Jesus was pictured in the center,
    more or less a center of gravity around which these little ones
    seem to orbit.
Perhaps the portrait of Jesus' strength
    is what made the children appear so much more needy;
    these were real sheep without a Shepherd.
In a certain way, as young as these children were,
    they looked old, gray and weary from their journey,

begging Jesus to provide comfort,
    an answer to life's burdens.
Children are like that:
    they are not afraid to admit to their needs.
It is only when we grow older
        that we start putting on masks of learning
        and cleverness to disguise our vulnerability.
But Jesus is like a child;
        he thanks his Father for revealing a mystery
        to the merest of children and hiding it from the wise.
There is a long history of spirituality that could be gleaned
        from this passage,
        a kind of repetition of an earlier Beatitude:
        "Blessed are the poor in spirit,
        for theirs is the kingdom of heaven" (Matt 5:3).
The children Jesus speaks of are the *anawim*, the lowly
        and humble in the Hebrew Scriptures;
        they are the ones most disposed to be dependent on God—
        without social rank, big degrees, a fancy office;
        nothing on their faces that could prompt a boast,
        like the familiar bumper sticker that proudly hails,
        "My child is a an honor roll student."
Humility knows nothing
        except honest-to-goodness dependence on God for everything.
The very self lives something like a rental car:
        to be a trusted vehicle at God's disposal.
This particular passage in Matthew's Gospel
        is also used for the Feast of St. Thérèse of Lisieux.
Well-known as St. Theresa of the Child Jesus,
        the popular Carmelite saint has become much sentimentalized
        since her painful death from tuberculosis in 1897.
Yet the recent edition of her famous autobiography, *The Story of a Soul,*
        reveals a depth of love characterized by deep simplicity.

She called her love for God the "Little Way."

It was a voyage—a short, acutely painful journey—about complete trust,
    and the cross,
        and love returned to God.

That humility took courage, passion, and great determination,
        qualities not often associated with childhood.

Yet these are the very gifts that we baptized adults claim
        in order to shake off our pretensions to sophistication
        and recognize our intense need for God.

We become holy often by shrinkage, by becoming little.

We are all vulnerable when we encounter Christ in sacramental love.

The sacraments of the Church often catch us "off guard," as it were;
        they discover us at liminal moments.

Edge moments.

I remember going to the hospital to anoint a man named Leonardo
        who was badly injured in a car wreck.

At seventy years old, he had just returned from Italy
        when his car was T-boned, broadsided.

He was hooked up to all sorts of machines, but he was conscious.

When his family gathered around his bedside,
        we celebrated the sacrament of the sick.

It was clearly an emotional moment for the entire family.

Just before we concluded our prayers,
        I traced a little cross on his forehead and said,
        "*Va bene*, Leonardo, *va bene*."

Suddenly, the man became very alert and looked at me with bright eyes.

Something came alive in that room.

Better put: *Someone* came alive:
        the risen Jesus.

We may not have to be completely down and out
        to experience the "easy yoke" that Jesus offers us
        in Word and Sacrament.

Ideally, couples who celebrate the sacrament of marriage
    transition to the state where they are no longer one but two.
That requires humility and the daunting strength of the "Little Way."

Msgr. Ronald Knox described, in a sermon "On Priesthood," reaching a
    state that was an emptying,
    even a rejection of rational thought for the blessed moment.
Knox writes that "the future priest stretched out at full length,
    face downwards, like a corpse, like a dummy,
    while the solemn chant of the litany rolled over his head…
    He was yielding his body to Christ to be his instrument, as if he had
    no life, no will of his own."*

Love demands no less:
    putting aside the self for the sake of the other.
That kind of love can best be described on a child's laughing face,
    which sparkles with confidence when she is lightly tossed
    into the air by a loving parent.
The thrill is not the leap itself;
    it is the certain, confident, complete knowledge
    that love has sure, big hands.

One of the Sunday Prefaces for Ordinary Time
    that is especially appropriate today recognizes God's children
    as wanderers,
    pilgrims looking for their true home.
The text says, "You gather them into your Church to be one as you, Father,
    are one with your Son and the Holy Spirit.
You call them to be your people, to praise your wisdom in all your works."
We pray this prayer all the while lifting up our hearts,
    allowing the Eucharist to gather us in so that our eyes
    can glimpse the promise that we will one day behold the great King.

---

*Ronald Knox, *Pastoral and Occasional Sermons* (San Francisco: Ignatius Press, 2002), 864.

We pray that all God's children will become one
    even as we put away all that separates us.
It is, after all, often the pretensions of the sophisticated that make divisions,
    and the segregation on buses,
    and the apartheid in whole communities.
I believe that today we call the polite, middle-class term
    "gated communities."
Hard to believe it, but it is true: what we think is progress
    may not be so progressive after all.
Some administrative people who thought they were clever once took a map
    of Africa,
    put it on a big oak table
    and drew lines dividing folks that had been living side by side
    for centuries.

Worldly "wisdom" like that has no place at the God's table.
But guided by the Spirit, God's children leave the maps home.
They come to rejoice in what Zechariah has seen:
    one God coming to us as a child himself;
    one God, meek and riding on an ass, not a stallion of war;
    one God, bringing his people only bread and the new wine
    of the covenant that he himself has made possible.

GD

Questions for Reflection

1. How can I let go of pretenses and become simply childlike?

2. Do I express a dependency on Almighty God? At what times? Only when things get really rough?

3. What did it feel like to be in God's merciful presence during a recent sacramental encounter? Have I changed because of this experience?

Other Directions for Preaching

1. The only true freedom we have is abandoning ourselves completely to God.

2. "Living according to the flesh" is really about my desire to be the author of my own destiny and it plays itself out in many expressions.

3. The Spirit dwells in us most fully when we come to know the Son in Word and Sacrament.

The Secret of the Seed
FIFTEENTH SUNDAY
IN ORDINARY TIME

Readings:
Isaiah 55:10–11; Romans 8:18–23; Matthew 13:1–23

When I was watching the television reports on Hurricane Bertha with her
    150 mph winds,
      I remember thinking to myself:
      "You really don't want to fool around with Mother Nature."
The scenes of trees bent double and houses being battered and heavy rain
    pelting the coast
      brought home to me once again the power of nature.
And yet in the face of all this, there are always people who want to go up
    on the beach
      and watch the storm come in.
Part of me says they are crazy and part of me would like to join them.
Such power puts me in awe of it.
One stands before it in wonder.

Jesus reminds us today of another symbol of power,
    one we do not usually stand in awe of:
      the power of a seed.
I put out some bowls in the back of church.
In the one on the right side, there are some seeds for a lavender plant;
    in the one on the left side, there are seeds for a cabbage plant;
      and in the bowl in the middle aisle are seeds for a mustard bush.

Behind each is the packet it came in with the picture of what results
    from a solitary seed.
Another kind of power is revealed when you take a moment
    and just look at that tiny seed on the tip of your finger.

The parable of the sower and the seed begins the third great discourse
    Matthew gives to Jesus in his Gospel.
This speech contains seven parables about the kingdom of God.
The first parable places before us a sower going out to sow seed.
Of course, the seed is nothing unless it lands in the right spot.
In Palestine, a sower would toss the seed all over, lavishly,
    and only after tossing was the earth plowed up and over the seed.
And so it would land in different settings: on the path, among weeds,
    in a shallow area, and sufficiently deep in the earth.
Thus a seed might be crushed underfoot, burnt up by the sun,
    or eaten by birds,
    or it might nestle securely in the earth that embraces it.
Seeds grow only when securely settled in soil.
If there's not satisfactory soil, no results.
If there's not sufficient soil, no growth.

This is a story that speaks of the power of God's word;
    but this seed must find a heart to rest in if there is to be any results.
Jesus told this parable at a time when many were rejecting his preaching.
And this story continues to speak to us and challenge us.
God's word has the power to change the world if it really takes root
    even in a single heart, much less in the heart of a community.
The seed carries the power that flows from knowing every person is part of
    God's creation.
It carries the power that comes from knowing this world was created
    out of love
    and was entrusted to us to see to its care and nurturing.
This seed proclaims that Jesus is the Lord of all life, calling us to allow him
to enter more fully into our lives so he can transform them.

This seed carries with it the presence of the Holy Spirit who is the Sanctifier,
  the one who makes us holy, who transforms all things
  into what God wants them to be.
This seed reminds us that we are all beloved, and it calls us to recognize
  that about each other,
  to come together in wonder and awe of each other
  and of the God in whom we live and move and have our being.
Just as the seed breaks apart into a form that seeks warmth and light,
  so too the Word of God moves us out of darkness
  into the fullness of life.

The obituary for newscaster John Chancellor
  in yesterday's *New York Times*
  quoted his final words on the last broadcast he made in 1993.
Mr. Chancellor said that the change that worried him most in our society
  was this:
  the isolation of so many Americans that has been brought about by
  television and computers.
He said that in households where so many members increasingly go
  to their own TV corners rather than talk,
  and in homes where the most time is spent
  with one's personal computer,
  you might begin to wonder what will be the capacity for human relationships in the future.

The seed that is God's Word calls forth life from us today.
Jesus plants this Word in each of our hearts in the hope that it will set down
  roots and grow,
  and we will know how much God loves us,
  and how much God wants us to recognize that together
  we are the branches
  that grow from the vine that is Jesus.
He plants his Word in us to draw us out of our selves, out of our homes,
  out of our churches, and into our world.

I can imagine no greater sorrow than when Jesus sees his word falling on
    hard hearts,

    as it did with so many of the Pharisees and the learned ones.
Or when he sees it welcomed for a while but then forgotten

    because of the worries

    that tend to overwhelm us all too often, as with the rich young man
    who seemed so eager at first.
Or when he sees a person begin to grow stronger in faith and hope and
    love, but then something happens and the life that was there is choked
    off, for one reason or another, as it was with Peter whose fear made
    him deny he even knew Jesus.
But there are also those times when people just opened wide to his message:
    like the young man who heard him and went off and got his brother
    and brought him to Jesus; the elderly widow who listened to him and
    then went to the temple and gave all she had to live on; the sister of
    his good friend, who would not leave his side when he came to visit;
    and the old man whose sight he had restored who followed him up the
    road.
You could see the light in all their eyes, that awareness they had found
    something so precious

    that only a fool would forget he or she had it.
The sower continues to go out and sow his seed.
And it continues to fall in different places.
What is growing within you?

                                                            JAW

Questions for Reflection

1. Have you ever watched something grow from seed to full size? What moved you about it?

2. What words of Scripture have given you life and drawn you to the light?

3. Where is God's Word moving you? How is God's Word speaking to this community?

Other Directions for Preaching

1. Isaiah's witness to the power of God's Word proclaims that it will achieve "the end for which I sent it." God's Word has a purpose that will not be denied.

2. The Letter to the Romans reminds us that, because of the presence of the Spirit and grace, we live in hope, despite the tension brought on by the reality of sin and corruption.

3. The purpose of the parables in Jesus' ministry and in our lives today as individuals and as a community is that we come to recognize the ongoing and active presence of God.

To Weed or Not To Weed
Sixteenth Sunday
in Ordinary Time

Readings:
Wisdom 12:13, 16–19; Romans 8:26–27;
Matthew 13:24–43

To be honest, on a gut level, I am in sympathy with a no-weeds approach
      to life.
You don't even need to have a garden to understand the desire to weed out.
I spent Friday morning weeding out my room, separating things
      into various piles,
      getting rid of things that had been laying about.
I had crossed the line of tolerance for holding onto articles I wanted to read,
      books that had been on the floor over a year, and files that should be
      sifted through.
There's a satisfying feeling of accomplishment when things are neat
      and ordered,
      a certain lightness of being when one gets rid of "clutter,"
      whether it's spam on the Internet, or the various accretions of the
      years that get stored in the various rooms of one's life.
So I sympathize with the servants in the parable we just heard.
When they saw weeds growing, they wanted to get rid of them—now!
And they had an even better reason: the weeds were growing around the
      wheat.

The problem comes when the "no weeds" approach becomes
    a life commitment.
It can move from influencing one's outlook on inanimate clutter to one's
    outlook on living beings.
For some people the liberals are weeds, for others the conservatives.
This holds whether you are discussing church matters
    or government politics.
In our country today, some treat the flow of immigrants as an influx
    of weeds,
        especially if they are illegal—forgetting how their own ancestors
        started out.
Weeding has been played out in what is called ethnic cleansing;
    this group decides *that* group is really not fit, nor worthy,
    not good enough, to live.
Sometimes it is done more subtly.
The Southern Baptist Conference recently decided to boycott Disney because
    that corporation was offering insurance to partners of gay workers.
I know there are times when action must be taken.
Jesus is not advocating a passive approach to life,
    a biblical version of "Don't worry, be happy."
Nor was he a proponent of "Let's wait and see—surely it won't get
    any worse."
Remember Neville Chamberlain!
Jesus was constantly preaching out of a sense of urgency,
    saying that now was the hour to turn from sin to new life.
So, what is the point of this parable?

First of all, parables give us a glimpse into the kingdom of God.
They speak about its coming into our world and into our lives.
While we can hear this parable in terms of what was happening
    in Jesus' ministry,
    and also in terms of the end of the world,
        I am going to treat it as it speaks to the life of the Church.
It is a story of about what should be our response when we find evil within.

The immediate response can be to tear it out.

But here is where the master of the parable is instructive.

Three things are interesting about the master here.

First he is more pro-wheat than anti-weeds:

> "If you pull up the weeds," he says, "you might uproot the wheat
> along with them."

He is committed to keeping the wheat alive so it can grow.

Second, he is into the long view.

He sees what is before him and recognizes an enemy has been at work,
> and that the weeds are right there with the wheat.

But he figures he can wait until the harvest and separate the wheat out then
> —again, lest the wheat be damaged.

Finally, in the master's approach, the present is a time for patience
> and forbearance.

Acting hastily now will bring about a future that holds no promise.

What wisdom does this parable hold for us?

It is not hard to see the God of Creation in this story:

> the God who waits for us to come to full growth,

> the God whose future includes a day or reckoning,

> but, most of all, the God whose present is marked by mercy.

Our God so loves this world that when the original gardener
> didn't work out,

> God gave his Son the job of bringing about a new creation.

And this Son, even though rejected and seemingly overwhelmed
> by the evil of those who put him to death,

> was not allowed to be conquered by death but was raised to new life.

This Son is now the source of our life for all who believe in him.

This parable raises some questions for us.

Are we more pro-wheat or anti-weed?

Do we allow people the time to grow by way of God's grace into goodness?

It can be very tempting to want to pull up and toss out.

Problem ended.

But pulling up weeds can lead to greater loss than anticipated.
Can we trust that the future belongs to God?
In the end God will be there to harvest all that is good.
In the meantime, with patience and forbearance, can we focus on the good?

In Martin Luther's catechism, we find the instruction that you should not
    tell lies about your neighbor,
        but should apologize for him, speak well of him, and interpret charita-
        bly all that he does.
What is most important is the good; God will care for what is evil
    among us.

This approach can be difficult to trust when one faces our world today.
When one lives with the real possibility of another terrorist attack—
        when one lives with the frequent occurrence of suicide bombers
        who turn restaurants into abattoirs, buildings into burial plots,
        and street corners into scenes of unforgettable suffering—
        is there anyone who would not want to weed out those
        who would bring about the destruction of innocent lives?
But the impulse to respond with equal devastation only incites more hatred
    and increases the likelihood of even greater violence.
Is it possible to transform the human heart when it has become what one
    might well imagine
        as the dwelling place of evil spirits?

Tomorrow we celebrate the feast of a woman who was certainly looked on
    as a weed
        by her own people: Mary Magdalene.
I am not talking about Mary Magdalene whom tradition has cast
    as a prostitute;
        there is really no historical basis for that, other than the imaginations
        of artists and preachers who identified her with the woman who came
        and wept at Jesus' feet and washed them with her hair.

What Scripture tells us of Magdalene is that she was the woman
from whom Jesus cast out seven demons.
What form this possession took we do not know;
such a description simply presents her as one held captive by the forces
of evil.
But Jesus saw something more, gazing at her with the eyes of love.
And this woman was among those who were most faithful to him,
who was there at the end when all the men ran,
who was the first to be sent to proclaim the resurrection of Jesus
to these same men.

Does this end up leaving us with a kind of holy indifference
towards what is evil?
Certainly not.
But it calls us to be careful what we decide to root up
and to consider how costly such action can be to the life growing
around it.
Most of all, we are called to live in the awareness that God will be there
when all is done,
to claim the good for life in the kingdom.
Today's Eucharist calls us to enter more fully into this promise and live out
of it.

JAW

Questions for Reflection

1. What weeds would you like to root out of our world? If you had the power to do so, would it affect any wheat growing up around it?

2. Do you trust in the wisdom of God that allows the just to live with sinners, not just tolerating them but reaching out in love?

3. Can you recognize your own life as a field of wheat and weeds and turn to God in hope rather than despair?

Other Directions for Preaching

1. Wisdom reveals that God's justice is different from ours.

2. The Spirit intercedes for us even when we do not know how to pray as we should.

3. The parables of the mustard seed and the leaven proclaim that the kingdom often comes in a surprising way that disarms us and maybe even disappoints us: not as a mighty cedar but as a shrub, not as something pure but as something marked by corruption.

Pursuing the Pearl
SEVENTEENTH SUNDAY IN ORDINARY TIME

Readings:
1 Kings 3:5, 7–12; Romans 8:28–30; Matthew 13:44–52

Four hundred thousand people waited on Thursday to catch a glimpse of
the Pope as World Youth Day began.
In the newspaper reports, you could hear the excitement.
One girl said, "I just saw the back of his head."
Another, "I saw his face. I couldn't see his hands, but I saw his face."
And yet another sighed, "I saw this much," indicating a span of two inches.
The press in its limited imagination could only compare him to a rock star.

There seems to be something a little deeper at work here.
"I felt peace, total peace, something I never experienced in my life,"
said an eighteen-year-old from Texas.
Sister Margaret from Boston commented, "People feel faith, just to be
in his presence."
Peace, faith, a sense of connection with what is holy, and with what is good—
whatever words people choose, they indicate they have found
something of value
when this man is present among them.
I think we can connect it with what Jesus is talking about in these stories,
a glimpse of the kingdom, a touch of the treasure
one suddenly stumbles over.

Or, to take up the imagery of the second parable, seeing from a distance
>the pope's round white skullcap, his zucchetto,
>one might imagine the gleam of a pearl.
But Pope John Paul is not the treasure in himself,
he is one who witnesses to the treasure he has found:
"Look to Christ.
With your gaze set firmly,
>you will discover the path of forgiveness and reconciliation
>in a world often laid waste by violence and terror.
Look to Christ.
Listen to Christ."

This morning, let us look to Christ, and listen to Christ.
We hear the voice of Jesus the teacher, speaking to his disciples.
Jesus is at work today forming us into a school of scribes,
>not, as we might have felt in recent days, a school for scandal.
In the conclusion of his third great speech in Matthew's Gospel,
>Jesus tells three final parables, offering wisdom in their images,
>taking us deeper into an understanding of the kingdom of God.

"The kingdom...is like a treasure buried in a field...," Jesus says.
"The kingdom...is like a merchant searching for fine pearls...," Jesus says.
The first two stories seem similar, tales of discovering something valuable
>and the joy
>that follows from such a discovery.
The usual way we hear these stories interpreted is that, when we come upon
>the kingdom,
>whether we accidentally stumble upon it, or deliberately go out and
>search for it,
>when it is finally there before us, we are to sell all we have
>to possess it.
Two stories, then, that appeal to our nature as consumers: "Buy wisely!"
We can also hear in them a call to take charge, take control,
>take possession of the kingdom of God, no matter what the cost.

This understanding has been around for awhile and does have its virtues
    as a call to action.
But another understanding is also possible:
The man who stumbles upon the field is one of Jesus' rascals, like the ser-
    vant who changes the amount owed to his master to win friends
    before he's sacked.
Here a man stumbles upon a treasure, then reburies it—why?
So no one else will get it.
The problem is: it doesn't belong to him.
The ethics of the Mosaic Law is not one of "finders, keepers."
According to the Law of Moses, the treasure would still belong
    to the original owner.
The man who stumbles over it would be obligated to turn it over to him.
If he did not, then his neighbors would consider him a thief when they
    found out.
So people hearing Jesus tell this tale would laugh at the ending.
The rascal is also a dumbo.
Selling all he had would leave him staring out onto a treasure he couldn't
    touch.
If he touched it, he would have to return it.

As for the merchant, he similarly sells all he has to gain the pearl.
But then what?
He will have to turn around and sell it again in order to live.
Diamonds may be a girl's best friend, but you can't eat a pearl.

What's the Gospel here, the good news?
Consider this:
Yes, the kingdom is a treasure, a pearl of great price.
And whether we stumble over or search for it and find it, this is the truth.
And yes, when we find it, it is a time of great joy, for this kingdom is God's
    presence,
        in our world and in our lives.
But here is the twist: do we really think we can *possess* it?

Because if we try to possess it, our joy is corrupted.
If we begin to think of it as "ours," this inevitably leads
    to its not being "theirs"—
    whoever "theirs" happens to refer to:
    sometimes another religious group,
    or an ethnic group, or any group that "we" don't think is worthy of
    "our" treasure.
We are called to receive the kingdom as a gift.
But while there is only one designated donor,
    the plan is that as many as possible shall have it.
Accept it as such, a gift given to whomever God pleases.
And God's pleasure is that it is for all God's children.

The final story about the fish in the net can be heard as reinforcing this.
It concerns the kingdom at the end of time.
The bottom line is this: whoever comes into the kingdom,
    the question of their worthiness to be there is not *our* concern.
The final judgment is up to God (Matthew uses the angels as stand-ins for
    God).
So, live lives worthy of the gift, for as Luther reminds us:
    "We are beggars all."

It is very human to want to possess what we value.
Two weeks ago, when the fires out west were burning,
    an online survey asked,
    "If you only had five minutes to leave your home,
    what would you take?"
You could check to see what people had written.
One woman wrote, "My husband, I think."
Others mentioned pets, record collections, stamp collections,
    "my tax records because the IRS doesn't care about fires."
But do you know what was the most common thing mentioned?

Photo albums, pictures—those pieces of the past, reminders
       of those we love,
              memories of places and times spent with others.
What struck me as a fellow photo-album-collector is that,
       while you can seize certain moments on celluloid,
              you can't possess, control, or safely secure what matters most –
              the people in the pictures, nor your relationship with them.
They are a gift, and some last a lifetime, and others don't.
Relationships are subject to change—due to death, distance, or different
       dreams.

The best things in life are free as the old song goes.
And that's true for the kingdom of God.
There is no need to grab at it when it comes to us.
Just put your hands out to receive it,
              as we do when we come to receive that taste of the kingdom
              in the Eucharist.
What is set into our open hand reminds us of the gift Jesus wishes us
       to have:
              peace, forgiveness, the nourishment necessary for the work
              of the kingdom.
So today, in coming to receive communion, we do what our life is meant
       to be about:
              We receive the kingdom of God, God's presence and love,
              into our lives,
              with open hands, giving thanks for the gift and going out to live in
              gratitude.
"Do you understand all these things?" Jesus asks.
Today he might put it this way: "Do you get it?
Do you have an understanding heart?"

JAW

Questions for Reflection

1. Has there been a treasure in your life that you have stumbled over? Or one that you have spent years pursuing?

2. What have you discovered about trying to possess a treasure?

3. Can you rejoice in God's desire for all to share in the kingdom?

Other Directions for Preaching

1. The young teen Solomon asks for "an understanding heart," and Jesus asks those listening, "Do you understand?" What is this gift of understanding and why is it so important?

2. "All things work for good for those who love God," writes Paul. How can this be true in the light of so much human sorrow and tragedy in our world today?

3. The note of delight and joy is sounded in the parables. Consider the difference between the joy that the kingdom brings and the joy held out to us by our consumer culture.

From Fear to Faith to Feeding
Eighteenth Sunday
in Ordinary Time

Readings:
Isaiah 55:1–3; Romans 8:35, 37–39; Matthew 14:13–21

It is easy to miss the first part of today's Gospel.
I don't often think of Jesus ever being afraid, but I guess he must have been.
There is the night before he died, of course, in the garden of Gethsemane.
But, beyond that, he always seems so forthright and willing to take on all
 comers.
This story of the feeding of the five thousand begins with Jesus hearing of
 the death of John the Baptist.
And he withdraws to a deserted place, to be by himself.
Luke tells us that John is his cousin, and all the Gospels record that Jesus
 underwent
the baptism of John.
There was a bond there to be sure.

John had sent word from prison, asking Jesus if he was the one who was to
 come.
And Jesus sent word back, quoting the prophet Isaiah,
 whom we heard this morning.
Jesus sent the message that the blind see, the deaf hear, the lame walk,
 and blessed is the person who didn't find him a stumbling block.
Did John laugh when he heard that; did his heart leap for joy as he had
 in his mother's womb a lifetime ago?

Jesus had turned to the crowd after saying this and said: "Among those
    born of women there has been none greater than John" (Matt 11:11).
Now John was dead and Jesus was...what? Depressed? Saddened?
In a state of grief and sorrow? Afraid?

But then the crowd shows up, needy, sick, and eventually hungry.
Matthew tells us that his heart was moved with pity for them.
He sees the longing in their eyes—for a better life, for relief from their
    poverty.
He sees the desires they bring with them out to the desert.
And he starts to touch them, to pray over them, to cure them.
And suddenly the day is nearly over and the disciples come to him.
The people should be sent away, they say to him.
It is late and they need to get to a town to buy food.

But Jesus says something strange:
"There is no need for them to go away; give them some food yourselves."
They must have wondered, What could he be thinking?
"Five loaves and two fish are all we have here."
But Jesus knows there is more than that here.
He has moved from fear to faith.
He has looked into the face of the people and seen the hungers of their
    heart and he has remembered why he has come.
The Father has sent him and he has work to do.
He and the Father have work to do.

So he takes the bread and the fish and blesses them.
Then he starts breaking the bread, and handing it out,
    breaking it and handing it out to the disciples,
    who passed it to the men present,
    who passed it to the women and the children.
And five thousand were fed that day, not counting women and children.

It is the inner movement of the story that speaks to me today:
>   from fear to faith to feeding.

I wonder if it is the movement that Jesus himself had to make more often
>   than we might imagine.

I think the starting point is fairly common these days.

So much to be afraid of.

Since 9/11, does anyone feel safe anymore?

Since 9/11, who can board a plane without checking who's waiting with you
>   to board the plane?

Since the sniper shootings, just a trip to fill up the car,
>   or the walk across the parking lot at the mall,
>   no longer seems like something to take for granted.

Since the anthrax scare, even going to the mailbox commands courage.

Then there are the gang shootings that have erupted here,
>   replacing the drive-by shootings that held the front page of the Metro
>   section now and again last summer: random acts of violence that
>   transform familiar places into grounds for grieving.

We come here every Sunday mindful of another kind of transformation.

The movement from fear to faith is made possible in the first part of every
>   liturgy.

We hear the Word of God speak to us as God's people.

Today, we hear the invitation sounded through Isaiah:
>   "All you who are thirsty,
>>   come to the water!...
>   Heed me, and you shall eat well....
>>   listen, that you may have life."

From fear to faith and from faith to feeding.

Bread and wine become the Body and Blood of Christ.

And we, despite our fears and failures, grow ever so gradually
>   into what the Word of God promises we already are:
>   the Body of Christ in the world.

Fear is not our future.
Faith carries us into the kingdom of God,
   a kingdom embodied in Jesus Christ, yesterday, today, and forever.
Faith sings out this morning in the passionate proclamation of Paul:
What will separate us from the love of Christ?
   Nothing, nothing, nothing!
Neither death, nor life, nor angels, nor principalities,
   nor present things, nor future things....
Nothing will be able to separate us from the love of God in Christ Jesus
   our Lord.

JAW

Questions for Reflection

1. Is there anything that gives fear power over your life?

2. What would you ask the risen Lord to heal so that you might have fullness of life?

3. How is Jesus sending you out to feed the world, even though you might feel like the apostles who only had a few loaves and two fish?

Other Directions for Preaching

1. Isaiah's words remind us that God does not charge us for the gifts lavished on us. Eucharist calls us to make thanksgiving a way of living.

2. Paul's confidence that neither earthly nor cosmic forces can come between us and Christ speaks to fears that today's world developments evoke.

3. What is the relationship of the eucharistic to the messianic banquet in the kingdom of God?

A Miracle Worth Celebrating
Nineteenth Sunday
in Ordinary Time

Readings:
1 Kings 19:9a, 11–13a; Romans 9:1–5;
Matthew 14:22–33

A few weeks ago the secular humanist magazine *Free Inquiry*
    revealed the results of its research
    on the religious beliefs of Americans.
The magazine had long been suspicious of the Gallup Polls that concluded
    that the overwhelming majority of Americans are religious.

The magazine had to admit that their findings were a surprise.
They came awfully close to Gallup:
More than 90 percent of Americans believe in God and have a religious
    affiliation.
And nearly 90 percent believe in a personal God who can answer prayer.

Just as I was beginning to feel smug over the results of *Free Inquiry's* poll,
    I spotted an interesting statistic:
    94 percent of Protestants and 89 percent of Catholics believe
    that even today
    God performs miracles.
Now I know that 5 points aren't much of a difference even in empirical
    studies, but I couldn't help wonder why we Catholics scored lower in
    the miracle question.

What about all those places of pilgrimages like Fatima, Lourdes,
Medjugorje, where people claim cancer cells were canceled and rosary
beads turned to gold?
Weren't we the ones into miracles?
Are we Catholics beginning to loose the miracle tradition?

There is perhaps no miracle in the Bible that has been so doubted than the
story of Jesus walking on the water.
You know all the jokes: Peter forgot to walk on the stones and fell in, etc.
One of my favorite is the parish known for its bitter factions
and constant complaining,
which was finally sent a pastor known for his dynamic personality and
his ability
to bring people together.
When he arrived, he invited the entire parish to a picnic during which he
announced:
"See that lake over there. Watch this, I'm going to walk on the water."
And to the people's amazement, he did. He walked on the water.
But there was still one suspicious parishioner who shook his head and
grumbled to a friend:
"I bet he couldn't do it again."

Maybe one of the reasons we're beginning to lose the miracle tradition
is that we, too, have become suspicious:
Suspicious of TV evangelists who guarantee miracles, as long as you provide
your *Visa* number.
Suspicious of politicians who in this season promise miracles
more powerful than walking on water, as long as you vote for them.
Suspicious of some of our Catholic practices, which have sometime bor-
dered on the superstitious
rather than the miraculous.
Suspicious even of God when we pray for a miracle for a cure for breast
cancer or AIDS,
and we don't hear from God even a tiny whispering sound.

And so when we hear proclaimed the story of Jesus walking on water,
    we are tempted to write it off
        since it doesn't seem to speak to our own experience of life,
        since it is contrary to what we know is the law of nature.

But the Bible has a different notion of miracle.
Miracles are not necessarily breaches of the laws of nature.
They are events in which God breaks through in our lives,
    demanding our obedience and our faith.
The biblical notion of miracles points to events where people of faith see
    acts of God.
It's from that perspective that we listen to our miracle story today.
When Peter left the boat, he made a leap of faith and in that leap, the disciples recognized an act of God.
While praying over this leap of faith,
    I couldn't help but think of the Olympic divers going for the gold.
Every time a diver does his or her thing, there is the voice of a sports
    reporter from the sidelines
    saying some extraordinary things like:
    "Oops, he had one centimeter of his left toe off balance" or
    "Too bad, she had too much splash!"
"What?" I would say. "How does she know that and know that
    so instantly?"
"Splash? Too much splash. Well, for heaven's sake, the woman is diving
    into water where you're supposed to splash!"

The real miracle that happened that morning on the Sea of Galilee is that
    Peter and his disciples
    recognized Jesus as the Son of God.
Peter, like any good captain, had always instructed the others never to leave
    the boat, no matter what happened.
But he abandoned all that worldly knowledge, his neat little rationales,
    the wisdom of his experience—
    everything that gave him comfort and security.

He transcended all that and jumped into the water because Jesus bid him to
    come.

I am usually amused when I read the religion section of Saturday's
    Washington Post.

The stories are often trivial, denominations squabbling over rights or power.

Few miracles are there.

But yesterday I spotted a photo in the religion section that surprised me.

It was a photo of Dietrich Bonhoeffer,
    one of the most significant Protestant theologians of this century.

The German theologian had been an outspoken critic of the Nazi regime,
    and so he was hanged in April 1945.

Fifty-one years later, Bonhoeffer made the news because last Tuesday
    justice officials in Berlin finally cleared him of charges of treason
    for allegedly plotting to kill Adolf Hitler.

While in prison Bonhoeffer wrote moving works.

In one of these, *The Cost of Discipleship*, he meditates on the meaning of
    today's miracle:

> Peter had to leave the ship and risk his life on the sea, in order to learn
> both his own weakness and the almighty power of his Lord. If Peter
> had not taken the risk, he would never have learned the meaning of
> faith....The road to faith passes through obedience to the call of Jesus.
> Unless a definite step is demanded, the call vanishes into thin air, and
> if [people] imagine that they can follow Jesus without taking this step,
> they are deluding themselves....*

With words like that it is no wonder that in the new Lutheran
    Book of Worship
    Dietrich Bonhoeffer has a special commemoration in the
    Feast of Saints.

---

*Dietrich Bonhoeffer, *Cost of Discipleship* (New York: Macmillan, 1979), 68.

We might not have to jump into the nasty waters to fight an evil empire
  as Bonhoeffer did.
But there is a sense in which today we're all being tossed by storms
    and holding on desperately to the security of our boats
    and the little faith we still have left.
But being a Christian always means taking risks.
God does not say to us from the sidelines:
    "Oops, you made a splash" but "Why aren't you making a bigger
    splash?"
Central to our miracle today is that Peter found his belief in Jesus
  in the terrifying splash in the water.
The challenge for us as individual Christians, as a parish, as a denomination,
    as a universal Church, is to listen to how we are being called to take
    some real risks
    in order to encounter our living God.
Now that's a miracle worth celebrating.

RPW

Questions for Reflection

1. Do you believe in miracles?
2. When have you last taken a risk to meet the living God?
3. How is the Church being called to walk on water today?

Other Directions for Preaching

1. The "tiny whispering voice" of God continues to come in places least expected.

2. The Letter to the Romans offers an opportunity to speak of the relationship between the Christian and Jewish communities.

3. Christ continually calls his followers to "get into the boat" and does not abandon them in times of storm.

Hard Bargaining
Twentieth Sunday in Ordinary Time

Readings:
Isaiah 56:1, 6–7; Romans 11:13–15, 29–32;
Matthew 15:21–28

Like many large cities, New York is famous for its neighborhoods.
There are the ethnic spaces, like Little Italy,
> with its enchanting fragrances of anise and oregano;
> or Williamsburg, with its religious fervor
> of black-suited, long-bearded Hassidic Jews.
Head to the upper East Side and you will find fashion and glamour.
Go down to SoHo and you will find remarkable galleries and outdoor cafes.
And so it is with many cities and their enclaves of diversity.
Indeed, our very identity or family of origin
> suggests only a part of a particular culture,
> a composite of nations, a hyphenated personality.
I am an Irish-Italian-Hungarian American
> and like many in this country,
> I am glad to discover my national heritage not in one, but in many.
> We are a nation of aggregates, marvelous pieces of a puzzle,
> still waiting to be assembled;
> figures in a tapestry that are not quite defined;
> faces in a fog-dimmed window emerging in twilight.

In modern times we have become used to absorbing
       other ethnic groups in North America—all the more so these days—
       but it could not have been otherwise in the formation of Israel.
Israel shaped its very being out of a particular set of laws and
       a covenant that was quite loathe to collaborate with other nations.
To read the early history of Israel is to be entranced by the accounting
       of a tribe becoming a clan evolving to a nation,
       finally ratified as such under King David.
The experience of exile that would later befall the Jews in Babylon
       was perhaps the worst event that could inflict itself on a people
       who saw themselves as chosen by a God, jealous for their well-being.
They had become familial and, of course, linked to a patriarchal lineage
       stemming from Abraham, Isaac, and Jacob.
The people had become a nation, and then a nation on the edge.
Over and over again, the people of Israel were defined and redefined
       according to what they were not:
Not worshipping other gods.
Not in the land of Egypt or of Babylon.
But rather, "a people sacred to the LORD" (Deut 7:6).

With this in mind, we can only imagine
       how difficult it was for the Jewish-Christian community
       living inside Matthew's Gospel to welcome outsiders, the *goy'im.*
Paul faced the same problem over and over in bringing the Gospel
       to the Gentiles
       but he boasts of his mission all the same.
So in his Letter to the Romans, for example, Paul reckons
       Abraham's connection with the Christian community
       not through blood or a religious practice, but through faith.
Faith is what joins the hyphenated people of God together.
Faith is what transcends ethnic and national boundaries.
And faith is uppermost in Matthew's mind when he tries
       to reconcile strangers into this new hybrid,
       Jewish-Christian experience.

It is no accident that in Matthew's account of Jesus' birth,
>   three visitors from the East, three non-Jews,
>   are among the first to greet the newborn king of Israel in Bethlehem.

Enter loudly—the Canaanite woman from today's Gospel.
From the point of view of ethnic origins,
>   Matthew could not have picked a worse problem for a pious Jew.
The Canaanites were precisely the group of people
>   from whom the Israelites were disengaging.
The Canaanites were famous for their idolatry and human sacrifices
>   and became, for the nation of Israel, an abomination.
To make matters worse, the person who was asking Jesus for help
>   was a woman.
A Canaanite woman!
As a Jew, Jesus becomes a lightning rod for an exposition
>   of a cultural and religious problem:
>   what to do with this alien, this Gentile woman, this unclean foreigner.
And indeed, this is one of the few moments when we can really
>   feel Our Lord's embarrassment and, most interesting of all, his silence
>   over what to do.
See what happens.
The disciples push for her exclusion,
>   but it is the woman's faith that finally wins Jesus over.
It is almost as if Our Lord is trying to force the woman
>   to articulate her passion for the kingdom in front of the Jews and
>   Pharisees:
>   "Have pity on me, Lord, Son of David," she says.
No fool, she distinctly announces Jesus' Jewish lineage.
But more importantly, it is faith, persistent and undefeated,
>   that triumphs over national boundaries.
As Isaiah says, "The foreigners who join themselves to the LORD,
>   ministering to him,
>   loving the name of the LORD,
>   and becoming his servants...

them I will bring to my holy mountain
        and make joyful in my house of prayer."
According to the Roman Missal, one of the prayers
        that we can invoke during the penitential rite
        at the beginning of the Eucharist is:
        "Lord Jesus, you came to gather the nations into the peace of God's
        Kingdom." What a marvelous way to set the tone for today's liturgy!
Clearly, Christ's mission and work on earth was for all people,
        and even all creatures on earth.
Everything is new in Christ.
There is a technical term for that, long written about
        and studied by theologians such as Christoph Barth;
        it is called in Greek *apokatastasis,* the restoration of all things,
        the transformation of all beings,
        the reordering of fallen creation in Christ.
And I tell you that this potential reunion is already present to us.
We have a glimpse of what is at stake
        and awaiting redemption in our own global economy.
There is at this time nation butchering nation over boundaries.
We have seen the horrors of war in the last century like no other
        based on ethnic cleansing.
Gas chambers.
Firing squads.
Anonymous graves.
There continues to be exploitation of poor countries
        with national resources by wealthy, industrialized nations.

And yet we know that the only way we can keep our eyes on a global,
        ecological restoration
        is to recall Christ's work on earth in making all things one.
Jesus came to make possible what looks impossible:
        that nations with self-interests might never take up their swords
        any more.

That, despite the natural order of decay,

    every thing on earth, all creation, will flourish beyond our imagining.

In a strange sort of way, the Canaanite woman is our prophetic guide here,

    albeit an unlikely one at that.

But that, after all, is the point:

    those whom we target as outsiders are often the ones

    who lead us to the doors of the kingdom.

For we know only that the kingdom is coming and it is being brought

    by Christ.

Now.

Here is the Eucharist before us, disclosing that banquet which is

    the foretaste and promise of the restoration of all things.

Christ has made the many one.

Let us once again give thanks together in this house of prayer,

    on this holy mountain,

    where all shall be made one.

GD

Questions for Reflection

1. Who are my friends? Are they usually drawn from my own racial or cultural background?

2. We have all heard the expression "Think outside the box." What does it mean to "believe outside the box"?

3. What would it take to help me make better connections with the members of my faith community? Beyond that?

Other Directions for Preaching

1. The gifts and the call of God are irrevocable—how so today?

2. Biblical spirituality calls us to be as bold as possible—with God and everyone else.

3. What we want most is often the key to who we really are at the core.

Today's Guest Preacher: Peter the Fisherman
Twenty-First Sunday in Ordinary Time

Readings:
Isaiah 22:19–23; Romans 11:33–36;
Matthew 16:13–20

When pastors in some Protestant churches take their summer vacations,
　　they invite retired pastors to deliver the Sunday sermon.
We saw St. Peter trying to walk on water two Sundays ago.
Today he's a central figure because he recognizes Jesus as the Messiah.
And next week St. Peter will return again in the Gospel story.
And so I thought it would be appropriate and hopefully refreshing to invite
　　a retired pastor,
　　　St. Peter himself, to be this summer's guest preacher.

(Pause)

Thank you, very much.
I am deeply honored to be asked to preach today and to get a chance to tell
　　my own story, especially about what happened that day in Caesarea
　　Philippi.
A lot of you probably know me only from those jokes people tell
　　about meeting me at the pearly gates.
But there's much more to my story than that!

Well, where do I start?
Forgive the pun, but I guess the best place is "B.C."

Before I even heard of Jesus, I was a fisherman living with my wife in
    Capernaum, where we shared a little house with my mother-in-law
    and my brother Andrew.
We had what you would call today a small business with a couple of part-
    ners named James and John.
It was smelly, hard, and frustrating work, but it was honest work.
We lived a good, peaceful life by the beautiful Sea of Galilee.
We had heard stories about a rabbi in the neighborhood preaching to
    people to repent because the kingdom of God was near.
But I had no time for such dreams.
I had fish to catch.
Mouths to feed.

But one day, just as Andrew and I were casting a net into the sea,
    there he was: the rabbi from Nazareth.
Now I had heard and given many orders in my life,
    but never had I heard an order like the one he gave to us:
    to follow him, and he would make us fishers of people.
It was the way he said it: a voice of certainty and authority
    but also a voice as gentle as the waves on the sea that day.
Well, you know what happened next.
Andrew and I left everything and so did James and John.
We followed him throughout Galilee where he taught in the synagogues
    in a way that made people marvel.
We followed him and saw for ourselves how he cured people of terrible
    diseases and liberated people long believed to be possessed
    or forgotten.
And all the while, that same voice of certainty, authority, and gentleness
    as he talked about the coming of God's kingdom in our midst.

Now I know as Catholics you have been taught that Jesus was both God
and human.
But I sometimes think that a lot of people, and that includes you,
forgot the human part.
Even in the early Church there were great theologians who downplayed the
humanity of Jesus.
The famous fourth-century bishop Hilary of Poitiers once preached:
"Our Lord felt the force of suffering but without its pain; the nails
pierced his flesh as an object passes through the air, painlessly."
No, dear Hilary, Jesus was God and man.
He felt *our* pain because he felt *his* pain.

I know that down the centuries I've been honored for recognizing Jesus as
the Son of God, but what people forget is that day in the city of
Caesarea Philippi
I first saw him as a man.
He looked at us, a motley group of fishermen, and simply asked,
"Who do people say that the Son of Man is?"
We couldn't believe our ears.
We were simple folk.
Our clothes and our hair smelled of fish.
Our hands were scarred from the rough rope of our nets.
Nobody ever asked our opinion about anything.

And that's why we started to quote the big shots: the Pharisees, the political
leaders, the important ones.
We started to quote who *they* thought the Son of Man was.
But he stopped us, and said no,
that he wanted to hear what *we* thought
I recognized there and then that Jesus was a man who was puzzled about
the impression
he was giving people,
what with the curing of the sick and all.

I could see that he needed the resolution and the enlightenment
    that only best friends can give one another.

I wanted at that moment to be Jesus' rock of support and so I blurted out:
    "You are the Christ, the Son of the Living God."
Now where did *that* come from?
What possessed me to say that in front of everyone?
That's when Jesus smiled and told me,
    "Blessed are you, Simon son of Jonah.
    For flesh and blood has not revealed ths to you,
    but my heavenly Father."
And that's when he named me Peter, which meant rock,
    and told us that he was going to build his Church upon *this* rock.

Now don't think I haven't noticed that the Church in your day is getting a
    little rock-*y*.
There are divisions on the left and the right that are draining the Church of
    her energies and creating distrust and fear.
Even the liturgy, which is meant to draw you together as a Christian com-
    munity, has become a partisan battleground.

Please don't think this is the only time in history that the Church has been
    rocky.
The Church has lived through sinful and conniving popes,
    drunken monks and jealous bishops,
    people burned at the stake who were more saint than witch,
    heresies, trials, persecutions, and dire predictions about the end,
    even, some say, from our gentle Blessed Mother.
In early 1970s a priest by the name of James Kavanaugh wrote a book,
    A Priest Looks at His Outdated Church.
Fr. Kavanaugh was featured on the cover of *Look* magazine, which
    predicted that in twenty years there would be no Catholic Church.
Over thirty years later there is still a Catholic Church, even though there is
    no more *Look* magazine.

Remember what Jesus said in today's Gospel:
Even the jaws of death will not prevail against the Church.

Through all the Church's rocky history, grace has always abounded.
There have always been spirited Christians who stood up tall
    when Peter's boat was tossed by storms.
Just as I became Jesus' rock that day in Caesarea Philippi,
    there are people in your day who step forward
    to announce in their own way that Jesus is still the Messiah,
    the Son of the Living God, and that we must put our faith in him,
    and not chain people but use the keys of the kingdom
    to open up new ways to be Church in your own day.

I was delighted when I read Chicago's Cardinal Bernardin's new initiative,
    the Catholic Common Ground Project, which issued the splendid
    statement: "Called to Be Catholic: Church in a Time of Peril."
The Cardinal and twenty-five other Catholic leaders call you to examine
    your divided Church
    with fresh eyes, open minds, and changed hearts.
I realize you don't have much time on your hands like I do,
    but if you get a chance,
    I urge you to find time to read the entire statement.*
But for now let me quote just two sentences from it:

> Jesus Christ, present in Scripture and sacrament, is central to all that
> we do; he must always be the measure and not what is measured.
> Around this central conviction, the church's leadership, both clerical
> and lay must affirm and promote the full range and demands of
> authentic unity, acceptable diversity and respectful dialogue, not just
> to dampen conflict but as a way to make our conflicts constructive.

---

*Available online at www.nplc.org/commonground/calledcatholic.htm.

How sad it is that some other Church leaders are suspicious
    about this marvelous document and its call for common ground.
I wonder what they are preaching about today from this Gospel?

Let me finally tell you about the last conversation I had with Jesus on earth.
It was after Jesus had died and risen.
And there I was, still trying to catch fish instead of people.
We were on the beach at daybreak where he had cooked us breakfast on a
    charcoal fire.
The Lord of all was still serving the least of all.
That's when he gave me my final order, still with the voice of authority, cer-
    tainty, and gentleness:
    "Feed my lambs....Feed my sheep" (John 21:15–17).
He didn't say, "Excommunicate my lambs, stifle my sheep, stop discussing
    the issues," but "feed them."
That is what I have tried to do today.
I urge you not to give in to despair or cynicism no matter
    how rocky things are.
As you struggle to be Church for and to one another,
    may you have fresh eyes, open minds, and changed hearts.

Well I had better stop or you'll never invite me back again.
Thanks for listening to an old fisherman.
Oh yes, if you ever do invite me back again to preach,
I just may bring back my wife and even my mother-in-law
    for a dialogue homily.
You'll be surprised to find what *they* have to say!

RPW

Questions for Reflection

1. Who do you say Jesus is?

2. Have there been people in your life who have been a "rock" for you, helping you to come to faith?

3. Are there people to whom you are sent to be a "rock," letting your faith support them in times of trouble and doubt?

Other Directions for Preaching

1. The symbol of the key is featured in both the reading from Isaiah and the Gospel, allowing preachers to consider the issue of authority as service, providing order and stability.

2. Paul stands in awe before the mystery of God. Our faith calls us to praise, wonder, and awe when we gather for Eucharist.

3. One's faith in Jesus is something that can deepen or diminish over the years. Peter is an example of one whose faith led him to make the ultimate commitment as a disciple by dying for Christ.

A Question of Love
Twenty-Second Sunday
in Ordinary Time

Readings:
Jeremiah 20:7–9; Romans 12:1–2; Matthew 16:21–27

With the close of the summer months, we bid farewell to the many wed-
dings that invariably adorn this season,
and also to the brides who will trade their silky white gowns
for navy-blue business dresses during the week
and thick gardening gloves on weekends.
We say goodbye to the long line of grooms who will hand in their cuff links
and bow ties for monthly commuter tickets, nightly chores, and struggles with toolboxes. Sobriety soon sets in after the honeymoon, as we
know.
He snores, and she can't get to sleep.
She gets home too late; it's not what he is used to.
They fight, then they apologize.

The long-running series *The Honeymooners* spoke to millions
about the ups and downs of relationships.
Ralph Kramden was forever trying a new scheme or doing something or
other that would bristle against his level-headed wife, Alice. Typically,
a fight would ensue in the course of each episode between husband
and wife, and then the misunderstanding would be resolved.
For all his gruffness, though, Ralph became more lovable when he said to
Alice at the end of the show, "Baby, you're the greatest."

246

Relationships are like that, although some "religious" people think
    that we are never supposed to be anything but sweetness and light.
Holy people never get angry, especially at God—
    so this version goes, anyway.
Far from it!
For these folks the Hebrew Scriptures were written and remembered.
The Old Testament prophets are a good example
    of people who were very real,
    as well as being very holy, and sometimes also tormented
    in their relationship with God
Being holy and being real always go together.
In a way, they are a protracted, living example
    of the kind of covenant that God has made with all of us.
They will always be the chosen people.
But sometimes that covenantal bond gets down to the nitty-gritty details
    of confusion, bewilderment, and anger.

Jeremiah had a tough job to do,
    and God seemed to make the prophet's task harder and harder.
He had to proclaim God's word to a people who would face exile,
    and to a leadership that was corrupt and hostile.
"The word of the LORD has brought me
    derision and reproach all the day."
This reads more like an intimate spiritual journal
    than what we are accustomed to seeing in the Old Testament,
    a kind of memoir of a tempestuous relationship with God.

Jeremiah is a very sympathetic character, a martyr for the Word.
As he anticipates the Suffering Servant, Jeremiah reminds us
    of Jesus himself.
Both were rejected and killed by the people God sent them to free.
And Jesus' words on the cross—"My God, my God,
    why have you forsaken me" (Matt 27:46)—
    are an echo of Jeremiah's own despair.

Through it all, though, we see the depths of the human soul
     as a place for a substantial relationship with God.

That "marriage" is echoed in Psalm 63 and its response
     to the Jeremiah text:
     "O God, you are my God—
          for you I long!
     For you my body yearns;
          for you my soul thirsts,
     Like a land parched, lifeless,
          and without water."
Despite our struggles, we are persistent, especially in our search for God.
St. Benedict might have had that psalm in mind
     when he says in the Rule that seeking God is often "harsh and bitter."
After all, the Letter to the Hebrews says that, "our God is a consuming
     fire" (Heb 12:29).

Human nature, though, often wants to take Peter's tactic:
     there has got to be a way out, a solution to this problem of pain!
There must be another way besides the cross!
In Robert Bolt's play *A Man for All Seasons*,
     Thomas More is caught in a question of conscience
     that ultimately becomes "a question of love."
After being badgered and persecuted for years,
     Thomas finds himself in the ultimate pressure point.
He must declare his loyalty to King Henry VIII
     as Sovereign Head of the Church of England, or be beheaded.
Thomas's own daughter asks him why he cannot take the oath
     and believe something else.
That sounds pretty reasonable—and a great way out of a difficult situation.
Thomas could not do it,
     not because he was a legalist,
     but because he knew that embracing the cross would
     necessarily be part of his love for Christ and the Church.

In my ministry I have seen remarkable people come to accept
    unimaginable suffering, even those who have been redeemed by it.
Sam came to my office in a parish at which I was assisting one summer.
An African American who had grown up in the Church as a youth,
    he had gotten mixed up with drugs and alcohol for over twenty-five
    years.
Now he had been sober for forty-two days and had been through hell.
He said, "I know that I can never in my life have another drink."
That is the reality of acceptance, or what Paul tells the Romans
    when he says, "Do not conform yourselves to this age but be
    transformed by the renewal of your mind, that you may discern
    what is the will of God,
    what is good and pleasing and perfect."

Renewal almost always involves more than a passing glance at discomfort.
Addictions that become second nature tear people apart
    when they have to let go of them.
Conversion happens because we stare our burden in the face
    and decide that we want to ask God to be transformed by divine love.
We may have some harsh words for the One
    who has mysteriously led us into suffering,
    but our journey to Jerusalem will lead us only the same way
    Jesus himself has taken.
"Whoever wishes to come after me must deny himself, take up his cross,
    and follow me." Easier said than done.

St. Thomas More was finally beheaded,
    having stayed true to his love.
But the man who perjured himself to criminalize the saint, Richard Rich,
    did so, as the play suggests, to obtain a nearby dukedom.
At the trial, St. Thomas faces his betrayer and says,
    "Richard, it profits a man nothing to gain the whole world
    and lose his immortal soul.
But for Wales?"

The Son of Man will come
>with his angels in his Father's glory
>and then he will repay all according to his conduct.

GD

Questions for Discussion

1. How do we witness the Gospel in our daily lives? Am I afraid?

2. Have I really gotten angry with God? What does it feel like when I do? Do I have hidden feelings of anger at God that I am afraid to express?

3. What do I do in the face of the mystery of human suffering?

Other Directions for Preaching

1. The cross is the source of strength that never fails to give life to those who embrace it.

2. We are called not to conform with this age but to transform it.

3. Searching for God is always relational and occasionally involves personal pain.

River of Mercy
TWENTY-THIRD SUNDAY IN ORDINARY TIME

Readings:
Ezekiel 33:7–9; Romans 13:8–10; Matthew 18:15–20

Buildings change because of their inhabitants.
That is especially true of churches.
My first visit to the newly dedicated Cathedral of Our Lady of the Angels
    in Los Angeles was to celebrate the tenth anniversary of the Igbo
    Catholic Community.
The Cathedral is surely an imposing structure.
Several words come to mind, but the vastness and complexity of the struc-
    ture is both difficult to describe and daunting to photograph.
Even the multiple textures—teak benches, stone, alabaster, ceramic,
    marble, cloth, and so on—only suggest the dizzying technique
    used to convey a dazzling sensory experience.
The communion of saints—depicted as they are in delightfully warm,
    earth-tone tapestries—stand in a magnificent procession
    on both walls of the cathedral, further suggesting a space that is far
    from static.

As the Eucharistic Liturgy began,
    the interior of this great church would shift again
    as the seven or so liturgical dancers from Nigeria, dressed in blazing,
    shocking, orange-yellow-blue, moved down the aisle with a bowl of

251

incense, all the while swaying to the chorus and drum, as did the
whole congregation.
Few buildings could have absorbed such a striking array of diversity.
And that afternoon the cathedral itself,
    albeit arresting in its angular lines and cement facing,
    became quite liquid.
In hindsight, I could not help but think that, during the sprinkling rite,
    the people of God became a great penitential river,
    changing stone walls to water, with the grace of the Holy Spirit.

That is what happens when we get together as a Church:
    stone changes to water.
When Jesus says, "where two or three are gathered together in my name"
    he means to invoke the power of his risen presence.
Everything, everything, everything is
    different because the Lord has risen.
Nothing will ever be the same again
    after God's Son entered human history, died, and rose.
All creation continues to be renewed by this singular, divine event.
And so the Church gathers to remember the paschal mystery;
    its unfolding among us is a very powerful witness
    to the transforming power of Christ Jesus risen indeed.

The glory of the resurrection lives in the Church's living,
    sacramental tradition to reconcile sinners in the community.
We are just plain disfigured by sin,
    turned to stone like Lot's unfortunate wife.
Around the turn of the nineteenth century,
    the English novelist and playwright Oscar Wilde
    wrote a novel about a man named Dorian Gray
    who made a pact to sell his soul in exchange for eternal youth.
But that was just the beginning.
For years Dorian got deeper and deeper into evil, deception, and murder.
His physical appearance remained unchanged.

But there was a record of his moral decay told in his portrait,
    which mysteriously became more and more ugly
    with each of Dorian's callously wicked acts.
At the end of the novel, we finally see the fruit of the unrepentant soul
    in decay:
    the picture of Dorian Gray had become a hideous man,
    hardly recognizable as a human being.

Dorian's agreement was more telling than he realized:
    he didn't want to change in more ways than one.
But Jesus' words to us are all about changing, experiencing conversion,
    becoming new.
That renewal happens in the community of love,
which "does no evil to the neighbor."
How else can we become something other than what we are?
It is the *other* that calls me out of myself.
It is my neighbor I have to thank for drawing me
    out of my tendency to be self-absorbed and egocentric.
So the Church's role as reconciler is nothing short of prophetic.
Like Virgil to our Dante, the Church guides us—calls us—
    out of our very selves into newness of life.
The Church calls people out of themselves
    to be healed in the community of the blessed,
    to cure the wounds of division amid God's people.
The words of God to the prophet Ezekiel
    directly concern the task of the prophet to confront, to be a watch-
    man, for the people.
But that is all the prophet can do.
The rest of the task of conversion is up to those whose lives are unloving.
We have to will to change and, as Cardinal Newman says, "change often."

The Church's liturgy continually reminds us
    of the need for healing and forgiveness.

Most obviously, we need to free ourselves
   from the bonds of sin through the sacrament of reconciliation.
But consider the Penitential Rite at the beginning of each and every
   Eucharist.
This "preparation" period is certainly a way
   for individuals to ask God for forgiveness.
But it is the community that is also being reconciled here as well:
   it is the "two or three gathering [in Jesus'] name"
   and celebrating the gift of God's love and peace.
This altar is the place of peace—perhaps the only place in the entire world
   where we can say true reconciliation happened—
   cosmic, saving atonement.
That peace continues on that same altar and will until eternity dawns.

Peace talks break down everywhere but God's table.
With nations continually at war,
   politicians bartering the bones of the young in foreign lands for the
   sake of power,
   and the globe increasingly driven by those who have all the wealth,
   we come at long last to the great equalizer: the altar of God.
It is, after all, those who refuse
   to give up power whom Jesus faults in the Gospel.
The powerful never feel they have to listen to anyone but themselves.
We know that the Church itself
   has gotten into trouble when it ceases to listen to the faithful,
   when it fails to be a poor Church that loves justice.
Yet what could be sweeter, brothers and sisters,
   than the voice of the Lord calling out to us here
   in this very voice of the Church;
   a voice which cries peace even as we break the bread that He broke
   and drink that cup overflowing with the new wine of the covenant.

Behold, that covenant is before us even now,
   a covenant of peace: bread broken; wine outpoured.

The long reign of sin has ended.
And peace will follow in his steps.

GD

Questions for Discussion

1. God asks us to be bold in our proclamation. What would it take to acknowledge my role as a prophet for my parish community?

2. Are there people that I still hold a grudge against even after many years?

3. During the Eucharist, do I find myself praying alone? Am I connected to the liturgical assembly?

Other Directions for Preaching

1. We are accountable for our witness of the Gospel, which includes painful confrontations with myself, others, and society.

2. Reconciliation requires the grace of honesty and love that is generated by the willingness to come together for the sake of the Gospel.

3. Everyone has failed to love except the God who loved us into creation.

Seizing by the Throat or Forgiving from the Heart?
TWENTY-FOURTH SUNDAY IN ORDINARY TIME

Readings:
Sirach 27:30—28:7; Romans 14:7–9; Matthew 18:21–35

Chapter 18 in Matthew's Gospel is about people in the community who sin.

Last week the focus was on those who sin but don't care.

What do we do? If no change, treat them as tax collectors.

Today we consider those who sin and ask to be forgiven,

      sin again and ask to be forgiven, sin again....

"How often [do we have to] forgive?" Peter wants to know.

And Jesus says—no limit.

Then he tells a story that explains why we forgive, the motive for mercy.

The story is really a three-act play:

The first act is a comedy.

A servant owes his king a preposterous amount: 10,000 talents.

One talent would have been fifteen years' wages for a servant.

King Herod made nine hundred talents a year; a Pharaoh could not have

      paid this back.

A "huge amount" is how it is translated.

The king realizes the impossibility and is going to sell the man and his

      family.

So when the servant asks for time and promises to pay everything back,
        it would have gotten a laugh. "Yeah—right."
But then the king suddenly says "Never mind, forget about it."
The servant is saved. Applause. Curtain down.

The second act is darker.
This same servant immediately comes on a fellow servant who owes three
        months' wages.
He grabs him by the throat and throttles him.
This servant makes the same request, to be given time and he will pay all
        back.
But the servant, who has just been given the gift of his life, throws the other
        man into jail.
"Pay back what you owe," he shouts, slamming the cell door shut.
The servant is doomed. Boos. Curtain down.

The third act is darkness itself.
The other servants report the whole sorry affair to the king, who is furious.
"You wicked servant! I forgave you your entire debt."
He tosses him toward the torturers who throw a bag over him and march
        him out.
Curtain down. Silence.

The puzzling thing is why the man didn't forgive the small debt owed him.
He had just come from being given the biggest gift of his life.
What was he thinking?
Is it the difference between how you act when you have no power,
        and when you have a modest amount of power?
We can be as meek as lambs when someone has power over us,
        but when we have power, we can turn into tyrants, godlings,
        a self-made divinity demanding a self-defined "justice."
I count two things Jesus wants to get across in this story:
First, we are to forgive because we have been forgiven.

God is merciful, and God wants mercy shown to others as mercy was
      shown to us.
Second, if we don't forgive, then God will act toward us as we act toward
      others.
If we do not act in God's image, God will act in ours.

I saw King Lear the other night.
You know the set-up:
The king announces his retirement.
As he is dividing up the kingdom among his three daughters,
      he asks each to say how much she loves Daddy.
The two older daughters gush: "More than life, more than anything else."
But the third one, his favorite, Cordelia, doesn't have anything to say.
He asks, "What have you to say, Cordelia?"
"Nothing," she replies, "I have nothing to say."
"From nothing comes nothing," he snaps back.
"I love you as you deserve—no more, no less," she replies, gently but firmly.
Lear is enraged, and he disowns and banishes her.

Lear acts like God, his own God who wants total love,
      and when that is refused, he is unforgiving.
But when the two sisters turn on him and cast him out,
      he eventually finds himself in darkness:
      the darkness of the storm that beats on him from without;
      and the darkness of madness which beats on his mind from within.
He comes to dwell in the darkness of total loss.
Eventually all three of his daughters die.
But in the last act, Lear is reunited for a short time with his beloved
      Cordelia.
He falls on his knees and begs, "Forgive, forgive, forgive, and forget."
He realizes he is just a man, not a god demanding his own
      determined "justice."
Forgiveness is all.

Years ago I remember reading the book *That Man Is You* from spiritual
    writer Louis Evely.
Evely said that "men don't forgive, they forget;
    women forgive, but they never forget."
I don't think it is so "gender divided";
    either alternative is possible for anyone.
Forgiveness is hard; sometimes we may even find it impossible.
When someone has hurt us so deeply by their lies, betrayal, deception,
        when a relationship has been broken not just in half but in pieces,
        there can seem little chance of anything ever mending.
And when hurt is perpetrated on a national level, or an international one,
        the odds are even greater against any possibility of healing.
Seizing another by the throat, even murderous rage seems
        far more satisfying.
But in all of this, we are called to live as the image of God, who is merciful.
This is where the Eucharist reminds us who we are.
And although *we* might not have the power to forgive,
        there is One who can give us this ability.
The Spirit who transforms bread and wine does this for *our* good.
        so that, day after day, week after week, month after month, *we* might
        be transformed.
The Spirit works in us so that we grow into the fullness of Christ's stature.
In our groanings, the Spirit is at work, praying, interceding for us.
And that Spirit, who has worked with chaos before,
        moves over the chaos of our wounded feelings, our savored grudges,
        and from the murk and mess of our lives shapes a new creation,
        blessed and touched by the healing finger of God, who calls to us:
        "Inherit the kingdom prepared for you from the foundation of the
        world" (Matt 25:34).
        We will be told to sit at the table with the other children because we
        have forgiven our brother and sister from our heart."

JAW

Questions for Reflection

1. Have you experienced what it is to be forgiven?

2. Have you experienced what it is to forgive another?

3. Consider how in our weakness the power of God's Spirit empowers us to forgive.

Other Directions for Preaching

1. The book of Sirach notes: "Wrath and anger are hateful things." Is anger always hateful? Isn't it possible that anger can be a gift, rather than a curse?

2. God's sovereignty extends over life and death. Romans 14:7–9 offers an opportunity to reflect on God's power over death: "Whether we live or die, we are the Lord's.

3. How do you reconcile God's mercy with the final words of Jesus in the parable: "So will my heavenly Father do to you, unless each of you forgives your brother from your heart."

Grumbling and Gratitude
Twenty-Fifth Sunday
in Ordinary Time

Readings:
Isaiah 55:6–9; Philippians 1:20c–24, 27a;
Matthew 20:1–16a

They grumbled.

They grumbled because they thought they had been treated unfairly.

But the owner simply said: "My friend, I am not cheating you."

The owner didn't say, "My friends, but my friend."

He addressed only one of them, perhaps the ringleader, the most articulate,
    the one who grumbled the loudest
    and who became the spokesperson for all the others who felt left out.

Last Tuesday in Ocean City, Maryland, a man died who history will note
    was the man who
    resigned as vice president of the United States
    under a cloud of personal scandal and corruption.

At the height of his political career, Spiro Agnew fashioned himself as the
    spokesperson
    of all the others who felt left out.

These were the millions of Americans in the late 1960s and early 1970s
    who felt alienated by the anti-Vietnam-war protestors, the antigovern-
    ment protestors, and the civil rights militants,
    those who seemed to stand around all day and work only an hour
    in the shade.

Vice President Agnew became the spokesperson of the people who grumbled
    and were known as the so-called silent majority.

He spoke out against the "effete corps of impudent snobs," "the nattering
    nabobs of negativism,"
    and "the hopeless, hysterical hypochondriacs of history."
Agnew called the protesters of the Poor People's Campaign
    encamped near the Lincoln Memorial
    "poor people with Cadillacs."
Such rhetorical outbursts made him not just the spokesman but the darling
    of the silent majority.
He and Richard Nixon were reelected in a 1972 landslide,
    carrying every state
    but Massachusetts and our own District of Columbia.

But his world crashed when faced with charges of corruption
    while governor of Maryland
    that forced him to resign a year after the landslide election.
He felt abandoned by Richard Nixon, who did nothing
    to defend his vice president.
He never again spoke to the former president,
    refusing to take several telephone calls from him.
But when Nixon died in 1994, Agnew went to his funeral.
He said in his book, "I decided after twenty years of resentment to put it all
    aside."

Just yesterday another man died.
For years he wrote popular spiritual books
    about dealing with the many resentments in our lives.
The Dutch priest Henri Nouwen insisted that
    whenever we face our losses, large or small, real or imagined,
    we have only two options, resentment or gratitude.
Just like those who grumbled to the owner of the vineyard, the first option
    is tempting.

In one of his books, Nouwen wrote:

> When we are hit by one loss after another,
>
> it is very easy to become disillusioned, angry,
>
> bitter, and increasingly resentful.
>
> The older we become, the greater the temptation to say:
>
> "Life has cheated me. There is no future for me, nothing to hope for.
>
> The only thing to do is to defend the little I have left, so that I won't
>
> lose it all."
>
> Resentment is one of the most destructive forces in our lives.*

If we were really honest with ourselves, we would have to admit that it is
 easier to relate

to the grumblers in today's parable than to the latecomers.

Who among us has not felt left out, cheated, abandoned, unfairly treated?

Our brother or sister seems to get a bigger chunk of pie, a better toy, a
 neater pair of jeans, even a better hug.

You stand there, a little runt on the playground, not the first pick but the
 last pick for the game.

That new gal or guy on the job gets the same salary, the same benefits, and
 better treatment
 from the boss than you.

The will is read after the death of a relative and someone in the family
 always feels cheated.

A U.N. statistic shows that women do three-fourths of the world's work but
 receive only one-tenth of the world's salary.

White people feel left out because of affirmative action.

Hispanic, Asian, and African Americans feel discrimination
 even with affirmative action.

Very often, life isn't fair.

---

*Henri J. M. Nouwen, *With Burning Hearts* (Maryknoll, NY: Orbis, 1995), 29.

When the parable of the vineyard was first told,
     it probably referred to the pious people
     who felt left out or cheated because Jesus was welcoming
     slobbering sinners
     and nasty tax collectors to the dinner table and to the reign of God.
When Matthew wrote the parable,
     it probably was told because good Christian Jews resented the fact
     that there were newcomers, converted Gentiles,
     who were given equal status in the Christian community.
Like ourselves, our biblical ancestors felt resentment toward the new kid on
     the block.

That is why this parable was told and is still told in the Christian assembly.
It's not about fair wages or even justice.
It's about grace.
It's about a God whose ways are not our ways,
     whose thoughts are not our thoughts.
It's about an invitation that God extends to everybody, not just those of us
     who feel entitled
     to special treatment.
It's about grace extended to all.

Henri Nouwen urged people to learn how to practice what he called the
     "discipline of gratitude."
Instead of focusing on our loses with resentment,
     he urged us to be grateful for the many gifts God has given us
     and also extends to all of our brothers and sisters.
We celebrate this Eucharist in memory of Jesus Christ, who on the night
     before he died
     (you can't get more left out than death)
     turned to God and praised and thanked God out of the very depths
     of his sorrow.

We mourn our losses at this Eucharist: Lord have mercy, Christ have mercy.
But we also lift up our hearts.
Eucharist—which means gratitude—comes from above.
Eucharist is a gift.
We can't fake it.
We can only receive it, welcome it, be in communion with it.
It is then that we can turn all our resentments into thanksgiving.

RPW

Questions for Reflection

1. With whom do I identify in the parable?

2. Is there any particular area where I need to move from resentment about what I do not have to gratitude for what I do?

3. Do I know and accept the God "whose ways are not our ways, whose thoughts are not our thoughts"?

Other Directions for Preaching

1. The idea of God calling us to worship (Isaiah) and to work (Matthew) allows for a message on the universal call to holiness and how it is carried out in life.

2. Paul's desire to be with Christ gives way to his commitment to the community, but overall there is the awareness of living in union with Christ.

3. The image of God as judge calls us to consider God's justice and how it relates to what we think of as justice in our world. The interplay of God's justice and God's mercy takes us into the mystery of God.

Even Popes Can Change
TWENTY-SIXTH SUNDAY IN ORDINARY TIME

Readings:
Ezekiel 18:25–28; Philippians 2:1–11; Matthew 21:28–32

I enjoy reading Richard Cohen in the *Washington Post*
    and often find myself in his camp.
But when it comes to his understanding of saints,
    frankly, he makes my teeth itch.
A few years ago, when Maximilian Kolbe, the Polish priest who offered his
    life in order to save a Jewish prisoner at Auschwitz, was made a saint,
    Cohen was outraged.
After all, hadn't Kolbe in his early priestly zeal published
    religious pamphlets that contained anti-Semitic statements?

Richard Cohen is once again agitated because Pope John Paul II seems to be
    on a fast track to canonize Pope Pius XII, whom Cohen believes did
    little to stop the Holocaust.
While scholars do find anti-Semitic statements published by St. Maximilian
    Kolbe in his early priestly years,
    the case against Pius XII is not as cut and dry.
A new book about Pius XII quotes his anti-Semitic views when he was
    Archbishop Pacelli,
    the papal ambassador to Munich in 1919.

A more balanced reading would say that Pacelli was passive
    about the emerging neo-Fascist movement in Germany
    because he was so bent against the rise of atheistic communism.
Besides, the so-called anti-Semitic quotes of Pius are highly suspect by some
    scholars.

My own beef with Richard Cohen is his misunderstanding of what it means
    when the Church elevates someone to sainthood.
When it does so, the Church is not declaring that the saint was *always* a
    saint, *always* holy,
    always pure, and *always* free from prejudice and sin,
    from the moment of birth until death.

At the heart of the gospel message is redemption, God's plan
    that we be saved,
    which means that salvation is always possible
    because it is always possible for sinners to change.
Saints are canonized not because they said yes to God and never wavered.
Saints are canonized because they often first said no to God but later
    changed.

The righteous son in today's parable seems like a good fellow,
    eager to please, always having just the right word to say like:
    "Yes, sir," or, as the Greek word *Kyrie* indicates, "Yes, Lord."
Notice that he doesn't just say "yes," but "Yes, sir!"
He is correctly polite and politically correct.

Not so the other son.
He is like… he is like…well, he is like *us*!
Sinful, biased, not yet complete in Christ.
He doesn't even have good manners.
"I will not," he says, not "No, sir!"

But then a remarkable thing takes place.

He changes.

It is not a major conversion.

The Greek word used here indicates not a major and complete conversion
    but regret...a change of mind.

And, then, he goes to do his father's will.

We are all challenged today to have the same attitude as Christ,
    to have that same attitude to the naysayers of our time:
    the tax collectors and prostitutes,
    the drunk drivers, the rebellious teenagers, the people in our lives and
    world whom we regard as less than polite, less than deserving and
    good.

Try to imagine this:

It is near the end of World War II.

You are a priest hearing confessions.

Into the confessional comes a man named Oscar Schindler,
    a German industrialist who during the war made a fortune
    from Jewish slave labor in Poland.

By all conventional standards, he was not a good man.

And so he confesses to you:

"I really don't know when my last confession was;
    it was a long, long time ago.

During that time I drank too much, gambled too much, was arrogant in the
    way I lived,
    and slept with many women other than my wife.

The only thing I did good was that I managed to trick the Nazis and thus
    saved thousands of Jews from going to gas chamber."

If you had heard Herr Schindler's confession, what would you say to him?

What penance would you give?

Think about it.

My prayer is that you would have remembered today's parable
  about the son who said "no" at first but then changed his mind.
My prayer is that today's parable will continue to sting us *Yes* people in the
  Church so that we will never forget what Jesus once said in his
  Sermon on the Mount:
  "Not every one who says to me, 'Lord, Lord,' will enter the kingdom
  of heaven, but only the one who does the will of my Father in heaven"
  (Matt 7:21).

RPW

Questions for Reflection

1. Which brother do you identify with? Why?

2. Do you think conversion is once and for all or a more gradual
process? How do you see yourself in the process of conversion?

3. Have you ever changed your perception of a person because of something he or she did that cast them in a totally different light?

Other Directions for Preaching

1. Often we hear people say, "It's just not fair!" How does the "fairness
doctrine" apply to God?

2. Paul calls on all members of the community to "Have in you the same
attitude that is in Christ Jesus." The passage that follows offers Paul's theology of kenosis (self-emptying), which is at the heart of Paul's Christology and
has implications for daily life in the world.

3. In what does true obedience consist? How can one judge if one is obedient to God's will?

The Layers of Meaning
TWENTY-SEVENTH SUNDAY IN ORDINARY TIME

Readings:
Isaiah 5:1–7; Philippians 4:6–9; Matthew 21:33–43

Last Monday night I was in St. Paul, Minnesota, giving a public lecture.
There was a period of questions that followed the lecture and they seemed
    to cover just about every hot topic people are wrestling with in the
    Church these days.
Toward the end of this session, one man raised his hand in frustration.
He was probably frustrated not just with the problems raised but also with
    my answers.
He said, in a no-nonsense Midwestern clipped voice:
    "Why can't the Church just say what is right or wrong
    in a simple, clear way?
    People are confused these days. They want to know.
    When Jesus spoke to the people of his day,
    he spoke in a clear way. People knew what he meant."

I didn't want to disturb the man anymore than was necessary.
But I did find myself saying to him:
    "Have you every heard the parables?"
They were anything but simple.
In fact, the reason why we continue to tell the parables of Jesus
    over and over again
    is because they help us to discover not one answer

but deep layers of meaning that shock us, perturb us,
and make us ponder.
When Jesus first told the parable of the wicked tenants,
it was in a shorter form.
He was trying to draw a lesson from the tenant's despicable behavior.
Something like:
"See how these evil vine dressers stopped at nothing?
They even murdered the heir in order to get possession
of the vineyard.
You, the children of light, must be just as determined
to get possession of the kingdom of God."
That's one layer of meaning.

But another layer of meaning was added to the parable when Matthew
retold it in light of the needs of his day.
Matthew allegorized the parable to make the point
that the Jewish religious authorities
rejected the prophets of old and finally rejected Jesus the Messiah by
crucifying him.
Now the vineyard of the Lord has been taken out of their hands
and placed in the hands of the Gentiles.

Unfortunately, this parable could be used to condemn our Jewish brothers
and sisters.
And that is how this parable and other sections of the New Testament are
used by some preachers.
The other night I was channel surfing and came upon
Minister Louis Farrakhan.
He was quoting certain verses from the Book of Revelation that speak
of God's rejection of the Jews.
Farrakhan was using these verses to preach a message of hate against the
Jews of our time.

We dare not gloat over the fact that the kingdom of God has been taken
away from the Jews
and now given to us, the righteous people.
Such a simplistic interpretation led to the ovens of Auschwitz in the past
and leads to the Jew-baiting and defacing of Jewish cemeteries
in our own day.

But there is yet another layer to this parable.
It is the most important layer of meaning in any parable that we hear pro-
claimed at Eucharist:
It is the layer that refers to us.
This Gospel is always about God's actions, God's love, God's challenge to
us
and not to those people "out there."
The challenge of the parable is for *us*.
The parable asks us:
Are we a people producing the fruits of the kingdom?

When I prayed over our parable this week, for some reason I remember the
pastor of our small Pennsylvania parish when I was a young man.
He was all fire and brimstone, cut and dry, black and white.
No tolerance for layers of meaning.
As kids we were literally petrified of him.
I hate to say this, but I do not remember one single incidence of human
kindness from the man.

But I do recall, not long after I was ordained, when he was old
and quite bitter,
one thing he said that did reveal a rare glimpse of pathos.
He said: "You know what is hurting our Church these days?
All this love stuff.
All this insistence on God's love and mercy and not his judgment.
All this love stuff came in with Vatican II and it is ruining us."

Our parable is not meant to be simple.

It presents both love and judgment.

The parable reminds us that God is in charge, that all things come from
    God, and that God is foremost a loving and merciful God
    who keeps reaching out to us, despite the stingy way we live our lives.

The tenants misread the landowner.

They thought the landowner's love and mercy was a sign of weakness and
    lack of concern.

Being a follower of Christ means to be open to both his love
    and his judgment.

The parable is not about *them*.

It is about *us*.

It is about our responsibility for God's vineyard.

It is about the harvest that is due to God.

The harvest of goodness, love, and care for all our sisters and brothers.

We come to Eucharist to confess our sins and to know God's love and
    mercy.

Anything else is too simplistic and dangerous.

We thank God for a precious Son who came not to show that life is simple
    but wonderfully complex.

We ask God for the courage to face all the layers of meaning.

RPW

Questions for Reflection

1. What layer of meaning speaks most to you today?

2. How do you feel called to tend God's vineyard?

3. Do you agree that we must be open to both God's mercy and God's judgment?

Other Directions for Preaching

1. The image of the vineyard and the vine have great meaning in both the Old Testament and the New Testament. In today's first reading and the Gospel, the vineyard refers to God's people and the responsibility of those charged with their care.

2. We can become so used to saying "The peace of the Lord be with you" during the Mass that we lose a sense of its meaning. The reading from Romans invites us to consider what God's peace means for our lives in such an anxious age.

3. Anti-Semitism is a constant danger even when reading the Gospel. This is one of those gospel readings that can unconsciously evoke such a response. A deliberate and sensitive consideration of the relationship Christians and Jews should have with each other because of their common heritage may be pastorally appropriate.

Jacket Required
Twenty-Eighth Sunday in Ordinary Time

Readings:
Isaiah 25:6–10a; Philippians 4:12–14, 19–20;
Matthew 22:1–14

We hate contradictions.
At first blush, our readings seem to be suggesting two vastly different,
    utterly distinct geographies.
The prophet Isaiah takes us high atop the holy mountain
        where the Lord will provide a banquet for all people—
        endless and rich.
And that is certainly very much to our liking.
Who could argue with a freebie?
Good old Isaiah!
He gives us the God who wipes away tears and bandages our knees.
I once heard a modern, intelligent actor answer this question,
        "What would you like to hear at the Day of Judgment?"
        by saying, "That everything is okay."
Fair enough. Maybe that is everybody's dream.
By contrast, Jesus seems strict.
He tells us a parable about some people refusing to partake in a feast
        and the call that then went out to everyone on the margins.
That is great, too, we might think at first.
Americans love victims and are none too thrilled with royal guests.

But then the glitch comes:
>   the new recruits are rejected because they are not wearing the correct
>   formal, starched-white eveningwear.
What's going on?

We are not the only ones confused by this parable.
It baffles experts too.
Some may even argue that the historical distance in the parable
>   makes it impossible for moderns to grasp its true meaning.
They say that the notion of the king's sending armies
>   to blot out their enemies cannot speak to a postindustrial, democratic
>   society.
Indeed, Jesus' parable certainly would have spoken
>   to sectarian concerns in the early Church,
>   all the more because of the symbol of the banquet,
>   frequently compared to the kingdom.
Those chosen people of Israel rejected the invitation while Jewish-Christians
>   accepted it. Yet just being invited will not suffice;
>   a garment of righteousness is required.
The lesson: even those who were asked to come from the highways and
>   byways must be prepared.
So let's face it: this parable, as confusing as it is,
>   would make anyone uncomfortable at anytime.
And it is meant to do so, to shake us up.
It is, after all, about judgment
>   and that will be more and more on the mind of the Church
>   in the remaining weeks of the liturgical year.

It may be best to keep the last sentence of this pericope as a backdrop:
>   "Many are invited but few are chosen."
From this perspective, the call issued in Isaiah
>   becomes refined in Matthew.
I like to think of this parable very much along the lines
>   of Jesus' call to discipleship and our response.

Jesus issues forth his call to everyone.

But not everyone responds.

In my mind, the "wedding garment" certainly suggests a baptismal robe,
    which becomes symbolic in our own context.

Many have been clothed in that garment,
    but not all have lived out its promises.

One of the most stunning and instructive sequences
    in American cinema is the baptism sequence
    in Francis Ford Coppola's *The Godfather*.

The ten minute clip is a favorite among film teachers
    because it shows the director's brilliant use of cinematic montage
    deployed to make a very theological and dramatic point.

Roughly three-quarters of the way through the film,
    Michael Corleone is gathered with his family
    for the baptism of his child.

He has also issued orders for several hit men
    to execute men from other warring clans.

Coppola contrasts the baptism with the slayings,
    as he intercuts the two events.

The priest asks Michael, "Do you renounce Satan?"

Then, cut to a shooting,
    and Michael says, "I do."

The rite ironically comments on precisely
    what it is supposed to be renouncing.

Several brutal juxtapositions of the sacred and profane occur.

In the end, the blood of Michael's enemies flows freely—
    on an elevator, on the street, in the bedroom—
    even as the priest pours the water on Michael's son,
    now washed in baptismal waters.

So much for turning away from what the baptismal rite calls "the glamour
    of evil."

For most of us, keeping our baptismal promises,
> or wearing our white garment, is not nearly so dramatic.
Thank God.
Instead, we proceed, as if by inches, to slip a little bit at a time:
> an unkind word here, a lie there;
>> something stolen, or perhaps we call it "creative borrowing";
>> a little infidelity—we might call it an indiscretion.
Somewhere along the line we may have lost our white garment or even
> given it away,
>> but for many folks it is more like an unraveling.
Before you know it, we are dressed in gaudy attire not fit for a wedding,
> but more for a lonely, dark bar lit only by flashing neon signs to see
> the way.

The parable, then, is a call to honesty—
> to live out what we have been given by grace.
It is also a reminder to live in the "now" of God's kingdom:
> we long for the day Isaiah describes
> but the banquet invoked by Jesus is happening now.
That is just as it should be.
The first reading and the Gospel position us in the middle of two worlds
> because the Christian community lives in a marvelous tension
> between the present and the almost:
> for the day when the God of all creation will come
> to set his people free.
But until then we must beg the Lord to fully supply whatever we need,
> "in accord with his glorious riches in Christ Jesus."
That means living on the edge of mercy.
That means finding Christ in the ordinary
> and treating it like the extraordinary.
That means coming to the banquet ready to emerge
> as prophets for the kingdom for the sake of the covenant.

Once I was at a parish assignment during the summer and was asked to
    come over
      and bless the Wednesday morning "outreach" ministry after the morn-
      ing Mass.
I was flabbergasted when I walked into the large cafeteria
    to see table after table crammed with bags of food
    and many parishioners ministering to the poor.
Later that morning, I saw a man crossing the street with a bag literally
    bursting with food.

That is what happens when the parish community ignites once again the
    burning flame
    given to them at baptism.
The unconditional love of God is made possible for others—
    for the poor and the needy—by the gifts that grace us.
We become the ones not who expect to be waited on
    but who have prepared and tended that holy mountain Isaiah
    describes.
So the invitation stands for all who intend to serve at this table.
The baptismal garment becomes an apron of love.

GD

Questions for Reflection

1. How do I live out my Christian vocation day to day?

2. If I died this evening, would I be ready to meet God? Would I do anything different for the next few hours?

3. Am I grateful for the invitation to dine at God's table? How do I show this thankfulness?

Other Directions for Preaching

1. The unconditional love of God is offered in a covenant of love that will never be broken.

2. The Lord is the Shepherd of all creation and will never lose one sheep—even in death.

3. The grace we received at our baptism asks us to cooperate with the works of mercy, making Christ visible on earth.

God's Currency
TWENTY-NINTH SUNDAY IN ORDINARY TIME

Readings:
Isaiah 45:1, 4–6; 1 Thessalonians 1:1–5b;
Matthew 22:15–21

Matthew's Gospel often presents Jesus in a struggle with the Pharisees.
As a matter of fact these laymen, educated in the way of Torah,
    are often presented negatively in the Gospels, particularly Matthew's.
Today as we end another political season,
and in the name of the Fairness Doctrine,
I thought we might allow a Pharisee to speak.
Perhaps he might bring a fresh perspective on the event we just heard.
And since the discussion then had political overtones,
    perhaps he will have some reflection for us in these days
    of political interest.
So I present to you this morning Eleazar, a disciple of the Pharisees,
    living in Jerusalem, not far from the Temple.

(Pause)

Shalom, my friends.
I must confess my surprise at being here this morning.
It is the first time I have been invited to speak in a Catholic Church,
    and a Jesuit one at that.
I have some questions about these Jesuits...but not today.

I am a Pharisee, of the tribe of Benjamin, the son of Jacob, the son of
     Baruch.
Also, since I am told you are interested in these things,
the son of Miriam, the daughter of Rachel, the daughter of Hannah.

Now this story you just heard is true.
I was there.
Right in the front of the group of my brother Pharisees, I must confess.
You must try to understand things from where we stood.
This Jesus worried us. What's more—he scared us.
He was saying things that threatened the traditions of Moses.
And he was doing things that made him a great favorite with the people,
     especially the country people.
The times called for great delicacy....
The Romans occupied Jerusalem; their foot was always on the back
     of our neck.
And this Jesus and his teachings could be the irritant to bring it down,
     crushing our windpipe.
He was not one to tailor the truth to suit the political winds.
In that, I must admit, I admired him.

Now on one side were the priests of the Temple (who were Sadducees)
     and the Herodians (who were supporters of Rome's puppet, Herod).
They both were looking to get the Romans to crucify this Jesus.
He had just taken a whip to the moneychangers in the Temple,
     turning over the tables that held their goods, doves flapping all over
     the place, and, now the priests were against him.
It wasn't just a matter of not upsetting the applecart,
     (literally *and* metaphorically speaking);
     it was much more than that.
No one wanted to see this Temple go the way of Solomon's.
Any sign of unrest would provide the Roman soldiers with an excuse
     to invade the sacred precincts.

Then, on the other side, were the Zealots—a bunch of terrorists who hated
     Rome, and were always ready to start a rebellion.
They wanted to co-opt Jesus as a Messiah.
He could be a rallying point against Rome;
          they even sent one of their own to infiltrate his inner circle—
     Simon, by name.
But, interestingly, he seemed to fall under the spell of Jesus.

We Pharisees stood in the middle—as virtue always does.
We thought we'd take a nonviolent approach.
We figured we could discredit him in some way and get him off the scene.
So I came up with this question about taxes. It was a no-win question.
If he said, "Pay the tax," the people would walk away,
     and the Zealots would lose their Messiah.
If he said, "Don't pay it," the priests could have the Roman soldiers arrest
     him for trying to overthrow the government.
So we staged a debate—something I notice you are quite familiar
     with these days.
Though, to tell the truth, I found Jesus far more impressive than any
     of your Republican or Democratic candidates in the last few weeks.

Jesus was clever, even politically astute,
     and slyly asked to be shown a coin.
Now, none of us *should* have.
The coin carried an image of Tiberius the Emperor
     and was inscribed with the titles Divus (the Divine One)
     and Pontifex Maximus (The Greatest Priest).
For a Jew to even carry one was blasphemy…well, Jesus got us there.
The words of the Torah came to our minds and hearts immediately:
     "The Lord is God alone; you shall have no graven images before Me."
Then Jesus said, almost as if it just occurred to him,
     "Repay to Caesar what belongs to Caesar, and to God what belongs
     to God."
Jesus didn't need a stable of script writers; he was very good on his feet.

Now, there are different ways you can hear this.

The obvious level, first of all:

     "The state has authority and so has God.

     Give each its due."

The question is: what is due to each?

And what happens when Caesar exercises power that belongs to God?

And how do you know when God might be working through Caesar,

     as God worked through Cyrus the Great of Persia,

      who freed us from our exile so many centuries ago,

      as you heard in the first reading this morning?

So there are problems when you try to find clear-cut divisions

     between Caesar's realm and God's.

But there was also a deeper level.

Jesus was holding the coin when he said, "Repay to Caesar"

     and we could see Tiberius's image on it.

In paying it back, we were giving Caesar's image back to Caesar.

Paying the tax brought us roads and security, a society of law and order,

     the purpose of good government.

But then he looked directly at us when he told us to repay to God what is

     God's—and there wasn't a person in the crowd who didn't think of

     Genesis and creation:

     "God created man in his image;

      in the divine image he created him;

      male and female he created them" (Gen 1:27).

In a nutshell, we are God's coins, God's currency, God's due.

And that is what God wants a return on:

     the divine image that is in you, in me;

     our hearts, our minds, our wills, our love, our bodies,

     given as a sacrificial offering.

That's the challenge, isn't it?

All of us carry God's image to the places we live and work, study and play,

We have been imprinted with God's spirit, who dwells in us,

and who can do more in us than we ask for or imagine.

According to Jesus, we should think of ourselves as God's ready cash,
and if it's true that "money is power," surely this money is.
Out of such wealth, a kingdom can be built—God's.

Well, enough from an old Pharisee.
Don't believe everything Matthew tells you about us.
Not all of us were hypocrites.
Remember Gamaliel, Hillel, and Shammai—good and godly men all.
We kept the flame of faith burning in Israel from the time the Temple was
    finally destroyed in the 60s (ours, not yours)
    and for hundreds of years after.
Shalom, my friends.
May the peace of God fill your hearts, and flow through you to touch the
    world our Creator has entrusted to us.

JAW

Questions for Reflection

1. How do you hear the call to render to Caesar what is Caesar's and to God what is God's?

2. Do you see yourself as one who carries the image of God into the world?

3. How are you investing yourself in the world for the sake of making God's presence known and felt?

Other Directions for Preaching

1. The reading from Isaiah recognizes God at work in a king who did not even know God. Can we recognize that God is not above politics but is to be found within political structures, working for the good of the world?

2. The Gospel comes not to us not only in human words but through the power of the Holy Spirit, ever at work in the world.

3. The separation of church and state invites us to ponder the relationship between God who is revealed in Christ and our political allegiances.

Religion: Trick or Treat?
Thirtieth Sunday
in Ordinary Time

Readings:
Exodus 22:20–26; 1 Thessalonians 1:5c–10;
Matthew 22:34–40

Sandy, my dental hygienist, seems to choose the most inopportune time
    to ask questions that need to be answered.
With hand and pick inside my wide-open mouth she asked the other day,
    "Is Halloween a Satanic holiday?"
I mustered up as much articulateness one can under such circumstances and
    shot back,
    "Where did you get such an idea?"
Sandy told me that her next-door neighbor,
    who is a fundamentalist Christian,
    was told in church how Halloween originated in ancient Satanic rites,
    and therefore she now forbids her kids to go out for trick or treat.

When the teeth were finally flossed and the mouth relatively workable,
    I told Sandy,
    "Actually the word *Halloween* comes from the English phrase
    All Hallow's Eve, since October 31st was the eve
    of the great feast of All Saints' Day on November 1st.
    Oh, it is true that in England and Ireland it once was a Druid holiday
    that honored Samhain, the Lord of the Dean,

287

and that the Druids believed
that it was the night when the spirits of the dead returned home.
But what's important is that Christians baptized this day
and saw it as a time
to celebrate the eve of All Hallows or All Saints."

"Then I can still allow my kids to dress up in weird costumes on
Halloween?" Sandy asked.
"Of course, as long as they do it in good fun and not hurt anybody
in the process,
let them enjoy.
But it might be wise for them not to do any damage to your neighbor's
house on Halloween."

As I drove home from the dentist's office,
I thought about how religion can often become more trick than treat.
What really made Jesus upset and angry was how the religious leaders in his
day burdened people with endless distinctions
between God's commandments in the Torah.
They argued over the 613 precepts in the Torah: 248 do's and 365 don'ts.
Of course, the don'ts usually won out over the do's.

Not all the Pharisees in Jesus' time were connivers.
Most of them were sincere and good people
who kept faith alive in Israel during its darkest hours.
But there were some like the legal theologian in today's Gospel
who were more concerned with trick than treat.
The legal theologian came to Jesus that day in order to play "Gotcha."
For this man, religion had become a game,
a clever debate, a way to put the other down.
Jesus' answer to the question "Which commandment in the law
is the greatest?"
is at once masterful and orthodox.

He reminds the Pharisee that Deuteronomy (6:5) says,
        "Love...God with all your heart."
But he also combines this with what was found in the book of Leviticus:
        "Love your neighbor as yourself."
Jesus doesn't throw out the 613 commandments;
        he simply says that all of the commandments hang on
        the Greatest Commandment: love of God and love of neighbor.

I confess to you that the group of people I am most challenged to love as
        neighbor are some religious people of our day
        who also seem to be more into trick than treat.
The school where I teach, Washington Theological Union, is situated in the
        heart of Seventh Day Adventist land.
In fact, our new building once served for many years
        as the International Headquarters of the Adventist Church.

We Catholics are the new kids on the block there and sometimes are chal-
        lenged with questions not unlike the one Jesus faced in today's Gospel.
The other day in our cafeteria, a young man who has just begun to work in
        the kitchen and who is either an Adventist
        or a member of some fundamentalist Christian sect, asked me,
        "How many books are there in the King James version of the Bible?"
A trick, no doubt, to see if a Catholic priest and seminary professor knows
        the Bible.
I'm sure I had a push from the Holy Spirit when I said to Reuben:
        "Catholics aren't into final exams about the Bible.
        We're more concerned with the meaning of the Bible."
Not only was I able to dodge a question for which I had no answer,
        but my answer seemed to catch him off guard.

I then told him the story of how the great Protestant theologian Karl Barth
        was asked what was the most important truth
        he had learned in his theological study.
Barth simply said, "Jesus loves me, this I know, for the Bible tells me so."

More and more religious groups are offering religious reasons to support
    nationalism, racism, and sexism
    in order to strangle the human rights of others.
They make religion not a treat, but a trick.
More and more, not just priests, but all of us as Catholics
    are going to be challenged
    by the rising tide of fundamentalist Christians in our nation.
They will more and more become not just our neighbor,
    but our next-door neighbor.
We can dismiss their trick questions or treat them with core answers,
    reminding them that at the heart of the biblical message
    is the challenge for all of us to treat ourselves to God's love.

God invites us to the treat of the banquet this morning: Eucharist.
Eucharist helps us as a community to know that the whole law
    is not about rules but about love,
    about really loving God and one's neighbor,
    not about figuring out how to avoid stepping on cracks in the legal
    sidewalk.
Eucharist helps us to have a whole new way of looking at our religion
    so that it never becomes a trick,
    so that it never gets in the way of our relationship with God
    and one another.

RPW

Questions for Reflection

1. Do you approach religion more as a "treat" or a "trick"?

2. Why do the whole law and the prophets depend on the two commandments Jesus quotes?

3. How does the law of love take shape in your life these days?

Other Directions for Preaching

1. Exodus 22 reminds us that God hears the cry of the poor and is particularly concerned how we treat the weak, the helpless, the needy.

2. The Thessalonians witnessed to the world that they had turned from idols to serve the living and true God. What are the forms of idolatry in our world and how does the community model the imitation of the Lord?

3. The law of love is at the center of the Church's practical theology, spirituality, and missionary activity.

Great Expectations
THIRTY-FIRST SUNDAY
IN ORDINARY TIME

Readings:
Malachi 1:14b—2:2b, 8–10; 1 Thessalonians 2:7b–9, 13;
Matthew 23:1–12

Again and again this year Matthew's Gospel comes across as having the
right words for the right time.
To a Church racked with explosive revelations about child abuse, we have
heard the teaching of Jesus as something that speaks directly
to our experience.
Both the words and stories of Jesus' ministry have been connecting
with our lives:
from the disciples caught in a boat during a fearful storm at sea,
to the parable of the weeds planted among the wheat,
to the words of Jesus today denouncing leaders who did not practice
what they preached—
Matthew's Gospel continues to call us to conversion and life as children of the kingdom.

Today's readings offer us several profiles of ministry.
Not all of these profiles are for direct imitation as you may have noticed.
They are more of what used to be called a "via negativa," a listing of what
not to do.

In this sad time, they remind us that failure on the part of those called
    to serve God's people is nothing new.
The Old Testament called them "bad shepherds,"
    just as Jesus referred to himself as the "Good Shepherd."
God's Word today also affirms that God's people have a right
    to have great expectations about their ministers—
    not be confused with unrealistic ones.

The prophet Malachi speaks in the name of the Lord when he chastises the
    priests of his day for not listening and taking to heart that they are to
    give glory to God.
These priests have turned aside from the way of the Torah, the law of the
    Lord, and they have led others astray.
You must wonder what Malachi would make of our situation today.
It's a safe bet he would not be a silent bystander.

And Jesus is no less severe in his blast at the scribes and Pharisees.
While not as bad as the priests of Malachi's day who led people astray
    with faulty teaching, the scribes and Pharisees only sounded good.
Jesus called them hypocrites, which could be translated as "actors."
They put on a show, but were not the genuine article.
They gave clear directions about the road to take,
    but they weren't too good at traveling there themselves.
Worst of all, they burdened others with the details and minutiae,
    while they themselves only went as far as looking good.
Only Paul offers us a positive picture of what it means
    to serve God's people.
It means being as gentle as a nursing mother.
It means sharing not only the words of the Gospel, but one's very self.
It means working to support oneself, causing no burden for others.
No wonder that the people received the Gospel Paul preached
    "not [as] a human word but, as it truly [was], the word of God."
Paul embodied the vision that he preached, a Gospel freely given,
    a message of grace and hope and life.

The power of a person to transform another life came home to me
>   when I was watching the old Broadway musical *Man of La Mancha**
Last week I went to the revival playing at the National Theater.
Like many of you, I had seen it years ago and had read Cervantes' book in
>   high school.
So, I was not at all expecting to be so caught up in its spell.
But the gently mad Don Quijote is a man whose mission embodies helping
>   others to see what the world might be.
And while he seems to fail miserably by the end of the play, he does not fail
>   completely.
Don Quijote has been taken back home to his relatives,
all his seeming illusions stripped away.
He is dying, a sad and broken old man.
Then, Aldonza the serving girl, whom he named Dulcinea, his Lady, comes
>   to see him.
At first the family tries to block her from entering,
>   but she forces her way in.
She kneels before him but he doesn't recognize her.
She who had described herself as "scum of the earth" and as a whore,
>   who had been so hardened to life, so unable to accept his kindness,
>   asks through her tears, "Don't you remember what you said to me?"
>   and she begins to recite the words Don Quijote had sung to her:
>   "To dream the impossible dream, to fight the unbeatable foe,
To bear with unbearable sorrow, to run where the brave dare not go...."

At first the dying man just looks at her, but then suddenly his memory is
>   jolted, and he rises out of his bed and for a few moments, he comes
>   back to life again and joins her in singing:

>   "This is my quest, to follow that star,
>   No matter how hopeless, no matter how far.

---

*Written by Dale Wasserman, with lyrics and music by Joe Darion and Mitch Leigh.

To fight for the right, without question or pause,

To be willing to march into hell for a heavenly cause.

And I know if I'll only be true to this glorious quest

That my heart will lie peaceful and calm when I'm laid to my rest..."

It is a song that I have heard countless times,

> but the other night was like hearing it for the first time.

If there were any hearts present that were weighed down,

> they surely would have been lifted up.

If anyone came in feeling cynical or hopeless about the world,

> they must have felt a light draft of encouragement drifting through the room.

It was not just because of the music, nor merely the combination of words and music.

It was because someone hopeless and spiritually dead had come back to life:

> Aldonza had heard his words and taken them to heart,

> and her life had changed.

His words had taken root in her heart.

She had entered into the vision his words had introduced,

> and she had begun to be transformed.

And now she could sing them in her own right.

When Paul writes that the Thessalonians have received not a human word,

> but the Word of God, which is now at work in those who believe,

> this is what God's word can do for a community.

It starts to work in us and change us.

This must be especially true for those who called to minister to the community.

The preachers of the Word must first of all be listeners to the Word.

The proclamation of the Gospel of God has to transform them.

Otherwise there is no credibility.

If the leaders, teachers, bishops, and priests of the Church are not
    embodiments of the Gospel of Jesus Christ,
        who will believe it?
Today's readings affirm that great expectations are to be held onto;
    we are to expect preachers who practice what they preach,
        who are not into merely looking good but being good, living humbly,
        and lightening burdens rather than lifting them onto people.
The phylacteries and fringes of one age can turn into the red piping and
    French cuffs of a later one.
We pray that all who follow Jesus can be worthy servants,
    learning from our teacher Jesus.
Only Jesus is teacher, and only God is father; all others are learners
    and children.
Greatness is found in service.

Paul's words to the community he founded in Thessalonica
    are quite touching.
He refers to himself in this chapter as both a nursing mother fondling her
    little ones and as a father caring for his children.
Later on again, Paul speaks of himself as an orphan when separated from
    them (2:17).
He offers us a positive profile of one who ministers as a gentle, affectionate,
    self-giving, loving, hardworking, proclaimer of the Gospel.
Both Paul and Jesus serve as models of mutuality.

The meaning of a name can change.
The name Pharisee went from meaning the "separate one" to meaning a
    hypocrite.
In our day, the name of priest and bishop has suffered a change.
Can they be redeemed again?
For some people, those who have suffered from abuse and lies, the answer
    is probably no.
But those who bear the name can transform it with the help of God.

JAW

Questions for Reflection

1. What has been your experience of bishops and priests?

2. What would you see as the most important qualities for leaders in the Church to have?

3. How can you help those who are providing leadership in your own parish?

Other Directions for Preaching

1. The readings highlight the ongoing need of reform in the Church, especially among those who would lead it.

2. The image of a nursing mother applies to both those in ministry and the God who sends them into ministry; the image offers an opportunity to reflect on a female image of God.

3. The law of God can be interpreted broadly or strictly. Each has its dangers. But Jesus' harshest words were for those who made life burdensome and used the law to crush their brothers and sisters.

Wise Up
THIRTY-SECOND SUNDAY
IN ORDINARY TIME

Readings:
Wisdom 6:12–16; 1 Thessalonians 4:13–18;
Matthew 25:1–13

As we head into the Christmas shopping season I am reminded of a song
from a musical called *She Loves Me.* *
The name of the song was "Twelve Days Till Christmas,"
and it cleverly created portraits of the different groups of Christmas
shoppers.
As you know, there are those who shop early, in good time, late,
and frantically late.
The second verse describes the moderate group like this:

Nine days to Christmas, nine days to Christmas,
Still enough time to do your Christmas shopping.
These are the people who shop in time, shop in time, still enough time.
Sensible people who organize the time at their disposal.
Nine days to Christmas, nine days to Christmas
Still enough time to do your Christmas shopping;
These are the people who plan their time wisely and well,
These are the people who shop in time and they can go to hell.

She Loves Me, music by Jerry Bock, lyrics by Sheldon Harnick, book by Joe Masteroff (original Broadway production at the Eugene O'Neill Theatre, 1963).

I think of the "nine-days-before-Christmas" shoppers whenever I hear this
    parable.
They are the wise virgins who, like the shoppers in the song, plan their time
    "wisely and well."
Not for them the last minute, frantic rush to the mall—
either at Christmas or any other time.
Not for them to be without oil when the bridegroom finally comes.
I admire them.
But my heart is not with them.
Rather, it goes out to the unwise virgins.

There they are, waiting all night, faithfully at hand.
Excited, hungry, then getting tired and, finally, sleepy.
And that's when the bridegroom comes.
So, they forgot their oil. Big deal. An honest mistake.
But when they turn to their friends, these wise virgins turn away.
Some friends!
Sounds more like a bunch of obsessive-compulsives
    who never make a mistake.
I wonder if any of the unwise started to look for a cow plop to toss.

Then there is the bridegroom.
He certainly wasn't transformed by the joy of the occasion.
When he comes to open the door, all they get from him is,
    "I do not know you."
Then we get this word of warning: "Stay awake, for you know
    neither the day nor the hour."
What was Jesus thinking? And why all the fuss about oil?

Some say this is an allegory, that Matthew was addressing those in his com-
    munity who were losing heart, and had begun to think Jesus might not
    be coming back.
So the wise virgins stand for those who confidently wait for Jesus to return;
    the unwise are those who have given up and who get shut out.

But, again, why the stress on the oil?

Some say the oil stands for the good works needed to get into the kingdom.

These are the good works that shine out for all to see, so there is light.

The Master locks out those who don't have oil because Jesus has said earlier,

> "Not everyone who says to me, 'Lord, Lord,' will enter...only the one
> who does the will of my Father" (Matt 7:21).

Matthew's moral: Don't fall asleep; live in light by doing good deeds
> until the Master returns.

I prefer the biblical scholar Pheme Perkins' take on this parable.

She says that this is one of Jesus' many stories about good and bad servants.

The bridesmaids are really servants, and the two groups are people
> we all know.

There are those folk who are always prepared and those who never are.

You meet them in school, at work, and even at home—

> "They are the ones who will be late for their own funeral,"
> as my grandmother used to say.

Jesus was using comedy here, but with a very important point.

There are those who are wise and those who are not...at least yet.

Note that those who are prepared don't lecture and harangue the others.

They are wise in not being nags, and not getting into self-righteousness.

But neither do they take responsibility for the others—
> no codependents here!

Rather, they send them off to the store.

Now when they get back late, the door is closed.

And they are scolded. Not sent to hell. Just scolded.

Hopefully, next time, they will have the oil.

Taken this way, it is a story about the possibility of change.

The emphasis is on becoming wise.

Being wise in terms of Jesus means knowing that we are all waiting,
> and that this waiting is with the assurance that he will come;

This waiting is not just a waste of time.

It is an important part of life, showing good faith in the promise of return.
And part of waiting is having the oil to greet the master.
All of this signals that one never wavers from waiting.
The wise live in an active awareness of waiting for the Lord to come.

Now waiting is not a cultural virtue in our day.
For most people I know, waiting is something they don't want
      to put up with.
I must confess that, if I can, I try to avoid it,
      gently accelerating through yellow lights,
      checking out various lines at the store for the shortest one
      and least purchases.
And for those unavoidable red lights,
      I bring out a little book of poetry to read, to occupy myself—
      anything to put aside the awareness that here I am stuck, waiting.

However, there are those who assure me that if I can begin to wait patiently
      and consciously, it begins to influence the present.
Having an eye on the future that is coming is meant to have an impact
      on how we live now.
The difference between being wise and foolish is not some unusual effort on
      the part of the wise, but a way of being that is habitual.
The wise have the oil that allows them to go on waiting until the bride-
      groom comes.
They remain in a state of living with an eye on the One who will come,
      even though they don't know when.
Falling asleep wasn't the problem; both groups did.
But whether awake or asleep, they were waiting.

So when we come here to give thanks, we are acting wisely.
Being here reminds us that we are waiting on the Lord:
      Christ has died, Christ is risen, Christ will come again.
We come to the meal that is a reminder of the heavenly banquet
      that awaits us.

And to come here today to be anointed with the oil of the sick is also
    to act wisely.
Doing this recognizes that while we wait for the Lord, we need support in
    our faith,
        especially at a time of illness or a threatening life disease,
        when not only our bodies but our spirits can weaken.
And while we wait, Jesus touches us through the signs of the laying on of
    hands and the anointing with oil,
And while we wait, the community's faith supports and encourages
    the faith of those who are sick.

To become wise is about more than accumulating knowledge—
Lady Wisdom comes to those who seek her.
She comes at dawn, bringing the light of faith in God.
When we are wise, we have her light burning within us.
Paul once wrote to Timothy to "stir into flame the gift of God that you
    have" (2 Tim 1:6).
When Christ comes, he wants to see us burning brightly,
    shedding the light of our faith on the world.
He wants to be greeted by wise men and women with their lamps lit.
And those waiting will enter into the wedding celebration with great joy.

JAW

Questions for Reflection

1. Do you consider yourself wise or foolish? Why?
2. What are you waiting for? What do you long for?
3. Do you give light to those around you?

Other Directions for Preaching

1. The biblical personification of wisdom promises much to those who seek her. In an age of searching, the image of God as wisdom may speak to many who are alienated from institutional religion.

2. During the month of November, when attention turns to those who have died, Paul's words about "those who have fallen asleep" offer hope.

3. The wedding banquet as a metaphor for the end time offers an opportunity to speak of what was traditionally called "the last things."

Investing Wisely
THIRTY-THIRD SUNDAY
IN ORDINARY TIME

Readings:
Proverbs 31:10–13, 19–20, 30–31;
1 Thessalonians 5:1–6; Matthew 25:14–30

People of biblical time would have been startled by how this story ends.
The third servant would have been seen not just as cautious, but as wise.
A talent was a lot of money—a year's wages.
To be entrusted with a year's wages was a great act of confidence.
Not to squander it carelessly certainly seems a praiseworthy response.
But only those who double the investment are welcomed into the joy of the
    kingdom.
Since it is called the parable of the talents or the parable of the silver pieces,
    the focus seems to fall on the valuables.
What are we to make of this?

This is not the beginning of the Investment House of Jesus of Nazareth,
    but it does have to do with what God has entrusted to us.
Often we hear this parable interpreted in terms of the talents we have been
    given, those gifts and abilities God gave us at birth.
But as precious as these gifts are, and as important as it is to make good use
    of them, there is another way to think about the true wealth the mas-
    ter has handed over.

All the parables are about the coming of the kingdom of God.

The wealth of the master has to do with the kingdom.

We are entrusted with this kingdom.

That is the greatest treasure: God's gift of God's presence in our lives.

Jesus came to bring about the kingdom through his preaching and healing
and finally through the giving of his very Body and Blood.

In Matthew's Gospel especially, the teaching of Jesus is the treasure.

Matthew presents Jesus as the teacher like Moses.

And the question today is: what have you done with this treasure?

How have you invested it in your life, in the life of the world?

What return have you made of the Gospel implanted in your mind and
heart?

This Gospel has five great speeches of Jesus that contain his teaching

There is the sermon on the mount with its teaching about membership
in the kingdom,
and what it means to be and act as a child of the kingdom.

There is the teaching given to the disciples sent out on mission:
those reminders that we are called to evangelize, bring the Gospel to
others through our words and through how we love and witness
to Jesus Christ.

There is the discourse of the kingdom of God, told in the seven parables:
speaking of how the kingdom comes into the world,
of the tension between the weeds and the wheat,
about the growth of the kingdom like a mustard seed.

There is the discourse on how the community is to live with each other:
loving others, especially caring for the least in our midst, forgiving one
another, reaching out to protect the little ones.

And there is the discourse we have been listening to these last weeks:
stories and teachings about waiting on the Lord to come again,
being a wise people who burn with the light of Christ,
investing what has been given, until the day of his return.

As we come to the end of the Church year and the end of the Gospel of
 Matthew, take some time over the next two weeks
  to read this Gospel again, slowly.
How has this treasure been invested?
What difference has it made in your life?
What return has his words and the stories about him brought about?

We all have different abilities to understand and implement the Gospel.
The difference in talents might be seen as corresponding to our varying abil-
 ities to comprehend and enact the message of the Gospel.
Some have a deeper, fuller, richer understanding.
But whatever we have, we are to use it for our own sake and the glory
 of the master.
The challenge is to find ways to bring the Gospel into life
 for the sake of life.

One way to invest in our world is to speak out when we witness violence in
 any form.
Yesterday in the *Washington Post* there was an article on the bishops'
 revised statement on domestic violence in the home.
A frightening and ongoing problem in our society, especially among the
 most helpless,
  there is never any justification for abuse in the home—physical or verbal.
Never.
Domestic violence is a sin—one of the greatest and most common in our
 society.
Statistics tell us that in a Church of sixty-three million, eight million women
 and girls suffer violence,
  either physical, sexual, psychological, or verbal.
One way the Gospel is buried is when we remain silent in the face of this,
 when we suspect such a thing is happening and do not help the victim.

There are many ways to care for those in need.
At this time of year, the collection for the Catholic Campaign
  for Human Development offers one way of responding.
The ongoing work of supporting those who have been abused as children
  as taken up by the Voice of the Faithful is another response
  to the call of the Gospel.
Any endeavor that works for peace and reconciliation in our world is a
  gospel venture.

I saw the movie *Bloody Sunday* last week.
It told the story of British troops who fired on peace marchers in
  Londonderry in 1972.
A number were mortally wounded.
At a press conference, the leader of the peace march says
  to the newspaper reporters:
  "They have just killed off the peace movement
  and they will reap the whirlwind.
  If you invest only in violence, primarily in it, or perhaps even any
  investment at all,
  it will come back to haunt you."
Investing wisely is the challenge we hear today.

God has invested in us in the person of Jesus,
  he is the treasure given for our salvation:
  God's gift offered to us this day in the Eucharist.
But once received, once absorbed into our being,
  where does his presence go in and through us?
How does that moment of grace flow through us into the world?
What are we doing with the great treasure entrusted to our care,
  the life of grace, meant to be lived out of and brought into the world,
  present both in the message of the Gospel,
  and in the very person of Jesus, Lord and Savior?
We receive a foretaste now of the joy that awaits us.

Let us give thanks and praise and ask for the wisdom to invest wisely all
   our days.

JAW

Questions for Reflection

1. Do you recognize in the words and stories of Jesus a treasure that
God has entrusted to you?

2. What parts of the Gospel of Matthew do you see as most valuable for
your personal life and for the life of the world? After rereading the Gospel,
can you find any other sections that speak to you?

3. Is there one particular way you might deepen your involvement in a
way that allows the call of the Gospel to bear fruit.

Other Directions for Preaching

1. The wife saluted at the end of the book of Proverbs has been called
the "capable wife," that is a woman with a capacity for wisdom. Her husband
has entrusted his heart to her and she responds wholeheartedly. She is a figure of the Church and of every person with a capacity for wisdom.

2. First Thessalonians invites us to address the "day of the Lord" that
comes like "a thief in the night." The image of the "thief" might be pondered—the suddenness of his arrival, what he has come to steal, what are we
to do in the face of it—and the need for vigilance and alertness.

3. God entrusts us with the Gospel ultimately to welcome us into the joy
of the kingdom. In this destiny we can find meaning and a reason for hope.

FEASTS

Signs from God
TRINITY SUNDAY

Readings:
Exodus 34:4b–6, 8–9; 2 Corinthians 13:11–13;
John 3:16–18

My father told me recently that he and my mother were asked to contribute
   a significant memory to a time capsule.
The occasion was a baby shower for my brother and sister-in-law,
   who were about to adopt a baby from China.
These "time traveling phrases" would greet my niece some eighteen years
   from now, when she would read the various greetings of relatives
   and friends written before she ever arrived in this country.
My parents and others had to generate a "bottom line" statement,
   a greeting that would sum up their lives in the last few years.
"So what did you write?" I asked.
My father said, "Oh, that was easy enough."
"Really?" I replied.
My father then explained that they wished the new member of the family
   love and joy as he and my mother celebrated
   their 50th wedding anniversary.
That was a milestone, I thought, fit for a time capsule.

John 3:16 is probably in a time capsule somewhere,
   maybe in a lot of different places.
In a way, that verse is the Gospel at ground zero,
   the bare bones of what God has done in Christ:

"God so loved the world that he gave his only Son, so that everyone
who believes in him might not perish but might have eternal life."
These words spoken to Nicodemus show up all over the place,
sometimes just the numbers for the chapter and verse themselves.
Somehow this proclamation of God's generosity,
mysteriously disclosed in Christ,
speaks to the multitude of fans in the football stadium
who hold it up on white cardboard signs.
It means something to the teenagers who wear the verse on their T-shirts.
It articulates volumes for the millions of drivers
who proudly display John 3:16 on bumper stickers.

God is in relationship with his people and has been from the beginning.
The Creator loves his creation.
That is reason enough to keep quoting John 3:16 as a kind of mantra.
God loves the world!
And these words are a reminder that this God has a personal relationship
with the people called His own.
God is linked to us as a ground of all being,
a center beyond all others.
At the same time, God is so inside us that he remains
outside of our own understanding.
The relationship between God and the world is so intense
that God wrapped himself around a human body in Christ.
And yet this mystery of the Incarnation was anticipated
in the care that God had for his people,
those he called again and again
in so many different ways to love him all the more.
"I have witnessed the affliction of my people in Egypt and have heard their
cry of complaint," the Lord God tells Moses from the burning bush
(Exod 3:7). That burning bush signifies what the poet Gerard Manley
Hopkins called the "dearest freshness of deep down things,"
God's presence that dwells in all things.

God reaches out to his creation in mercy and in love and definitively
    in his Son.
Jesus is the manifestation of God's love, and the work that the Son
    accomplished on earth—by his passion, death, and resurrection—
    sealed that divine love forever.
Jesus: grabbing the lame legs to make them straight.
Jesus: touching the eyes of the blind so that they might see.
Jesus: suffering and dying all for the restoration of creation and covenant.

God on a cross!
That is as bare bones as it gets.
God, literally stripped down to the essentials, reveals the essence
    of sacrificial love,
      so blindingly great that we can never hope
      to grasp its mystery but see it only dimly.
If we want to know how much God loved the world,
    think about the manifestation of the infinite God
    as a poor infant child.
If we want to know how much God loved the world,
    remember the works Jesus revealed as signs of God's love—
    the healing, the forgiving, the raising to new life.
And if we want to know how much God loved the world,
    behold the wood of the cross, on which hung the Savior of the world.
    That is Good Friday language:
    God in the flesh: naked, bloody, and dead.
Jesus Christ is a character study of the unfathomable God.
The Son had his Father's eyes;
    they were for the world that only God could find lovely.

You can often tell a lot about a person from how they behave
    during difficult times, crucifixion times.
Who could forget those famous, heroic last words of Todd Beamer on Flight
    93 on 9/11 when he showed the whole world what he was made of?

That utterance should be in every time capsule on earth
   as a reminder of the grace and strength that human beings are capable
   of even in the face of impossible danger:
   "Let's roll!"
"Let's roll," he said.
I've seen people in hospitals with cancer so advanced they can hardly speak,
   yet they manage to comfort the person in the bed next to them,
   who is in much better shape than their comforter.
And priests who muster hour after hour of service,
   running off to an emergency room to anoint someone,
   even after they thought they just answered the last night call.
And mothers in war-torn countries whose pain is so great
   because they have no milk left to feed their starving children.
When people are stretched to the limit, we see what they are made of.
Their deepest humanity is exposed.
There is the crucifixion;
   there God gives again his only Son.
And that is what was revealed on the cross:
   God at the edges of his own creation, revealing that he is entirely,
   utterly, and completely oriented in love.
God cannot *but* love.
As it says in the Alternative Opening Prayer for this Trinity Sunday,
   "You reveal yourself in the depths of our being,
   drawing us to share in your life and your love."
Perfect love knows no limits.

The movement of that life and love is happening even now.
That Spirit of love can only overflow into the very creation
   that it continues to animate, celebrated at this liturgy.
That Spirit is living and active here and everywhere in the world
   because the love God shows for all creation in Christ
   is still vital and vibrant.
Can you hear it?

It is whispered in the hopes and prayers of all of us in this church—
> a song of thanksgiving told in the Spirit.

We are ready to give back to the Father the love he has shown us in Christ.

Blessed Trinity.

We are at its center, its stillpoint.

God continues to love us in Christ through the Spirit.

How many times do we pray during the liturgy without thinking:
> "We ask this through our Lord Jesus Christ"?

We do so throughout the ages and forever to the glory of God the Father,
> and through Christ his Son and by the work of the Spirit,
> in whom we live and breathe and have our very being.

And that is who we are as individuals, as Church, as creation,
> at ground zero.

Lovely.

GD

Questions for Reflection

1. God is a mystery. Have I ever tried to make God over in my own image?

2. Where in the Gospel does Jesus strike you as most personable, most loving, and most tender?

3. Paul tells the Corinthians that they should "encourage one another, agree with one another, live in peace." Do I do this?

Other Directions for Preaching

1. The Spirit of God is at work in the Church that prays continually through Christ to the Father—meaning what?

2. Moses interceded for the people of Israel and we should make our prayers heartfelt and humble.

3. God renews his covenant and that means we are called to an even closer relationship than before.

Gazing or Becoming?
THE SOLEMNITY OF THE MOST HOLY BODY AND BLOOD OF CHRIST

Readings:
Deuteronomy 8:2–3, 14b–16a; 1 Corinthians 10:16–17; John 6:51–58

A faculty colleague of mine told me that when she went to communion at a
parish in this archdiocese last summer,
the eucharistic minister held the host high up in the air and said:
"Here is the Body of Christ."
After that, the minister of the cup announced to her:
"Receive the Blood of Christ, and have a nice day!"
My colleague is a very astute theologian.
She was dumbfounded and asked me:
"How on earth do they train these people when they become
eucharistic ministers?"

We are fortunate indeed here at Holy Trinity to have eucharistic ministers
who are well-trained and exemplary, and I mean that in all honesty.
They know their Catholic theology and tradition.
They know that in the Order of Mass, the eucharistic minister is not sup-
posed to say, "Here is the Body of Christ" or "Here is the Blood of
Christ," but simply "The Body of Christ" and "The Blood of Christ."

Communion time is not a time for gazing or for checkout-counter
    best wishes.
It is a time for becoming the Body and Blood of Christ.
This solemnity which we celebrate today used to be called Corpus Christi,
    Latin for the Body of Christ.
It dates back to the thirteenth century when for many historical reasons
    believers went from altar to altar to look at the consecrated host.
Many expected favors and answers to prayers by participating
    in this private devotion.
These believers became so wrapped up in gazing on the Body of Christ
    that they stopped receiving the Body of Christ.

At the beginning of this century, the practice of frequent communion
    was reintroduced into our Church.
Then came the reforms of the Second Vatican Council
    that invited us not just to look at the Body of Christ,
    but to receive and become the Body of Christ.
Eucharist is not a devotion when we enter into private communion with
    Jesus, but a time to receive and become the Body of Christ.

A few years ago, Pope John Paul II made this theological insight forceful
    in his encyclical on the Eucharist.
This is what he wrote:

> All of us who take part in the Eucharist are called to discover, through
> this sacrament, the profound meaning of our actions in the world in
> favor of development and peace, and to receive from it the strength to
> commit ourselves ever more generously, following the example of
> Christ who in this sacrament lays down his life for his friends.*

The Pope reminded us that it is not enough to gaze upon the Body of
    Christ, not enough to receive the Body of Christ.
We are invited to become the Body of Christ.

Sollicitudo Rei Socialis, § 49.

There are many in recent weeks after the tragedy of Littleton who are
      demanding that we hang up the Ten Commandments
      in our classrooms and courts.
Richard Cohen, in the *Washington Post* this week, challenged this simplistic
      notion of religion.
He recalled as a kid coming home after school, dreading to pass the local
      Catholic grade school because the kids from that school were the ones
      who threw the rocks and beat up all the non-Catholic kids.
Yes, they had the Ten Commandments and lots of other religious teachings
      on the wall but what was in their hearts?
Spirituality does not mean simply gazing at something on the wall
      but becoming what we eat and drink.

The Christians of St. Paul's day were receiving the Body of Christ
      but not becoming the Body of Christ.
The church in Corinth had great liturgies.
They were probably reported to the chancery from time to time.
But the problem with the church in Corinth was not their liturgies,
      but that it was a scandalous community:
      the rich did not share with the poor and the strong did not reach out
      to the weak.
St. Paul encouraged the Corinthian church not just to receive the Body of
      Christ but to become the Body of Christ.

In John's Gospel, Jesus told the people something new about the food that
      God gave them.
As wonderful and heavenly as the manna in the desert was, Jesus was the
      new manna, God's final food.
When they received his Body and Blood, they shared God's own life.

One of the great privileges of being a eucharistic minister is that
      over and over again
      we announce to those who approach God's table:
      "The Body of Christ. The Blood of Christ."

Gradually those of us who are privileged to distribute this sacred food
    begin to realize
        they are not just giving the Body and Blood of Christ to others;
        they are gazing into the eyes of the living bread come down from
        heaven.

I wish that every member of a parish could be designated
    a eucharistic minister.
People of all ages and colors and levels of faith could take turns on Sunday
    in this service to God's people in church and to the elderly and sick in
    their homes.
Then so many more of us would begin to see one another
    as the Body of Christ.
We would begin to think less of ourselves and more of others.
If such a day would come, we would become more of a Church
    of the Real Presence;
        a Church not just receiving the Body and Blood of Christ but
        becoming the Body and Blood of Christ.
It would give a whole new meaning to the word "communion."

RPW

Questions for Reflection

1. Can you think of ways that you could become more fully the Body of Christ?

2. How does your parish take seriously the words of Pope John Paul II to commit ourselves ever more seriously to the work of development and peace?

3. How can devotion to the Blessed Sacrament lead you to become what you behold?

Other Directions for Preaching

1. As he fed the Israelites in the desert, God continues to feed us with the bread come down from heaven to show us that "not by bread alone does one live, but by every word that comes forth from the mouth of the Lord." We are nourished as much at the table of the Word as at the table of the Eucharist.

2. Participation in the Eucharist is participation in the Body and Blood of Christ, so that when we receive, we accept and commit ourselves more fully to living out the paschal mystery of the Lord, the dying and rising so others might have new life.

3. The Sequence, "Laud, O Zion," offers food for meditation and preaching.

The Fisherman
and the Tentmaker
SAINTS PETER AND
PAUL, APOSTLES

Readings:
Acts 12:1–11; 2 Timothy 4:6–8, 17–18;
Matthew 16:13–19

When you think about it, there is a touch of irony in this feast.
Here in Washington, DC, the capital of the country,
    the center of world power, the modern Rome,
        we pause to honor two men who were put to death by the Rome of
        their day.
Here in this city of power and the powerful, we honor two
    who were powerless.
Here after two thousand years of human progress and scientific achieve-
    ment, we gather to honor a fisherman and a tentmaker.

Of course, that is not why we honor them.
The feast is called Saints Peter and Paul, Apostles.
These two are remembered as the two great pillars of the Church in those
    first days.
Peter brought the community from the country to the city,
    staying on in Jerusalem after Pentecost, then moving on to Antioch.
Paul took the Church from Jerusalem to the world.
And we honor them as martyrs.

When we think of martyrdom, we think of a bloody death and that holds
    true.
Tradition tells us:
    Peter was crucified, supposedly upside down;
    Paul was beheaded, his right as a Roman citizen.
And so as pillars and martyrs they become larger than life.
But it is also good to remember their human side, for they were human
    like us.
Peter, the first to be called, was impetuous, headstrong, argumentative:
    When Jesus says he will die in Jerusalem Peter answers, "God forbid,
    Lord! No such thing shall ever happen to you" (Matt 16:22).
    When Jesus says he will wash Peter's feet, Peter says, "You will never
    wash my feet" (John 13:8).
Even after the resurrection, in the Book of Acts, when he is in the house of
    Simon and receives a vision that tells him to take and eat,
    Peter says—and you can hear his self-righteousness—
    "Certainly not, sir. For I never have I eaten anything profane and
    unclean" (Acts 10:13–16).
Three times he is told to take and eat. Three times he argues with the vision.
And the greatest No of all was in that courtyard in Jerusalem after they
    arrested Jesus:
    Three times, "I do not know the man" he shouted (Matt 26:72, 74).
    And Peter wept.
But Peter also atoned. "Simon, son of John, do you love me?" Jesus asked.
Three times asked and three times answered: "Yes. Yes. Yes"
    (John 21:15–17).

Saul, a Jew of the diaspora, was born in Tarsus and was trained
    in rabbinic thought.
He persecuted with great zeal the young Christian community.
And then something happened on the road to Damascus.
Saul of Tarsus became Paul the Apostle:
The zealous persecutor of the Christian community became
    the zealous proclaimer

of the Gospel and great lover of Jesus Christ.

The one who oversaw the martyrdom of Stephen became the most articulate defender of the message Stephen preached.

The Paul of the letters is revealed as a profoundly passionate and pastoral man tending the flock as both a mother and father, and witnessing for the ages:

"For [Christ's] sake I have accpeted the loss of all things and I consider them so much rubbish, that I may gain Christ" (Phil 3:8).

Both Peter and Paul remind us that it is never too late to change,
    that there is nothing we have done that is so awful
    that God's grace cannot help us move beyond it,
    and that when we do, with God's help, wonderful things can happen in and through us.

We remember them both as human and as graced, touched by God's hand.

In today's readings, both are threatened with death.

In Acts, King Herod is flexing his political muscles—
    putting to death James and arresting Peter:
    two squads of soldiers, double chains.

Luke notes it is the feast of the Unleavened Bread—the Passover—that time when Jesus died.

The Church is praying that Peter be delivered.

Peter goes to bed and is sleeping so soundly the angel has to shake him awake.

It is made clear that it is God who has done this—
    God who raised Peter up to live another day.

And in the Gospel, the initiative of God is brought out once again.

After Peter confesses, "You are the Christ, the Son of the living God."
    Jesus says: "Blessed are you Simon, son of Jonah.
    For flesh and blood has not revealed this to you,
    but my heavenly Father."

The Second Letter to Timothy has Paul also in prison, waiting for death.

He sees his time is running out and yet there is no sign of fear.

He knows God is with him.

After noting that *all* had deserted—Demas especially—and Alexander had
   harmed him,
      Paul writes: "[Yet] the Lord stood by me and gave me strength....
      I was rescued from the lion's mouth. The Lord *will* rescue me
      from every evil threat and bring me safe to his heavenly kingdom."

Paul is very careful in his letters how he refers to himself:
      again and again he points out what God did to, for, and through him,
      what God in Christ Jesus is doing for all of creation, in the power of
      the Spirit.

God is at work in them and in us, Paul asserts, again and again—
      which brings us to the response they made
      and the question of our own response.

Today we celebrate Peter and Paul as *apostles* and *martyrs*—
      the words mean: one who is sent and one who witnesses, respectively.

Both end their days in Rome, far from their homes,
      witnessing to Jesus Christ.

Paul is presented as encouraging his protégé Timothy by speaking of his life
      as a libation poured out, that is, a cup of wine
      poured out to honor the gods before a journey;
      for Paul it was a life poured out for Jesus Christ;

Paul also speaks of himself as an athlete who has run the race,
      fought the good fight, kept the faith.

Peter is given the power of the keys, to bind and loose, Jesus declaring him
      the steward
      of the Church, entrusting him with the role
      of leadership and authority.

And so Peter and Paul speak to us today,
      we who are also human, graced, and called to a life of witness.

They call us to testify to the world and to one another,
      to speak always for the holiness of life—of all life—even in the face of
      a world where it often seems impossible to effect much change.

Today's *Washington Post* told us that nine million Americans are unem-
   ployed or underemployed;
      that since the Palestinian uprising started almost three years ago,
      almost three thousand people have been killed;
      and that, since May, sixty-one American soldiers have been killed and
      countless Iraqis.
In the face of this you can feel pretty helpless.

Yet we are called to let the power of God's Spirit work in and through us,
As these two men did—a fisherman and a tentmaker.
We are invited to let the Spirit of the risen Christ continue to transform us
      into witnesses to a power that can transform the world
      and bring about the kingdom of God.
We do that this morning in an act of anointing our sick.
Those who come forward to receive an anointing with oil and the Holy
      Spirit witness to us their faith and trust in the Lord
      who saves and raises us up to fullness of life.
And we witness to them and assure them of our prayer, that our faith will
      support them should their own falter.
As the oil is spread upon their heads and hands, let us pray with conviction
      that through this holy anointing, the Lord in his love and mercy,
      will help them with the grace of the Holy Spirit,
      and that the Lord who frees them from sin, will save them
      and raise them up.
And may we continue in our day to do the work that God has appointed us
      to do, doing in our time what Peter and Paul did in theirs:
      witnessing to the living, risen Lord.
May God be with us and keep us faithful.

                                                                    JAW

Questions for Reflection

1. Have you known what it was like for God to free you from your chains as God did with Peter in prison?

2. How is God calling you to witness to him in your life, at your job, with your family?

3. "Who do you say that I am?" Jesus asks.

Other Directions for Preaching

1. Consider the meaning of the keys of the kingdom that were entrusted to Peter and how that affects the life of the Church today.

2. The Lord remains our strength no matter what, whether we are freed from our prison like Peter or remain there like Paul. "The angel of the Lord encamps around those who fear him and delivers them," as Psalm 34 reminds us.

3. God continues to raise up men and women in the spirit of Peter and Paul, fearless and convinced of the truth of the Gospel, and sends them out to proclaim the good news of Jesus Christ.

A Holy Distraction
All Saints

Readings
Revelation 7:2–4, 9–14; 1 John 3:1–3; Matthew 5:1–12a

The church where I was baptized and worshiped as a boy was a veritable
    Polish pantheon.
It had many statues and paintings.
When the sermon and rites were dry and unintelligible,
    as most often they were,
    there was always a place to gaze:
    the statue of St. Lucy, her eyes on a plate;
    Thérèse de Lisieux, her roses and cross in hand;
    Anthony of Padua, ready to help us find not only our lost souls but
    our lost car keys.
And high above the main altar a mural of our parish's patron saint,
    Stanislaus, Bishop of Cracow, being murdered in the cathedral
    by King Boleslaw and his goon squad.
The saints for me were a refuge, a wild and wonderful communion.
But then came the liturgical reforms of Vatican II,
    the *necessary* reforms of Vatican II where we returned
    to the center of our liturgical life,
    the paschal mystery of Christ.

Despite these necessary reforms, we must admit that there are still times
    when the homily and rites are dry and unintelligible.
So, now where do we gaze?

Perhaps on a banner with too many words glued on felt.
Perhaps on the exit sign over the door.
Perhaps on a giant potted palm in the sanctuary whose droopy leaves
 remind us of our own dry spirits and our need for refreshment.

In our return to what is central to our Christian lives have we not
 robbed ourselves of what the Russian Orthodox call
 their iconography: "holy distraction?"
The Orthodox believe that it's necessary to distract ourselves from time to
 time from the principal liturgical action by allowing our gaze
 to wander, as it were,
 through the art of angels and saints that surround us in a sacred place.
Such "holy distraction" they believe actually brings us back to the great
 prayer of the Church
 because such art is always a reminder that helps our thoughts return
 to God.

From the earliest of times Christians were surrounded by art which
 reminded them
 that they were not alone in their journey of faith;
 that they were part of something larger,
 something called "the communion of saints."

The baptistery of St. John Lateran in Rome was the first major baptismal
 space in Christendom.
What a pity that it is now stripped down from its immense beauty
 and original designs.
When neophytes first emerged from the font to be presented to the assembly
 of the baptized,
 they were surrounded with images of the heavenly court
 in a triumphant procession.
Enormous statues—including deer as symbols of baptized souls—filled the
 baptismal space.

These images were the first signs to impress the imagination of the neo-
    phytes emerging from the font, welcoming them to the heavenly com-
    munion of those who had
    "washed their robes...in the blood of the Lamb."

For all our contemporary demythologizing and our iconoclasm,
    the saints still keep marching into our worship and imagination.
The Solemnity of All Saints is a persistent reminder of our need
    for holy distraction.
And if we allow ourselves the freedom and the imagination to gaze upon
    our sisters and brothers
    who once were poor in spirit, sorrowing, lowly, single-hearted,
    and persecuted,
    we will do what liturgy is supposed to do:
    lead us to thank and praise God.

The early martyrs, the noble lady Perpetua and her slave Felicity,
    walked with such graceful bearing into the amphitheater filled with
    lions that the people said it seemed that they were entering heaven—
Blessed be God!
Saints Perpetua and Felicity, pray for us!
The illegitimate mulatto Martin de Porres once asked his Dominican
    superior to sell him into slavery so that the money could be spent
    on the poor and the wretched.
He did so because he saw in every human being not a color but a Christ,
    not festering sores but the wounds of his Lord.
For Martin de Porres, let us give thanks to God!
St. Martin, pray for us!

Elizabeth Ann Bayley Seton struggled through two Christian traditions and
    two vocations.
She loved the sentimental piety she found in Italy while nursing
    her dying husband.
But she was also a take-charge woman.

One Sunday, after hearing a young priest deliver a poorly prepared sermon,
     she took him aside, whipped out her motherly finger, and sternly
     warned him:
     "Young man, don't you ever dare to preach a sermon without being
     prepared!"
I know I may be biased but for that statement alone, she deserved
     to be canonized.
For the courage of Mother Seton, blessed be God!
St. Elizabeth Ann, pray for us!

Thomas Aquinas, heady doctor of the Church, wrote great Summas
     but was also not afraid to write great hymns like
     "Lost, all lost, in wonder at the God thou art."
For Aquinas, who reminds us that theologians can have a heart
     as well as a head,
     let us give thanks to God!
St. Thomas, pray for us!

And today we gaze upon those we once knew not just as saints but as
     friends.
I remember today Stan Rother, priest of the Archdiocese of Oklahoma.
He was one year ahead of me in the seminary, a quiet guy, who once was
     warned that he probably would never be ordained
     because he couldn't master Latin.
Stan went on to join a mission team in Guatemala and mastered not only
     Spanish but translated the Gospels
     into the difficult Indian Tzuthil dialect of his people,
     the first time it had ever been done.
Because he taught the women to boil water and wear shoes in order to
     avoid deadly parasites,
     because he sharply decreased the infant mortality rate,
     because he organized the poor and dispossessed,
     on July 28, 1981, government hoods tied him to a chair, tortured him,
     and shot him twice in the head.

When his family requested that his body be sent back to Oklahoma,
  his parishioners pleaded that Stan's heart and guts be buried at the
  altar in their local church.
His family acquiesced.
For Stanley Rother, let us pray "Blessed be God!"
St. Stanley, pray for us!

Blessed be God for all the saints, the zany ones, the forgotten ones, the
  ancient ones, the saints in our midst.
Blessed be God for angels and saints who are our heavenly companions in
  prayer.
Blessed be God for this holy distraction!

RPW

Questions for Reflection

1. Have any of the canonized saints ever played a part in your life? Who were they and what did they witness to you?

2. Would you add anyone you have known in your life to the listing of the saints?

3. How do you want to be remembered as a holy one after you have passed over to God?

Other Directions for Preaching

1. When Robert Ellsberg wrote his book *All Saints* (New York: Crossroad, 1998), he included not only saints recognized by the Catholic Church, not only other Christians, but also Jews, Moslems, and even those without any faith affiliation. The reading from Revelation sets before us a crowd that represents all peoples of the earth, a new Israel made up of Gentile and Jew. The feast of All Saints can draw our attention beyond our own "borders" to include all those whom Elizabeth Johnson terms "friends of God and prophets."

2. The author of First John writes that "we are God's children now; what we shall be has not yet been revealed. We know that when it is revealed we shall be like him, for we shall see him as he is." This feast reminds us that the future is built on the present.

3. The Beatitudes hold up portraits of those who belong to the kingdom of heaven. It encourages us to see ways in which the kingdom is present now in our world as it has been in the past. Consideration might be given to how this parish enters into the work of the Beatitudes

Judging Amy...and Phil and Emily and You and Me
CHRIST, THE KING

Readings:
Ezekiel 34:11–12, 15–17; 1 Corinthians 15:20–26, 28;
Matthew 25:31–46

Today's Gospel can evoke a surprising shiver from us.
The image of gentle Jesus, laughing Jesus, Jesus meek and mild, is nowhere
      to be found.
Instead we have Jesus presenting a vision of the end time
      with the Son of Man coming in glory and power as a judge,
      to hand down two clear-cut and "non-appealable" verdicts:
      "Inherit the kingdom" or
      "Depart from me, you accursed, into the eternal fire...."
How did we get to this image of the God who came in Christ to save us?
And can we substitute something else for it?
Not if you take seriously the God of our ancestors in the faith.

The Son of Man who judges us is the Shepherd King of all the nations.
He is the one who judges in the name of the Father who sent him.
The prophet Ezekiel reminds us today that God spoke of himself
      as a shepherd:
"I myself will look after and tend my sheep....I will rescue them
      from every place

where they were scattered when it was cloudy and dark.

I myself will pasture my sheep…give them rest…"

And God describes who receives his special attention:

"The lost I will seek out, the strayed I will bring back,

the injured I will bind up, the sick I will heal."

God is a shepherd who attends especially to the weak and the powerless.

But, from the beginning, God the shepherd is also God the judge:

"…but the sleek and the strong I will destroy…

I will judge between one sheep and another, between rams and goats."

This note of judgment carries over into the vision that Jesus presents today.

The Son of Man who returns in glory comes to judge all the nations,

separating them "as a shepherd separates the sheep from the goats."

And the basis for separation?

Have we cared for those in need?

Have we entered into the work of rescuing the weak, the weary,

the wounded?

Have we been attentive to those that we find on our path as we walk

through life?

Of particular interest is that, when the verdict is handed down,

both groups ask, "Lord, when did we see you hungry or thirsty or a

stranger or naked or ill or in prison?"

Neither group knew that when they cared for one of the least they cared

for Jesus.

All anyone saw was a person in need—hungry, thirsty, alone, alienated, sick,

imprisoned—maybe holding a hand out, maybe too beaten down even

for that.

It wasn't a case of the deserving poor, the falsely accused, or the morally

acceptable.

It was simply a matter of a person in need, without resources,

a case of responding to what was right before one's eyes, ears,

and nose.

Nobody "saw Christ" in the hungry or naked.

No special mystical vision is recorded.

It comes as a surprise to all concerned.
The base for judgment is response to what is in front of your face,
    in all its unglamorous, smelly, little-to-be-gained-from—
    not even gratitude—reality.

The vision Jesus describes has to do with the Son of Man judging the
    nations.
It can project a forbidding image, evoking fear, guilt, and even hopelessness,
    especially when each of us considers all the missed opportunities we
    have had.
But the One who will judge is the One who has saved, and who continues
    to save.
Jesus came to continue the work of the Shepherd King
    whom Ezekiel pictured for us:
    The God who rescued Israel from Egypt
    and led the people back from the exile in Babylon
    is the God who sent Jesus to rescue all who have been enslaved
    by sin and death, fear and selfishness,
    and to break the grasp of all those forces that imprison
    the human spirit.

Jesus came to bring freedom, not just *from* darkness and death,
    but *for* light and life.
And it is this Jesus who continues to come,
    to enlighten us by his Word,
    to feed us in the Eucharist,
    and to lead us out the door to take our part
    in the ongoing development of our world.
As we approach the national holiday that calls us to give thanks for all we
    have received,
    as we remember that all we now know shall end,
    as we prepare to enter into the season of Advent that proclaims the
    return of the One who was born and who died for us,
    and who will then hand over the kingdom to his Father,

may we wholeheartedly give ourselves to the work that is at hand,
furthering the peaceful coexistence and development
of all God's people.
May we live out our days dedicated to this task,
in the hope of hearing the words of promise addressed to those
who have brought life and light into the world:
"Come, you who are blessed by my Father.
Inherit the kingdom prepared for you from the foundation of the world."

JAW

Questions for Reflection

1. What do you think of when you hear God spoken of as a judge?

2. How will it feel to have Jesus say, "Come, you who are blessed by my Father. Inherit the kingdom prepared for you from the foundation of the world"?

3. Who are the hungry, thirsty, stranger, naked, ill, and imprisoned in your world? How are you responding to them?

Other Directions for Preaching

1. The God who tends his flock in Ezekiel voices a preference for the lost and wounded. Jesus expresses this same preference in the parable in Matthew's Gospel. This preferential option for the poor continues to challenge all the nations of the first world, especially the United States.

2. First Corinthians offers the preacher an opportunity to preach on Christ as the firstfruits of those who have fallen asleep and of the end time when all will be subjected to Christ and he is subjected to God.

3. The Last Judgment is a topic one seldom hears much reflection on. The feast offers an opportunity to bring it to bear on how we live our lives in the present. Can this be done without resorting to fear tactics that only threaten with an updated version of fire and brimstone?